Piaget's Theory of Intellectual Development

third edition

HERBERT P. GINSBURG
Teachers College, Columbia University

SYLVIA OPPER
University of Hong Kong

PRENTICE HALL   *Englewood Cliffs, New Jersey 07632*

Library of Congress Cataloging-in-Publication Data

GINSBURG, HERBERT.
   Piaget's theory of intellectual development / Herbert P. Ginsburg,
Sylvia Opper.—3rd ed.
      p.   cm.
   Bibliography: p. 257
   Includes index.
   ISBN   0-13-675166-0   ISBN   0-13-675158-X (pbk.)
   1. Cognition in children.   2. Intellect.   3. Education-
-Philosophy.   4. Piaget, Jean, 1896–1980.   I. Brandt, Sylvia Opper.
II. Title.
BF723.C5G56 1988
155.4'13'0924—dc19   87-17353
                                                        CIP

To the memory of Jean Piaget

Editorial/production supervision and
   interior design: Lisa A. Domínguez
Cover design: Diane Saxe
Manufacturing buyer: Ray Keating

©1988, 1979, 1969 by Prentice Hall
A Division of Simon & Schuster
Englewood Cliffs, New Jersey 07632

Cover photograph reprinted courtesy of the Bettmann Archive, Inc.

Printed in the United States of America

10   9   8   7   6   5   4   3   2   1

ISBN 0-13-675158-X (paper)   01
ISBN 0-13-675166-0 (case)   01

Prentice-Hall International (UK) Limited, *London*
Prentice-Hall of Australia Pty. Limited, *Sydney*
Prentice-Hall Canada Inc., *Toronto*
Prentice-Hall Hispanoamericana, S. A., *Mexico*
Prentice-Hall of India Private Limited, *New Delhi*
Prentice-Hall of Japan, Inc., *Tokyo*
Simon & Schuster Asia Pte. Ltd., *Singapore*
Editora Prentice-Hall do Brasil, Ltda., *Rio de Janeiro*

Contents

Foreword

Today Piaget seems to be *the* child psychologist in the eyes of the American public. His name crops up in countless publications, and his ideas are discussed in many different circles—psychological, educational, philosophical, psychiatric. In spite of his popularity, however, he remains a difficult author, especially for an English-speaking reader. *Piaget's Theory of Intellectual Development* is therefore very welcome. Thanks to the joint efforts of a Piagetian-trained psychologist and an American professor of developmental psychology, we now have a book that brings out and explains the difficulties so often encountered by students of Piaget. Not to feel disturbed at any misinterpretation of his thought is a rare pleasure when reading a book about Piaget, and I was delighted to find that the authors have not fallen into the two most common pitfalls: they have not oversimplified, nor have they been content to adopt the difficult Piagetian terminology without adequate explanation.

The undergraduate students of Piagetian theory, for whom this book is intended, are really fortunate to have this book to help them understand some of the more abstruse concepts; even our Genevan students do not find his theory easy to grasp. Each time Piaget comes across a behavior, however trivial it may seem, he seeks to explain it with reference to his theoretical framework, which is thus continuously being refined and enriched; with Piaget, the empirical is never separated from the theoretical. It is this continuing development that students find difficult, and that is so clearly brought to light in this book. The authors in fact adopt this technique, passing from theory to example, and vice versa, in a way which is both clear and comprehensible. Their examples of children's behavior have been most carefully selected, and I particularly like the use of various aspects of one example to illustrate different theoretical points. I also think it useful that the authors have included other interpretations of some Piagetian concepts, thus giving the reader an idea of Piaget's position in contemporary psychology.

In fact, although this well-written book is primarily destined for students, it is quite clear that it will enable many readers already well acquainted with Piaget's theory to explore his reasoning more deeply. It is not concerned with lengthy discussion or criticism, but provides, as it was intended to, a concise description and clear analysis of Piaget's thought and work.

Geneva, Switzerland

BÄRBEL INHELDER
Professor of
Developmental Psychology

iv

Preface

Since the early 1950s, Piaget's theory has dominated the field of intellectual development. From 1920 until his death in 1980, Piaget and his collaborators produced more worthwhile research and theory than any other individual or group of investigators in child psychology. The sheer volume of Piaget's output is staggering. He published more than forty full-length books and more than a hundred articles in the field of child psychology.

But numbers alone do not tell the story. Piaget captured the interest of modern psychologists and educators for several important reasons. First, he introduced a score of new and interesting problems which previously went unnoticed. For example, it was Piaget who discovered the profoundly complex problem of *conservation,* which has caught the imagination of many investigators. This problem taps one aspect of the child's ability to construct a reality which transcends the mere appearance of things. Second, Piaget's theories have reoriented current conceptions of the child's development. His ideas are novel, imaginative, and comprehensive. They have substantially supplanted the stimulus-response behaviorist theory as the most influential point of view in developmental psychology. And finally, of all theories of development, Piaget's is the one most securely founded upon the study of the child. None of the investigators whose theories have been used to explain the development of children—Freud, Lewin, Hull, Miller and Dollard, Skinner, Werner—has studied children as extensively as has Piaget. In fact, some of these figures—for example, Freud, Hull, Skinner—hardly studied children at all. Gesell did study children, but did not produce a viable theory. By contrast, for nearly sixty years Piaget observed, interviewed, and tested children of all ages, and this enormous set of empirical data is the foundation of his theory.

Clearly, then, persons interested in human development should at the least be familiar with Piaget's work. Unfortunately, this is no simple task. For the most part, Piaget is an extremely difficult writer: his ideas are novel and hard to assimilate; his style of writing is not the ultimate in lucidity; many of his theoretical terms sound strange to the ears of the professional psychologist or educator, and certainly to the novice; and his later contributions are stated in terms of symbolic logic and mathematics. These difficulties have several unfortunate consequences. One is that the job of learning about Piaget is very onerous indeed. The interested reader seems to require a text introducing Piaget's ideas before he or she is able to profit from the primary sources themselves.

We have written this book in the hope of assisting the beginning student of Piaget. It is a brief introduction to his basic ideas and findings concerning the child's intellectual development. We hope that the book will be useful to students, particularly undergraduates, in psychology, education, and allied fields. The book may be used as supplementary reading, in whole or in part, in courses dealing with child psychology, cognition, educational psychology, and so on. We hope, too, that the book may be read with profit by the general reader.

Despite the fact that the book is an introduction, and a brief one at that, we have tried to present the material in some depth. That is, we have assumed that the reader, although knowing little about psychology and Piaget, is intelligent and willing to work a bit to understand Piaget's ideas. Second, we have assumed that the reader should not be shielded from difficult aspects of Piaget's theory, like the use of symbolic logic.

Naturally, in a book of this type, we have had to be selective. No doubt readers familiar with Piaget will notice that we have omitted a number of important topics. For example, we do not describe the work on perception, or the research on concepts of geometry. We make no pretense at offering a comprehensive treatment of Piaget's work. Rather, we have tried to present, as lucidly as possible, Piaget's major theoretical notions concerning intellectual development, as well as some of the research on which they are based. Since the aim of this book is to present clearly the basics of Piaget's ideas, we have kept our own critique to a minimum. For the same reason, and also to avoid a *very* long book, we have not referred extensively to independent investigators' research on Piaget's ideas. So this book is neither a critique nor a review of the literature; it is an introduction to Piaget.

The aim of this third edition is to update the second. Since the writing of the second edition, Piaget and his collaborators produced new research and theory on a variety of topics, mainly concerning development and learning. It is quite remarkable that during the last ten years of his life—when he was in his seventies and early eighties—Piaget was engaged in a major expansion and even revision of his theory. In this edition, we outline these major changes and thereby complete our account of Piaget's theory. (For a detailed exposition of late developments in Piaget's theory, see Gallagher and Reid, 1981.) While introducing this new material, we have attempted to retain features that we think made the book valuable to many readers, namely, an exposition which is simple and clear and yet faithful to the depth of Piaget's ideas.

Chapter 1 begins with a brief biography of Piaget and outlines some of his basic ideas. Chapter 2 deals with his account of development in infancy. The focus is on an aspect of the theory which has not been sufficiently stressed, namely, the account of learning and motivation. Chapter 3 describes Piaget's early research and theory concerning the child from about 2 to 11 years of age. Among the topics covered are the development of symbolism, the child's methods of communication, and moral judgment. Chapter 4 presents Piaget's research on children from about 2 or 3 to 11 or 12 years of age and covers the classic work on classes, relations, number, and conservation, as well as newer research on functions, imagery, and memory. We include cross-cultural work, where pertinent. Chapter 5 discusses adolescent thought, describing Piaget's use of logic as a model for adolescent thought and his notion of adolescent competence. Chapter 6 presents a discussion of learning and development and covers materials from Piaget's last works, published during the period from the mid-1970s onward. It includes descriptions of his revised model of the equilibration process, the role of disturbances and disequilibria, the spiral of knowing, and possibility and necessity. We have followed this with an expanded discussion of the implications of Piaget's work for education. We hope that by the end of the book students will have some insight into Piaget's views and will appreciate the magnitude of his contribution.

Finally, we have employed several bibliographic conventions. If a book of Piaget's has been translated into English, we use its English title and publication date; otherwise, we use the French. If a book is frequently cited, we refer to it by its initials. Thus, for easy reference, *The Origins of Intelligence in Children* becomes *OI*.

H. P. G.
S. O.

Acknowledgments

The authors wish to thank the following publishers for permission to reprint in this book copyrighted materials by Piaget:

Adaptation Vitale et Psychologie de l'Intelligence: Selection Organique et Phénocopie (Paris: Hermann, 1974), Figure of the spiral of knowing, reprinted by permission of Hermann.

The Child's Conception of Number (with Alina Szeminska), translated by C. Gattegno and F. M. Hodgson (London: Routledge & Kegan Paul Ltd., 1952), pp. 45, 50, 75, 79, 82, 124–125, reprinted by permission of Routledge & Kegan Paul Ltd. and W. W. Norton & Co., Inc.

The Child's Conception of the World, translated by J. and A. Tomlinson (New York: Harcourt, Brace & World, Inc., 1929), pp. 258–259, 274, reprinted by permission of Routledge & Kegan Paul Ltd. and Humanities Press, Inc.

The Construction of Reality in the Child, translated by M. Cook (New York: Basic Books, Inc., Publishers, 1954), pp. 14, 25, 51, 76, 77, 79–80, reprinted by permission of Routledge & Kegan Paul Ltd. and Basic Books, Inc., Publishers.

The Early Growth of Logic in the Child, translated by E. A. Lunzer and D. Papert (London: Routledge & Kegan Paul Ltd., 1964), pp. 21, 102, 109, reprinted by permission of Routledge & Kegan Paul Ltd. and Harper & Row, Publishers.

"Equilibration and the Development of Logical Structures," in *Discussions on Child Development: The Fourth Meeting of the World Health Organization, Study Group on the Psychobiological Development of the Child,* edited by J. M. Tanner and B. Inhelder (London: Tavistock Publications Ltd., 1956), p. 102, reprinted by permission of the World Health Organization.

The Growth of Logical Thinking from Childhood to Adolescence, translated by A. Parsons and S. Seagrin (New York: Basic Books, Inc., Publishers, 1958), pp. 56, 60, 70–71, 75, 103, 116–17, 129, 130, reprinted by permission of Routledge & Kegan Paul Ltd. and Basic Books, Inc., Publishers.

Judgment and Reasoning in the Child, translated by M. Warden (New York: Harcourt, Brace & World, Inc., 1926), pp. 17–18, 87, 88, 123, reprinted by permission of Routledge & Kegan Paul Ltd. and Humanities Press, Inc.

The Language and Thought of the Child, translated by M. Gabain (London: Routledge & Kegan Paul Ltd., 1926), pp. 35, 37, 41, 126, 130, 149, reprinted by permission of Routledge & Kegan Paul Ltd. and Humanities Press, Inc.

The Moral Judgment of the Child, translated by M. Gabain (New York: Harcourt, Brace &

World, Inc., 1932), pp. 55, 60, 122, 126, 141, reprinted by permission of Routledge & Kegan Paul Ltd. and Crowell-Collier, Inc.

The Origins of Intelligence in Children, translated by M. Cook (New York: International University Press, 1952), reprinted by permission of Delachaux & Niestlé.

Play, Dreams, and Imitation in Childhood, translated by C. Gattegno and F. M. Hodgson (New York: W. W. Norton & Co., Inc., 1951, 1962), pp. 10, 30, 31, 46–47, 55–56, 63, 65, 96, 218, 222, 224, 225, 231, 232, by permission of Routledge & Kegan Paul Ltd. and W. W. Norton & Co., Inc.

The Psychology of Intelligence, translated by M. Percy and D. E. Berlyne (London: Routledge & Kegan Paul Ltd., 1950), pp. 6, 7, reprinted by permission of Routledge & Kegan Paul Ltd. and Humanities Press, Inc.

1

Biography and Basic Ideas

We shall begin by reviewing Jean Piaget's life to give the reader an idea of the influences affecting his work and of the wide scope of his activities; then we shall discuss in a preliminary way some basic ideas and themes that underlie his theory of intellectual development.

BIOGRAPHY[1]

Jean Piaget was born on August 9, 1896, in the small university town of Neuchâtel, Switzerland. His father was a historian who specialized in medieval literature, and his mother was a dynamic, intelligent, and religious woman. Piaget showed an early interest in nature; he enjoyed observing birds, fish, and animals in their natural habitat. At school, too, his leanings were toward the biological sciences. But his was no ordinary schoolboy enthusiasm: when he was only 10 years old, a natural history magazine published his first article, describing an albino sparrow seen in the

[1]Piaget has written short autobiographies in several volumes. One, although outdated, appears in English: J. Piaget, "Autobiography," in E. G. Boring et al., eds., *History of Psychology in Autobiography*, Vol. IV (Worcester, Mass.: Clark University Press, 1952), pp. 237–56. See also Chapter 1 in J. Piaget, *Insights and Illusions in Philosophy*, trans. W. Mays (New York: World Publishing Co., 1971).

park. Soon he was able to help the director of the natural history museum of Neuchâtel, where his task was to assist in the classification of the museum's zoology collection. At this time, he began to study molluscs and, from 15 to 18 years of age, published a series of articles on these shellfish. One of the papers, written when Piaget was only 15 years old, resulted in the offer of the post of curator of the mollusc collection at the Geneva natural history museum. Piaget had to decline the position to complete his high school studies.

As an adolescent he spent a vacation with his godfather, Samuel Cornut, a Swiss scholar, who was to have a considerable influence on his intellectual development. Cornut felt that Piaget's horizons were too restricted in the direction of the biological sciences and decided to introduce the young man to philosophy, particularly to the work of Bergson. Consequently, Piaget, who until then had given his main attention to the study of biology and the natural behavior of organisms, now turned his thoughts to other pursuits. His readings broadened to include philosophy, religion, and logic. Contact with these subjects led eventually to a special interest in epistemology, the branch of philosophy concerned with the study of knowledge. He became curious to discover the answers to some of the basic questions of the discipline: What is knowledge? How is it acquired? Can one gain an objective understanding of external reality, or is one's knowledge of the world colored and distorted by internal factors? Although fascinated by these issues, Piaget felt that their solution could not be provided solely by philosophy. In comparing the attributes of philosophy and science, Piaget's conclusion was that "an idea is only an idea, while a fact is only a fact" (*Insights and Illusions in Philosophy,* 1971b). In other words, he was convinced that the philosophical approach is too speculative, and the scientific approach is sometimes too factual. What is needed is a linkage between the two: an experimental philosophy, as it were.

We see, then, that during his adolescence Piaget concentrated on two major intellectual pursuits: biology and epistemology. There is, of course, a great gap between the two disciplines. One is concerned with life and the other with knowledge. One employs scientific methods and the other relies on speculation. Piaget began to wonder whether it might not be possible to bridge this gap between the two disciplines and to find some way of integrating his biological and epistemological interests. How could one investigate the very fascinating problems of knowledge, and at the same time utilize the scientific framework of biology?

Although interested in epistemological questions, Piaget put his major efforts into the study of biology. In 1916 he completed his undergraduate studies in natural sciences at the university of his hometown, Neuchâtel. Only two years later, at the age of 21, he submitted to the same

university his dissertation on the molluscs of the Valais region of Switzerland and received the degree of Doctor of Philosophy.

After finishing his formal studies, Piaget decided to explore psychology. He left Neuchâtel for Zurich to work in two psychological laboratories and at Bleuler's psychiatric clinic. He then discovered psychoanalysis and the ideas of Freud, Jung, and others and later published an article on the relations between psychoanalysis and child psychology. In 1919 he left Zurich for Paris, where he spent two years at the Sorbonne University, studying clinical psychology as well as logic, epistemology, and the philosophy of science. His encounter with philosophy once more convinced him that it is necessary to supplement pure speculation with the scientific approach.

It was during his stay in Paris that an opportunity arose which was to shape the direction of his future work. In 1920 he accepted a post with Dr. Theophile Simon in the Binet Laboratory in Paris. (With Alfred Binet, Simon had earlier constructed the first successful intelligence test.) Piaget's task was to develop a standardized French version of certain English reasoning tests. In a standardized test the wording of the questions and their order of presentation are precisely defined, and the examiner must not deviate from the preestablished procedure. The aim of a standardized test is to present each subject with the same problems so that the subsequent differences in performance can be attributed not to variations in the questions, but to differences in the subjects' intelligence (or other traits being measured).

At the outset, Piaget was not very enthusiastic about the work. Standardizing a test can be a very mechanical and tedious process. But then three major events occurred. First, although intelligence testing usually focuses on the child's ability to produce *correct* responses, Piaget felt that, on the contrary, the child's *incorrect* answers were far more fascinating. When questioning the children, Piaget found that the same wrong answers occurred frequently in children of about the same age. Moreover, there were different kinds of common wrong answers at different ages. Piaget puzzled on the meaning of these mistakes. He came to the conclusion that older children are not just "brighter" than younger ones; instead, the thought of younger children is *qualitatively different* from that of older ones. In other words, Piaget came to reject a quantitative definition of intelligence—a definition based on the number of correct responses on a test. The real problem of intelligence, Piaget felt, was to discover the different methods of thinking used by children of various ages.

Second, Piaget sought a different method for the study of intelligence. He immediately rejected the standardized test procedure. Such an approach, he felt, was too rigid: for example, it might lead to a considerable loss of information if the child did not understand the questions. Consequently, he sought a less structured method which would give him more freedom to question the child. His solution was to apply to the task his previous experience in clinical psychology: he modified psychiatric interview techniques to make them suitable for the study of children's thought. The new method was extremely flexible. It involved letting the child's answers (and not some preconceived plan) determine the course of questioning. If the child said something interesting, then it would immediately be pursued, without regard for a standardized procedure. The aim of this "clinical method" was to follow the child's own line of thought, without imposing any direction on it, to comprehend the underlying causes of the child's responses.

At about the same time as his work in the Binet Laboratory, Piaget was also studying abnormal children at the Salpetrière Hospital in Paris. He felt, like Freud, that knowledge of abnormal functioning might provide insight into the normal working of the mind. Piaget therefore applied the "clinical method" developed at the Binet Laboratory to his study of abnormal children. However, he found that the method was not adequate since abnormal children's verbal abilities were deficient. Consequently, for these children he added an important procedure: the child was required not only to answer questions, but also to manipulate certain materials. Unfortunately, Piaget did not immediately apply the supplemented clinical method—free verbal questioning plus materials for manipulation—to the testing of normal children. It was only after the exclusively verbal procedure proved inadequate that Piaget later made use of his experience at Salpetrière.

Third, while using the clinical method to study children's thought, Piaget was reading extensively in logic. It occurred to him that abstract logic might be relevant in several ways to children's thinking. He noticed, for instance, that children younger than about 11 years were unable to carry out certain elementary logical operations. The possibility of extensively investigating this apparent deficiency immediately presented itself. Also, Piaget felt that thought processes form an integrated structure (not a conglomeration of isolated units) whose basic properties can be described in logical terms. For example, the logical operations involved in deduction seemed to correspond to certain mental structures in older children. He set himself the goal of discovering how closely thought approximates logic. This was a distinctive conception of the psychology of intelligence.

The years at the Binet Laboratory were very fruitful. Piaget published several accounts of his psychological research on children. But, more important, the stay in Paris taught Piaget that the problem of intelligence must be defined in terms of discovering children's ways of thinking, that the clinical method is useful for the study of thought, and that logic, rather than the imprecise natural language, might be an efficient way of describing thought. Furthermore, Piaget had now discovered a way in which he might integrate his biological and epistemological interests. As he saw it, the first step was to pursue the psychology of human intelligence. As a psychologist, he could study the individual's knowledge of the world, his attempts to comprehend reality. This kind of psychology, in other words, would be directed at epistemological issues. Also, it would be biologically oriented. For Piaget, this meant several things. First, psychological theory might make use of biological concepts. For instance, intelligence could be viewed in terms of an organism's adaptation to its environment. Second, psychology might focus on the process of intellectual growth in the individual. He believed that a full understanding of human knowledge could be gained only through the study of its formation and evolution in childhood. How could one comprehend the final product without knowing how it developed? For these reasons, then, Piaget decided to engage first in the psychological study of the child's understanding of reality. His initial intention was to spend a few years in experimental studies of the child's intelligence and then turn to a second project, namely, the application of his psychological discoveries to the theoretical problems of epistemology. He felt that he could clarify epistemological issues only after he had developed an understanding of the individual's cognitive growth. As we shall see, Piaget spent more than a "few years" at his first task. It was only after some thirty years of psychological study that Piaget was able to turn his attention to theoretical questions of epistemology.

In 1921, the director of the Jean-Jacques Rousseau Institute in Geneva, Edouard Claparède, who had been impressed by Piaget's early articles on children, offered him the post of director of research at the Institute. Piaget accepted the offer, which gave him an excellent opportunity to carry on his study of child thought. The outcome of his research was a series of articles and the publication, from 1923 to 1932, of his first five books on children. The first one, *Language and Thought in the Child* (1926b), provides naturalistic and experimental observations on the child's use of language. Piaget found, for instance, that the young child's speech is substantially egocentric and that this tendency decreases gradually as the child grows older. *Judgment and Reasoning in the Child* (1926a) deals with the changes in certain types of reasoning from early to late childhood. *The Child's Conception of the World* (1929) uses the exclusively verbal clinical method to provide data on how the child views the surrounding world, and on what he believes to be the origins of dreams, of trees, the sun, and the moon. In *The Child's Conception of Physical Causality* (1960a), Piaget describes the child's ideas on the causes of certain natural phenomena, such as the movement of the clouds and of rivers, the problem of shadows, or the displacement of water when an object is immersed. Finally, *The Moral Judgment of the Child* (1932) provides information on the development of moral behavior and judgment. Here Piaget maintains that children show two types of moral judgment: the young child holds to a predominantly authoritarian moral code, whereas the older child develops a morality of social concern and cooperation.

Contact with psychoanalysis is evident in the early works: Piaget's theories make use of Freudian ideas and are sometimes even stated in Freudian terms. The books also give a brief indication of what Piaget was later to expand upon: a view of intellectual development as consisting of a series of stages. Through his research, Piaget was becoming increasingly aware of the differences between the child's and the adult's thought processes. He realized that the child is not merely a miniature replica of the adult: not only does the child think less efficiently than the adult, but he also thinks differently. Thus, Piaget became convinced that it was necessary to conceive of intellectual development in terms of an evolution through qualitatively different stages of thought.

Piaget also attempted to discover the causes of this intellectual evolution. His first interpretation was that intellectual development resulted particularly from social factors, like language and contact with parents and peers. Later, after his study of infancy, where the role of language is negligible but where on the contrary the child's own activity is paramount, he changed his interpretation of the nature of intellectual development: he deemphasized the influence of social factors and stressed action as the source of thought.

Much to Piaget's astonishment, the first five books, which he himself calls his ''adolescent'' works, gained him considerable fame, particularly among child psychologists. Piaget, who had never in his life passed an examination in psychology, suddenly became an authority on the subject. The stir caused by the books disturbed him somewhat since he considered them to be only preliminary and tentative, and not an expression of his definitive views on the nature of intelligence. He was well aware of the books' deficiencies. Nevertheless, he agreed to publish the volumes, mainly because he felt they might lead others to further research eventually resulting in a fuller understanding of child thought.

In the United States, the books were at first received enthusiastically, and during the 1920s and 1930s, Piaget's work was highly regarded in this country. Then followed a period, lasting until the middle 1950s, when his views, as expressed in the early books, came under much criticism. Some investigators felt that Piaget's findings could not be replicated. But with the publication in the early 1950s of English translations of several of Piaget's later books, interest in his work revived.

During the period from 1920 to 1930, Piaget's time was fully occupied. He performed a great deal of research and at the same time also taught various courses in psychology, sociology, and scientific thought at Geneva and Neuchâtel. His three children were born during these years: a daughter in 1925, a second daughter in 1927, and a son in 1931. Piaget and his wife, one of his former students, became close observers of their children's behavior. The results of their study, which covered the "senso-rimotor period" from birth until about the age of 2, were published in two volumes: *The Origins of Intelligence in Children* (1952c) and *The Construction of Reality in the Child* (1954). Piaget's study of infancy convinced him that thought derived from the child's action, and not from his language. This increased emphasis on action led Piaget to modify his testing technique for older children. He remembered his past experience at the Salpetrière Hospital and his solution to the difficulties encountered in trying to apply an exclusively verbal method to abnormal children. Consequently, he made the manipulation of concrete materials an essential aspect of the clinical method for children of all ages. The emphasis was no longer on language alone, but on manipulation supplemented by language.

From 1929 to 1939 Piaget's professional life became even more active. He was appointed professor of history of scientific thought at Geneva University. He became assistant director, and shortly afterward co-director, of the Jean-Jacques Rousseau Institute, which he helped to reorganize when it became attached to Geneva University. He taught experimental psychology at Lausanne University. Also, Piaget became involved in international affairs and accepted the chairmanship of the International Bureau of Education, later to become affiliated with UNESCO.

Piaget's experiences led to several changes in his thinking. The studies of infancy influenced him to modify his techniques of research, and to place greater emphasis on the role of the child's activity in the formation of thought. Also, his teaching opened up new areas for research and experiment. The course on the history of scientific thought directed him toward the study of the child's understanding of certain scientific notions. With two important collaborators, Bärbel Inhelder and Alina Szeminska, he set out to explore this field, and in 1941 published two books on their research. The first, written with B. Inhelder was *The Child's Construction of Quantities* (1974). It shows how the child gradually comes to recognize that certain physical attributes of an object, like its substance or weight, do not vary when the object merely changes shape. Surprisingly, young children fail to *conserve* these invariants. The second book, written with A. Szeminska was *The Child's Conception of Number* (1952). Here Piaget describes the evolution of the child's efforts to master the notion of number.

The next book, published in 1942, *Classes, Relations, et Nombres*, deals with the correspondence between certain operations of formal logic and mental operations. Piaget uses logic to describe the mental operations available to the child from 7 to 11 in the stage of "concrete operations." The book is thus a fulfillment of Piaget's early intention at the Binet Laboratory in Paris to use a formal language for psychological purposes.

Piaget then became interested in the perceptual research of the "Gestalt" psychologists. His lack of agreement with some of their theories, however, led him and his collaborators to a lengthy series of experiments into the nature of perception. At first Piaget replicated the experiments of the Gestalt psychologists. Later his studies were extended to cover perception not only as an isolated process, but also its relation to intelligence. For some twenty years, from 1943 onward, Piaget and his associates produced a number of articles and monographs on perception. The culmination was the publication in 1961 of his book, *The Mechanisms of Perception* (1969), which describes perceptual structures and processes and relates them to intellectual ones.

In the early 1940s, Albert Einstein suggested to Piaget that it might be of interest to epistemology if he were to investigate the child's understanding of time, velocity, and movement. Piaget followed the suggestion and in 1946 published two books on these matters: *The Child's Conception of Time* (1970b) and *The Child's Conception of Movement and Speed* (1970a). In the same year, 1946, Piaget also published his book on symbolic thought, *Play, Dreams, and Imitation* (1951), which contains observations on his own children, from 2 to 4 years of age.

After the Second World War, appreciation of Piaget's work began to spread throughout the world. He received honorary degrees from several universities, including Harvard, the Sorbonne in Paris, Brussels, and the University of Brazil. In the United States, however, Piaget was honored but not fully understood; only his first five books had been translated. During the 1940s, he continued his activities in the International Bureau of Education and was appointed head of the Swiss delegation to UNESCO. In 1947 Piaget published a small volume entitled *The Psychology of Intelligence* (1950b). The book is a collection of lectures Piaget had given in 1942 to the College de France in Paris and sets out, for the first time at any length, an overview of Piaget's theory of mental development.

During this time, Piaget continued his research into various aspects of cognition. From the experiments on perception grew the study of two closely allied fields: the child's understanding of space and of geometry. In collaboration with Inhelder and Szeminska, he published in 1948 *The Child's Conception of Space* (1956) and *The Child's Conception of Geometry* (1960). In 1949 Piaget wrote *Traité de Logique,* a book dealing with the basic operations involved in logic. The book is the first full summary of his logical system: it expands upon the logical models already used in previous research and introduces additional logical models which he was later to apply to adolescent thought.

From about 1920 to 1950, Piaget had been engaged in experimental work with children in an attempt to understand the evolution of human intelligence. Now he felt prepared to apply the results of his psychological research to the epistemological problems which had originally motivated his interest in psychology. In 1950 he published a three-volume series on "genetic epistemology" entitled *Introduction à l'Epistémologie Génétique* (1950a). The books are a synthesis of his thinking on various aspects of knowledge, including mathematics, physics, psychology, sociology, biology, and logic. Piaget analyzes these facets of knowledge in terms of the relation between the individual and his environment—between the knower and the known. He tries to determine whether this relationship is affected by the type of knowledge involved, for instance, whether mathematical knowledge involves a different kind of interaction with the environment from that of physical knowledge. Piaget also draws a parallel between the historical and individual development of knowledge, and he finds that the evolution of individual thought sometimes follows the same progression as the history of scientific thought.

Next Piaget turned to the study of chance and the elementary concepts of probability. In 1951, he and Inhelder published a book entitled *The Origin of the Idea of Chance in the Child* (1975), which deals with the child's understanding of random events in his environment. In 1952 Piaget was appointed Professor of Genetic Psychology at the University of Paris (Sorbonne), where he remained until 1962. At the same time he continued to teach at Geneva University and to head the Jean-Jacques Rousseau Institute. He also pursued his research into both perception and logical thought. In 1952 he published a book called *Essai sur les Transformations des Opérations Logiques* (1952b), dealing with propositional logic and various logical structures, like the group and lattice, which he used as models for adolescent and adult thought. After having studied the period of early and middle childhood, Piaget turned to the next phase of intellectual development: the thought of the adolescent and the adult. In 1955 Piaget and Inhelder published a book on this subject, *The Growth of Logical Thinking from Childhood to Adolescence* (1958), which compared, again in logical terms, the thought processes of the adolescent with those of the younger child.

The year 1956 was important for Piaget, for he was able to initiate a project that he had been contemplating for some time. With his broad scope of interests, including biology, zoology, logic, mathematics, psychology, philosophy, and epistemology, Piaget had always dreamed of the possibility of an interdisciplinary approach to basic problems of cognition. The idea had initially encountered a certain amount of skepticism, but Piaget finally managed to establish an institution where such interdisciplinary cooperation was possible. An international Center for Genetic Epistemology was created within the Faculty of Science of Geneva University. The aim of the Center was to gather together each year a number of eminent scholars in various fields—biologists, psychologists, mathematicians, and others—who would combine their efforts to study a given problem. Each person would treat the problem from the point of view of his specialty, but the research was to be coordinated through regular discussions. At the end of the year, a symposium would be held, where the researchers' conclusions would be discussed. The deliberations of each symposium would be published in a series of monographs, entitled *Studies in Genetic Epistemology*. Over the past thirty years, approximately forty of these volumes have already been published, and have dealt with a variety of subjects such as the notion of causality, the learning processes, and mathematical thinking.

In 1959 Piaget published with Inhelder *The Early Growth of Logic in the Child* (1964). The book again uses logical models to describe the mental operations of the child from 7 to 11 years. It treats in particular the child's method of classifying and of ordering objects. In 1964 a small book containing six short essays on various psychological topics was published (*Six Psychological Studies,* 1967) and the following year, 1965, Piaget published *Insights and Illusions of Philosophy* (1971b). In this book he discusses the essential differences between philosophy, which leads to subjective "wisdom," and science, which leads to objective knowledge. He also explains why he turned away from his early preference for the former toward the latter. In the same year, 1965, he also published a book of four sociological studies entitled *Etudes Sociologiques,* which is a collection of some of the lectures he had given in his courses on sociology.

The titles of Piaget's books indicate that the contents deal in general with highly specialized aspects of thinking or cognition. Each book treats a particular topic, like geometry or number, in a similar manner. That is, the notion is studied from its origins in the child to the point, usually in late childhood or adolescence, where it reaches a mature status. Although such an approach is of interest to psychologists and educators, difficulties are presented for the person who wishes only to get a general understanding of Piaget's overall system. In 1966, therefore, recognizing the need for a short introductory work on his system, Piaget and Inhelder published a short book entitled *The Psychology of the Child* (1969), which was intended for the general public. The book gives a brief summary of Piaget's theory of intellectual development and also deals with related matters such as perception. In the same year, 1966, these two authors also published a book on mental imagery, *Mental Imagery in the Child* (1971), which describes the development of mental images and relates it to the growth of intelligence. In 1967 he published *Biology and Knowledge* (1971a), which deals with the relations between biological factors and the cognitive processes. He then turned his interests in another direction and in 1968 with Inhelder published *Memory and Intelligence* (1973). In this book, Piaget introduces a new approach to the study of memory: he examines the relations between memory and the development of intellectual functioning. He finds, for example, that memory does not always deteriorate over time; paradoxically, memory can improve as a result of the development of certain related intellectual skills. Another book published in 1968, *Structuralism* (1970d), reflects Piaget's continuing interest in the application of structural models to many different disciplines, and in particular to the operations of intelligence.

In the 1960s and 1970s Piaget's fame continued to spread, and his books were translated into many languages. In America, where his work had at first been received with a certain amount of skepticism, he was now recognized as a leader in his field. In 1969 he was honored by the American Psychological Association. In 1971, at the age of 75, Piaget retired as director of the Rousseau Institute, although he still actively pursued his research activities as head of the Center for Genetic Epistemology. He continued to be prolific in his writings and publications. A great many new books and articles, as well as reeditions of earlier works, were published in the 1970s. Some of the major titles include two books dealing with education, *Science of Education and the Psychology of the Child* (1970c) and *To Understand Is to Invent: The Future of Education* (1973b) and two books on genetic psychology, *Psychology and Epistemology: Towards a Theory of Knowledge* (1972b) and *The Child and Reality: Problems of Genetic Psychology* (1973a). In *Adaptation Vitale et Psychologie de l'Intelligence: Selection Organique et Phénocopie* (1974a), Piaget returned to his early interest in biology and tried to relate a biological model of development to the intellectual processes.

Piaget also conducted studies with Garcia into the notion of causality (*Understanding Causality,* 1974). Stemming from this research has been Piaget's work on the child's growing awareness of his actions. Studies in this area have been published in three books, *The Grasp of Consciousness: Action and Concept in the Young Child* (1976b), *Réussir et Comprendre* (1974b), and *Le Comportement, Moteur de l'Evolution* (1976a). At the end of his life, Piaget published several important books dealing with issues of development and learning. These include *The Equilibration of Cognitive Structures* (1985), *Success and Understanding* (1978), *Experiments in Contradiction* (1981a), and *Le Possible et le Nécessaire* (1981b, 1983).

The evolution of Piaget's interests is clearly illustrated by the titles and contents of his books and other publications. From his early work in biology, particularly the study of molluscs, he gradually turned to the psychological development of the child. His intention was to find a link between the biological study of life and the philosophical study of knowledge. His first few books on children's thought were exploratory, setting forth his preliminary theory of intellectual development. Later, however, he began to state his theories in terms of a formal language: logic. The subject matter of his books also began to change; he became attracted to the study of the child's understanding of scientific and mathematical notions, as well as to other aspects of the cognitive processes: perception, mental imagery, memory, consciousness. Once he had achieved a good measure of understanding of the child's intellectual processes, Piaget then wished to place his psychological theories within a larger framework. He returned, after more than forty years of psychological research, to his original interests—

theoretical problems in epistemology and biology—and attempted to view the development of intelligence as the link between the two. Toward the end of his life, Piaget became involved in the problem of the relations among reality, necessity, and possibility and in the issues of development and learning. It is quite remarkable that, into his eighties, Piaget pursued his professional work with great vigor. He died on September 16, 1980.

BASIC IDEAS

In the present section, we will introduce several basic ideas that have shaped Piaget's approach to the study of intellectual development. A scientist usually employs a theoretical framework to guide experimentation and theorizing. The framework is not a detailed theory but a point of view or a set of attitudes which orients the scientist's activities. A psychologist, for example, may be basically committed both to Freudian ideas and to the personality test approach, which are then likely to give direction to research and analysis. For example, this framework may influence the scientist to choose to study the familial causes of neurosis rather than possible physical bases of the disorder. Further, this orientation might lead the scientist to investigate the matter by giving paper-and-pencil tests, which might produce results different from those which could be obtained by the direct observation of the child in the home. This is not to deny, of course, that scientists do change their opinions as a result of conflicting research evidence. It is nevertheless true that orienting attitudes can be influential; the scientist does not begin work without preconceptions, and these then organize the interpretation of research data.[2]

Piaget's orienting attitudes, stated quite explicitly, are concerned with the nature of intelligence and with its structure and functions.

Intelligence

First, how does Piaget define the nature of intelligence? The reader should be aware that Piaget had almost complete freedom in this regard. Previous to the 1920s, when he began his investigations, there had been little research or theorizing on intelligence. The mental testing approach was in evidence, as exemplified by the Binet-Simon IQ test, and there were also scattered experimental investigations of intellectual processes like memory in the adult. However, neither of these approaches had been developed extensively, and psychologists had hardly agreed, and do not concur even today, on the proper subject matter for the psychology of in-

---

[2]For a discussion of these and related matters, see T. S. Kuhn, *The Structure of Scientific Revolutions,* 2nd ed. (Chicago: University of Chicago Press, 1970).

telligence.[3] Does intelligence refer to rote memory, to creativity, to IQ test performance, to the child's reasoning, or to other matters? Because Piaget began his studies during a pioneering era, he was free to conceive of intelligence in terms of his unique perspective. He was careful not to begin by proposing too rigid or precise a definition of intelligence. Piaget did not want to fall into the trap of too narrowly circumscribing the subject matter when so little was known about it. To lay down an overly restrictive definition at the outset would have been to curtail investigation and impede discovery. In fact, the major aim of Piaget's research was to discover what actually constitutes intelligence.

Desiring to avoid premature restrictions, Piaget offered several definitions of intelligence, all couched in general terms. These definitions reflect Piaget's biological orientation. For example, "intelligence is a particular instance of biological adaptation . . ." (*Origins of Intelligence,* pp. 3-4). This states quite clearly that human intelligence is one kind of biological achievement, which allows the individual to interact effectively with the environment at a psychological level. Another definition states that intelligence "is the form of equilibrium towards which the successive adaptations and exchanges between the organism and his environment are directed" (*Psychology of Intelligence,* p. 6). The use of the term "equilibrium," borrowed from physics, suggests a balance, a harmonious adjustment between at least two factors—in this case between the person or his cognitive structures and his environment. Although the balance may be disturbed, the individual can perform actions to restore it. Intelligence is the "instrument" which enables the individual to achieve this equilibrium or to adapt by means of certain actions carried out on the environment. The definition also implies that equilibrium is not immediately achieved: as the child develops, the type of actions that he is able to carry out on the environment will change and so, too, will the resulting equilibrium. Thus, for Piaget, there is no single and final intelligence, but rather a succession of intellectual stages. It is of special interest to the psychologist to study the evolution of attempts at equilibrium and the dynamic processes underlying it. Piaget's primary goal, then, could be defined as the study of children's gradual attainment of intellectual structures which allow for increasingly effective interactions with the environment.

Another definition stresses that intelligence is "a system of living and acting operations" (*Psychology of Intelligence,* 1950b, p. 7). Piaget is interested in mental activity, in what the individual *does* in his interaction with

[3]In this connection, it is interesting to compare two sources. One is a 1921 symposium in which leading psychologists attempted, with considerable difficulty, to define intelligence: L. E. Tyler, ed., *Intelligence: Some Recurring Issues* (New York: Van Nostrand Reinhold Company, 1969). A second is a similar symposium, held in 1974: L. B. Resnick, ed., *The Nature of Intelligence* (Hillsdale, N.J.: L. Erlbaum Associates, 1976). How much progress in defining intelligence has been made in the past fifty years?

the world. Piaget believes that knowledge is not given to a passive observer; rather, knowledge of reality must be discovered and constructed by the activity of the child. As we shall see later, this position is at odds with the behaviorist view which for a long time dominated American psychology.

Finally, Piaget's definition of intelligence involves intellectual competence. He is interested in the individual's optimum level of functioning at his current developmental stage. For Piaget, intelligence does not necessarily refer to the individual's ordinary or habitual activities, but to the best that he can do. This competence may of course be obscured by all kinds of conditions, both temporary and long-lasting—for example, fatigue, boredom, illness. Factors like these may produce *performance* that falls short of possible *competence*. While it is important to understand how and why this happens, Piaget's main interest is in what the individual *can* do, whether or not this is what he ordinarily does.

Thus far, we have seen that intelligence involves biological adaptation, equilibrium between the individual and the environment, gradual evolution, mental activity, and competence. These definitions are intentionally quite general. It is also instructive to take note of what the definitions do *not* stress. They do not emphasize individual differences in intelligence. While such an emphasis would be quite consonant with a biological approach, Piaget is not concerned with whether one person is more intelligent or more clever than another, or why. Piaget, of course, recognizes that differences in intellectual ability do exist, but he is not particularly interested in their analysis; instead, he seeks to abstract from the various idiosyncratic manifestations of behavior a description of the general form of thought. Thus, for Piaget, the issue is not why one baby starts to talk at 18 months and another at 22 months; the issue is rather what words mean to both babies once they do talk. Similarly, for Piaget, the question is not why one child can remember the names of twenty-four states while another child remembers twenty-eight; it is rather what mental processes allow each child to remember whatever he does. So Piaget is less concerned with explaining intellectual differences than understanding the mental processes which we all share.

It is important to note that the definitions place little emphasis on the emotions. Piaget, of course, recognizes that the emotions influence thought, and in fact, he repeatedly states that no act of intelligence is complete without emotions. They represent the energetic or motivational aspect of intellectual activity. Nevertheless, Piaget's empirical investigations and detailed theories substantially ignore the emotions in favor of the structure of intellect.

Piaget has chosen one of several available strategies with which to investigate the psychology of intelligence. He deemphasizes individual differences and the effects of emotions on thought and, instead, focuses on the optimum level of functioning. Many psychologists, particularly British and American, have concentrated on individual differences by means of the test approach to investigate intellectual activity. Others have attempted from the outset to consider the influence of the emotions, especially anxiety, on intellectual performance. Which strategy is best? The answer seems to be that all are of interest. All view the problem of intelligence from different angles and deal with somewhat different issues. Unable to study everything, the scientist usually settles on one approach to accomplish anything at all. As we shall see in the pages that follow, Piaget's approach seems to have amply demonstrated its merits.

In addition to proposing general definitions, Piaget has structured the psychology of intelligence by the selection of the particular subject matter he has investigated. As we saw in the biographical review, Piaget's early works were concerned with such matters as verbal communication and moral judgment. With the passage of time Piaget has come to stress the child's understanding of various scientific and mathematical ideas like velocity and one-to-one correspondence. To understand Piaget's conception of intelligence, therefore, we must not only consider his definitions, but the nature of his research activities. The latter, especially in recent years, reveal rather unique scientific and epistemological concerns.

In conclusion, we have seen how Piaget's two major interests—biology and epistemology—have shaped his approach to the psychology of intelligence. The biological concern resulted in definitions of intelligence in general terms of growth, stages, adaptation, equilibrium, and similar factors. The epistemological focus has resulted in the empirical investigation of the child's understanding of space, time, causality, and similar notions. Piaget looks at intelligence in terms of content, structure, and function. We will consider aspects of these in the following sections.

Content

One simple aspect of thought is its manifest content. This refers to what the individual is thinking about, what interests him at the moment, or the terms in which he contemplates a given problem. For instance, when asked what makes a car go, the mechanic gives an answer in terms of the explosion of gas, the movement of pistons, the transfer of power from one point to another. These statements reflect the contents of his thought. If a young child were posed the same question, the response would be quite different. Ignorant of the workings of the motor, he might suppose that the car's movement results from all the horses inside. Obviously, the content of his thought is quite different from that of the adult.

During the early portion of his career, Piaget's research focused on the contents of the child's thought. *The Child's Conception of the World* and *The Child's Conception of Physical Causality*, both written in the 1920s, paid particular attention to the child's views of the physical world. The clinical method was used to obtain the child's answers to such questions as: Where do shadows come from? What causes rivers to flow or the clouds to move? Despite these initial investigations, Piaget felt that the study of content was only a minor goal for the psychology of intelligence. While descriptions of content may have some interest, they do not get at the heart of the matter; they do not explain why thought takes the form it does. For Piaget, therefore, the primary goal of the psychology of intelligence is not the mere description of the content of thought but the understanding of basic processes underlying and determining the content. Piaget has therefore devoted the greater part of his career in psychology to the study of the structures and functions of intelligence.

Specific Heredity

It should come as no surprise that Piaget's theoretical framework deals with the role of biological factors in the development of intelligence. These factors operate in several ways: one of them is defined as the *hereditary transmission of physical structures,* or *specific heredity.* Different species are, of course, endowed by heredity with different physical structures. The nervous system, for example, varies considerably from worm to human, and the effects of this variation are obvious. The inherited physical structures both permit certain intellectual achievements and prohibit others. The eye is one example of such a structure. Gibson (1966) points out that predatory animals are generally endowed by heredity with frontal eyes which allow them to see clearly what is ahead and therefore what can be pounced upon. By contrast, preyed-upon animals are generally endowed by heredity with lateral eyes which allow wide peripheral vision so that potential enemies can be identified. Indeed, the rabbit can even see *behind* its own head. The physical structure of the organism quite literally determines its basic view of the world.

Another form of specific heredity is the *automatic behavioral reaction.* For example, members of many species possess various *reflexes* from birth. When a specified event in the environment (a *stimulus*) occurs, the organism automatically responds with a particular behavior. No learning or training or other experience with the environment is usually necessary for the reflex response to occur. Moreover, all members of the species, unless they are in some way defective, possess the reflex. The basis for this automatic behavior is an inherited physical mechanism. When the stimulus occurs it activates this mechanism which produces the response. One example of automatic behavior is the sucking reflex, which is necessary for survival. When any object (the stimulus) touches an infant's lips, the automatic response is to suck. The newborn does not need to be taught to make an elementary sucking response. A further example is the ability to cry.

The newborn's physical structure is such that when hungry he automatically signals discomfort with a wail. Often the reflexes are adaptive: they help the organism in its interaction with the environment.

Piaget feels that in the case of human intelligence, reflexes and other automatic patterns of behavior play only a minor role. It is only the infant, and more specifically the newborn, whose behavior is heavily dependent on the elementary behavioral reactions of the type described. Piaget's research has shown that after the first few days of life, the reflexes are modified by the infant's experience and are transformed into a new type of mechanism—the psychological structure—which is not directly and simply provided by heredity. As we shall see, psychological structures form the basis for intellectual activity and are the product of a complex interaction between biological and experiential factors.

A third aspect of specific heredity is physical maturation. The genetic code provides the basis for the growth of physical structures along certain paths. For example, as the child grows older, the brain grows larger, and the muscles of the legs become stronger. Such physical maturation is often associated with various psychological activities: as the brain grows, speech emerges; as the leg muscles strengthen, permitting greater mobility, the child expands his exploration of the world. Maturation alone is not sufficient to cause the development of these and other activities, but appears to be necessary for many, if not all, of them. We shall see shortly that, in Piaget's view, experience and other factors are also necessary.

General Heredity

We have seen that specific heredity affects intelligence in three ways: (1) inherited physical structures set broad limits on intellectual functioning, (2) inherited behavioral reactions have an influence during the first few days of human life but afterward are extensively modified as the infant interacts with his environment, and (3) the maturation of physical structures may have psychological correlates. Piaget's theoretical framework postulates that biological factors affect intelligence in a fourth way: all species inherit two basic tendencies or "invariant functions": *organization* and *adaptation*. This is general heredity.

Let us first consider organization. This term refers to the tendency for all species to systematize or organize their processes into coherent systems which may be either physical or psychological. In the former case, fish possess a number of structures which allow functioning in the water, for example, gills, a particular circulatory system, and temperature mechanisms. All these structures interact and are coordinated into an efficient system. This coordination is the result of the organization tendency. It should be emphasized that organization refers not to gills or the circulatory structure in particular, but to the tendency observed in all life to integrate their structures into a composite system (or higher-order structure).

At a psychological level, too, the tendency to organize is present. In his interaction with the world, the individual tends to integrate his psychological structures into coherent systems. For example, the very young infant has available the separate behavioral structures of either looking at objects or of grasping them. He does not initially combine the two. After a period of development, he organizes these two separate structures into a higher-order structure which enables him to grasp something while looking at it. Organization, then, is the tendency common to all forms of life to integrate structures, both physical and psychological, into higher-order systems or structures.

The second general principle of functioning is *adaptation*. All organisms are born with a tendency to adapt to the environment. The ways in which adaptation occurs differ from species to species, from individual to individual within a species, or from stage to stage within any one individual. Nevertheless, the tendency to adapt in some way or another is an invariant function and therefore considered an aspect of biology. Adaptation may be considered in terms of two complementary processes: *assimilation* and *accommodation*.

We will illustrate these processes first by means of a simple physiological example, namely, digestion. When a person eats something his digestive system reacts to the substances incorporated. To deal with the foreign substance, the muscles of the stomach contract in various ways, certain organs release acids, and so on. Putting the matter in general terms, we may say that the person's physical structures (the stomach and related organs) *accommodate* to the environmental event (the food). In other words, the process of accommodation describes the individual's tendency to change in response to environmental demands. The functional invariant of *assimilation* is the complementary process by which the individual deals with an environmental event in terms of current structures. In the case of digestion, the acids transform the food into a form which the body can use. Thus the individual not only modifies structures in reaction to external demands (accommodation), he also uses his structures to incorporate elements of the external world (assimilation).

For Piaget, intellectual adaptation is also an interaction, or an exchange, between a person and his environment and involves the same two processes—assimilation and accommodation—as are found in biology. On the one hand, the person incorporates or assimilates features of external reality into his own psychological structures; on the other hand, he modifies or accommodates his psychological structures to meet the pressures of the environment. Consider an example of adaptation in infancy. Suppose an infant of 4 months is presented with a rattle. He has never before had the opportunity to play with rattles or similar toys. The rattle, then, is a feature of the environment to which he needs to adapt. His subsequent behavior reveals the tendencies of assimilation and accommodation. The infant tries to grasp the rattle. To do this successfully he must accommodate in more ways than are immediately apparent. First, he must accommodate his visual activities to perceive the rattle correctly, for example, by locating it in space. Then he must reach out, adjusting his arm movements to the distance between himself and the rattle. In grasping the rattle, he must mold his fingers to its shape; in lifting the rattle he must accommodate his muscular exertion to its weight. In sum, the grasping of the rattle involves a series of acts of accommodation, or modifications of the infant's behavioral structures, to suit the demands of the environment.

At the same time, grasping the rattle also involves assimilation. In the past the infant has already grasped things; for him, grasping is a well-formed structure of behavior. When he sees the rattle for the first time, he tries to deal with the novel object by incorporating it into a habitual pattern of behavior. In a sense he tries to transform the novel object to something with which he is familiar, namely, a thing to be grasped. We can say, therefore, that he assimilates the object into his framework and thereby assigns the object a "meaning."

Adaptation, then, is a basic tendency of the organism and consists of the two processes of assimilation and accommodation. How do the two relate to one another? First, it is clear that they are complementary processes. Assimilation involves the person's dealing with the environment in terms of his structures, while accommodation involves the transformation of his structures in response to the environment. Moreover, the processes are simultaneously present in every act. When the infant grasps the rattle, his fingers accommodate to its shape; at the same time he is assimilating the rattle into his framework, the grasping structure.

In sum, Piaget postulates that there are two general principles of functioning which affect intelligence: *organization* and *adaptation* (assimilation and accommodation). These biological factors, aspects of general heredity, are common to all species. While organization and adaptation are inherited, they are not structures (like reflexes) but *tendencies*. The particular ways in which an organism adapts and organizes its processes depend also on its environment and its learning history. In Piaget's view, human beings inherit few particular intellectual reactions; rather, they inherit a tendency to organize their intellectual processes and to develop particular adaptations to their environment.

Psychological Structures

We have seen that the individual tends to organize his behavior and thought and to adapt to the environment. These tendencies result in a number of psychological structures which take different forms at different ages. The child progresses through a series of stages, each characterized by different psychological structures, before attaining adult intelligence. From birth to about 2 years, the infant is unable to think and can only perform overt action. For example, if a toy falls apart he cannot first think how it might best be put together again; instead, he might immediately act on the toy and try to reassemble it. His activities, however, are not random, but display order and coherence. Almost immediately after birth the infant shows organized behavior. As we have seen, some of these patterns of action, like the reflex, are due mainly to hereditary factors. However, specific heredity cannot explain all the orderliness in the infant's behavior. For example, the 2-month-old infant usually sucks his thumb or a finger. When put in the crib he regularly brings his hand to the mouth in a relatively quick and efficient way. In the common language we would probably say that the infant has acquired the "habit" of thumb-sucking. The word "habit" implies a regularity, a coherence, in the infant's actions. It is clear that thumb-sucking is not based entirely on inherited physical structures. While there is a reflex to suck any object touching the lips, there is no innate tendency to bring the hand to the mouth; this activity must be learned. In Piaget's theory, such an organized pattern of behavior is termed a *scheme*.[4] The concept of scheme is used in a very broad way. It can refer to the reflexes and other kinds of innate behavior already discussed. It is in this way that Piaget speaks of the "sucking scheme." But the vast majority of schemes are not innate; instead, they are in some way based on experience, as in the case of the thumb-sucking scheme.

Thus far we have spoken of the scheme only as a pattern of behavior, or as an action which displays coherence and order. However, there are a number of additional aspects of the scheme. First, it involves activity on the part of the child; the concept is used to describe things he *does*. Most often, use of the term in this way presents no difficulties. Occasionally, however, scheme is used to describe actions which are not immediately obvious. For example, Piaget speaks of the "looking scheme." The use of "scheme" here is quite deliberate since he means to imply that vision is an active process; the child's eyes move as they actively *search* the environment. Second, scheme refers to the basic structure underlying the child's overt actions. Scheme is used to designate the essence of the child's behavior. Let us take thumb-sucking as an example. If we examine the infant's behavior in detail, we will see that no two acts of thumb-sucking performed by one child are precisely the same. On one occasion the activity

---

[4]Piaget's French term *scheme* has usually been translated into English as *schema* (plural, *schemata*). We do not follow this practice since Piaget had been using the French word *schema* for another purpose. Also, the reader should be aware that scheme need not refer only to behavior; there are mental schemes too.

starts when the thumb is 10 inches from the mouth, on another when it is 11 inches away. At one time the thumb travels in almost a straight line to the mouth; at another time its trajectory is quite irregular. In short, if we describe behavior in sufficient detail, we find that there are no two identical actions. There is no one act of thumb-sucking, but many; in fact there are as many as the number of times the child brings the thumb to the mouth. At first glance this situation might seem to pose insurmountable difficulties for the psychologist. How can she describe and explain behavior if each act is different from every other? Fortunately, the difficulty is only apparent, since most psychologists are not really interested in the fine details of behavior. What is important, especially for Piaget, is the structure of behavior, that is, an abstraction of the features common to a wide variety of acts which differ in detail. In the case of thumb-sucking, whether or not the act starts from a distance of 10 or 11 inches is of no significance. What is crucial is that the infant has acquired a regular way of getting the thumb into the mouth. This "regular way" is an abstraction furnished by the psychologist. The infant puts the hand into his mouth in many particular ways, no two being identical, and the psychologist detects in these specific actions a certain regularity which she then calls a scheme.

Let us now consider another type of psychological structure: that of the *classifying operations* of the older child from about 7 to 11 years. Suppose an examiner presents the child with a collection of red and blue beads mixed together. Confronted with this situation the older child first thinks of the objects as being members of classes. There is the class of red beads and the class of blue ones. Further, unlike the younger child, he realizes that the class of red beads is included in a larger class, that of beads in general. Another way of putting the matter is to say that he groups the red beads into one class and conceives of it as being a part of a hierarchy of classes. The class immediately "above" the red beads (that is, the more inclusive class) is that of beads-in-general. Of course, the class of beads-in-general may also be located in a classification hierarchy. The class of solid objects contains the class of beads.

Obviously, the older child's operational schemes are quite different from the infant's behavioral schemes. The latter involve patterns of behavior; the infant acts overtly on the world. Although the older child's schemes also involve acting on the world, this is done intellectually. He considers, for example, the relatively abstract problem of whether given classes are contained in others. Piaget describes this aspect of the older child's thought in terms of the operations of classification. What is important for Piaget is not that the child can answer questions about beads (that, of course, is trivial), but that his activities reveal the existence of a basic thought structure, namely, the operations of putting things together, of placing them in classes, of forming hierarchies of classes, and so on. Classification, then, is composed of a series of intellectual activities which constitute a psychological structure. Of course, the child does not realize that he has such a structure and may not even know what the word "classification" means. The classification structure and "schemes" both describe an observer's conception of the basic processes underlying the child's activities; the child himself is certainly not aware of these structures.

The Description of Structures

How can we describe the psychological structures so basic to Piaget's theory? One way is by using common language. We can say that the child classifies objects or that his moral judgment is "objective," and so forth. Sometimes the common language adequately conveys meaning, but sometimes it does not. Unfortunately, there are occasions when an ordinary word means different things to different people. When this occurs the scientist is in danger of being misunderstood. Consequently, the sciences have tended to develop various formal languages to guarantee precise communication. The physicist does not say that objects "fall very fast" or "pick up speed as they go along." Instead, he writes a formula in which each term is precisely defined and in which the relations among the terms are completely specified by the formal language of mathematics. If the reader of the formula knows what the terms mean and understands the requisite mathematics, then the physicist's meaning can be accurately transmitted without the danger of misinterpretation.

Piaget feels that psychology, too, should attempt to use formal languages in describing the structures underlying thought. Psychological words in particular are quite ambiguous. While the theorist may intend a particular meaning for words like "habit," or "thought," or "classification," it is extremely probable that these terms will signify to others a wide variety of alternative interpretations. Consequently, Piaget has attempted to use formal languages—particularly aspects of logic and of mathematics—to describe the structures underlying the child's activities. In later chapters we shall consider in detail both the formal description of the structures and Piaget's rationale for using it.

Functions, Structures, and Equilibrium

We cannot emphasize sufficiently the extent to which Piaget believes that the functional invariants—organization and adaptation (assimilation and accommodation)—and the psychological structures are inextricably intertwined. As we have seen, assimilation and accommodation, although complementary, nevertheless occur simultaneously. A balance between the two is necessary for adaptation. Moreover, adaptation is not separate from organization. In the process of organizing his activities the individual assimilates novel events into preexisting structures, and at the same time accommodates preexisting structures to meet the demands of the new situation.

Furthermore, the functional invariants (organization and adaptation) are closely related to the structures of intelligence. As a result of the tendencies toward adaptation and organization, new structures are continually being created out of the old ones and are employed to assist the individual in interaction with the world. Looking at the matter another way, structures are necessary for adaptation and organization. One could neither adapt to the environment nor organize one's processes if there were no basic structures available at the outset. On the other hand, the very existence of a structure, which by Piaget's definition is an organized totality, entails the necessity for organization and adaptation.

There are, however, important differences between the invariant functions and the structures. As the individual progresses through the life span, the functions remain the same but the structures vary, and appear in a fairly regular sequence. Another way of saying this is that intellectual development proceeds through a series of *stages* with each stage characterized by a different kind of psychological structure and a different type of interaction between the individual and the environment. An individual of any age must adapt to the environment and must organize his responses continually, but the instruments by which the person accomplishes this— the psychological structures—change from one age level to another. Both the infant and adult organize and adapt, but the resulting psychological structures are quite different for the two periods.

Piaget further proposes that organisms tend toward equilibrium with the environment. The organism—whether a human being or some other form of life—tends to organize structures into coherent and stable patterns. These ways of dealing with the world tend toward a certain balance. The organism tries to develop structures which are effective in interaction with reality. This means that when a new event occurs the organism can apply to it the lessons of the past (or assimilate the events into already existing structures) and easily modify current patterns of behavior to respond to the requirements of the new situation. With increasing experience the organism acquires more and more structures and therefore adapts more readily to an increasing number of situations.

SUMMARY AND CONCLUSIONS

Early in his life Piaget developed two major intellectual interests: biology, the study of life, and epistemology, the study of knowledge. After devoting a number of years to each of these disciplines, Piaget sought a way to integrate them. In the course of his work at the Binet Laboratory in Paris, he came to the conclusion that psychology might provide the link between biology and epistemology. Piaget decided to spend a few years studying the evolution of knowledge in the child and then apply the fruits of this research to the solution of the theoretical problems which initially motivated him. Fortunately for child psychology, the few years became many, and in their course Piaget has produced over forty volumes reporting his investigations into such matters as the child's moral judgment, the infant's patterns of behavior, and the adolescent's solution of scientific problems. Only in the 1950s was Piaget able to return to theoretical issues in epistemology. Late in life, Piaget continued his contributions to psychology, and published works on causality, consciousness, and development and learning. He died in 1980.

Piaget's research and theory have been guided by a framework which can be defined as a set of orienting attitudes. His definition of intelligence is not restrictive, but states that intelligence involves biological adaptation, equilibrium between the individual and his environment, and a set of mental operations which permit this balance. Piaget's research activities also have increasingly come to focus on the growth of the child's understanding of the basic concepts of science, mathematics, and similar disciplines. Piaget is less interested in studying the contents of the child's thought than the basic organization underlying it.

The individual inherits physical structures which set broad limits on intellectual functioning. Many of these are influenced by physical maturation. The individual also inherits a few automatic behavioral reactions or reflexes which have their greatest influence on functioning in the first few days of life. These reflexes are rapidly transformed into structures which incorporate the results of experience. Another aspect of inheritance involves the general principles of functioning. One general principle of functioning is organization; all species have the tendency to organize their processes.

A second aspect of general functioning is adaptation, which may be further subdivided into assimilation and accommodation. Accommodation refers to the organism's tendency to modify its structures according to the pressures of the environment, while assimilation involves using current structures to deal with the environment. The result of the principles of functioning is a series of psychological structures which differ qualitatively from one another throughout a person's lifetime. For example, the infant employs behavioral schemes or patterns of action, while the child from about 7 to 11 uses mental operations. What is important for Piaget is not the child's behavior in all its detail but the structure underlying his activities. For the purpose of clarity, Piaget has made an attempt to describe these structures in terms of formal languages—logic and mathematics. The general tendencies—adaptation and organization—and the structures are all related to one another.

Assimilation and accommodation are complementary, whereas organization and adaptation are interwoven. For instance, one assimilates an environmental event into a structure, and one accommodates a structure to the demands of the environment. Eventually the organism tends toward equilibrium, aiming at a balance between existing structures and the requirements of the world. In this balance the structures are sufficiently developed so that the organism need exert little effort either to accommodate them to reality or to assimilate events into them.

Piaget's framework is quite general, and at this point the reader must find it hard to evaluate. In the following pages we will see the fruitfulness of Piaget's orienting attitudes. We will review, for example, the evolution of the psychological structures underlying the child's intelligence, we will examine the ways in which assimilation and accommodation affect the child's interaction with the world, and we will consider Piaget's theory of equilibration.

2

Infancy

Piaget's theory divides intellectual development into four major periods: sensorimotor (birth to 2 years), preoperational (2 years to 7 years), concrete operational (7 years to 11 years), and formal operational (11 years and above). (As we shall see shortly, these ages are only rough estimates; they vary from individual to individual, and from culture to culture.) This chapter treats the first of these periods, the sensorimotor, which occurs during infancy.

The account of infancy is novel and sometimes surprising. The surprises usually take one of two forms: cases where, according to Piaget, the infant is capable of much more sophisticated and elaborate forms of behavior than we would have expected and, conversely, cases where the infant shows unexpected deficiencies. Consider an example of the first case.

The untrained observer of an infant in the first few months of life usually reports several impressions. The baby, who is much smaller than anticipated, appears weak and fragile, and extraordinarily passive. He does not seem to *do* much of anything. The newborn spends most of the time in sleep, and usually wakes only to be fed. Even during the feeding, he does not seem very alert, and sometimes, in fact, falls asleep during the meal. Since the infant seems to show little reaction to people or things, our observer may even suspect that the newborn does not *see* the world clearly, if at all. Apparently such an infant is capable of learning almost nothing.

Piaget's view offers a strong contrast to this conception of the newborn as a predominantly helpless and inactive creature, for he characterizes the newborn as active and as an initiator of behavior. The infant quickly learns to distinguish among various features of the immediate environment and to modify his behavior in accordance with their demands. In fact, his activity reveals the *origins of intelligence.*

One of the first questions we should ask about these surprising findings (or indeed about *any* findings) is, how does he know? What are the methods which allow Piaget to penetrate beyond the commonly held assumptions and to propose a new and startling view of infancy? The question is particularly germane in the case of Piaget since he is methodologically unorthodox, at least by some standards.

METHOD

In the course of his psychological investigations, Piaget has employed a variety of methods. The assumption has been that methods must be tailored to meet the requirements of different problems and age groups. In the case of infancy, the methodology employed is partly naturalistic and partly informal-experimental.

For much of the time, Piaget carefully observed the behavior of his own three infants—Lucienne, Laurent, and Jacqueline—as it occurred naturally. For instance, he would sit by the crib and make careful notes of the infant's play, or he would direct his attention to the infant's eye movements and try to determine the direction of the infant's gaze. In these instances Piaget did not make use of special scientific instruments or experimental apparatus. He did not use another observer to check the reliability of the observations. In general, the intention was to employ careful observation, unaided by instrumentation, to learn as much as possible about the behavior of the infant in the natural habitat. The procedure is obviously different from the usual experimental approach in which the child's behavior or physiological reactions are observed, often with special instruments, under carefully controlled conditions in the laboratory. But Piaget's approach is hardly unique or scientifically taboo. Naturalistic methods are used in zoology, for example, by ethologists interested in the behavior of animals in their natural surroundings. It has been used, too, in child psychology, by the "baby biographers" who observed their own children and who included such notable figures as Charles Darwin.

Piaget's procedure has its unique advantages and disadvantages. The latter have often been stressed at the expense of the former. For example, Piaget based his conclusions on a sample of only three children, hardly a sufficient number to ensure the generality of the results. Piaget and his wife made all the observations themselves. Although both Piaget and his wife were trained psychologists, it is the general feeling that parents are notoriously poor evaluators of their own children's performance. Also, when naturalistic observation is used, it is impossible to identify cause-and-effect relations with certainty. While some event may have seemed to be the cause, other uncontrolled events may in fact have been involved too. Further, the standard statistical tests were not used, although today they are usually seen as indispensable tools of research.

Despite these apparent deficiencies, Piaget's methods offer a number of advantages. First and foremost, Piaget is an exceedingly sensitive observer of children. Some people, probably regardless of formal training, have this ability and some people do not; Piaget does. The acuity of Piaget's observations is confirmed by their generally successful replication by independent investigators.[1] Second, Piaget's intimate contact with his subjects allowed him to *discover* phenomena which might have gone unobserved or unnoticed in the laboratory. The controlled experiment tends to focus the investigator's attention on the limited class of behavior of interest, and indeed, often makes it impossible for other kinds of behavior to occur or be noticed. These other events, of course, may be of greater interest than those which the experimenter is studying. Third, Piaget's great familiarity with his children often gave him the insight to resolve certain delicate issues of interpretation. If, for example, one of his children was unable to wind up a toy, Piaget's extensive knowledge of the child was likely to give good grounds for deciding whether the failure was due to lack of interest, or fatigue, or real inability. An experimenter, on the other hand, not knowing the subjects well, often is unable to make such reasonable decisions.

Fourth, Piaget was able to observe his subjects over a long period of time. Such longitudinal studies are rare in psychology and provide a perspective which is notably absent from most experimental designs. Fifth, Piaget feels that at the initial stages of research the use of statistics may be premature. One's aim at the outset is to explore and describe. The intention is to discover and identify the significant processes and problems which at a later stage of investigation may be subject to rigorous statistical test. Sixth, Piaget attempted to compensate for the obvious deficiencies of the naturalistic procedure by performing informal experiments. If, for example, observation suggests that the child cannot deal with certain kinds of obstacles, Piaget may intervene in the natural course of events by imposing these obstacles on the child and then observe the results. These experiments are, of course, informal, since a very small number of subjects—three at most—is involved, and since the controls are often incomplete. Nevertheless, Piaget is sensitive to the limitations of naturalistic ob-

---

[1]For example, see Ina C. Uzgiris, ''Organization of Sensorimotor Intelligence,'' in M. Lewis, ed., *Origins of Intelligence* (New York: Plenum Press, 1976).

servation and whenever possible tries to supplement it with experimental techniques. We see then that Piaget's unorthodox procedure for studying infants has a good deal to recommend it and cannot be summarily dismissed.[2]

The result of these investigations is an account of infancy in terms of six "sensorimotor" stages. It should be emphasized that the age limits of each stage are only approximate, and subject to wide individual variations. Piaget stresses the flexibility of the age norms which are probably influenced by individual differences in physical and social environment, physiological factors, and so on. What is important is the regular order of succession of the stages, regardless of the particular ages at which they appear.

STAGE 1: BIRTH TO 1 MONTH

The newborn is not a completely helpless creature, but arrives in the world with certain abilities which are provided by heredity. (In fact, over the past several years research has shown that the newborn is far more skilled, visually, for example, than was ever supposed.[3]) One innate skill that the newborn possesses is the sucking reflex. When the lips are touched, the newborn in all cultures responds automatically with unlearned sucking movements. In describing the newborn's behavior, Piaget's central themes are, first, that the sucking reflex, and others too, are not simply activated by external stimuli; instead, the newborn often initiates activity himself. Second, although the physical structure of the infant provides ready-made mechanisms, like the sucking reflex which functions from birth and which is of obvious utility, these furnish only a basis for future development. Even in the first month of life experience plays an important role in modifying and supplementing the inherited mechanisms.

Consider the following observation.

> During the second day also Laurent again begins to make sucking-movements between meals. . . . His lips open and close as if to receive a real

[2]Indeed, the reader should recognize that unorthodox procedures have led to many of the great discoveries in psychology, including Freud's free association technique, Wertheimer's demonstration experiments, Chomsky's introspective analyses of language, Brown's naturalistic observations of the language of three children, Skinner's studies of individual pigeons, and the Gardner's examination of Washoe's sign language.

[3]For example, see T. Appleton, R. Clifton, and S. Goldberg, "The Development of Behavioral Competence in Infancy," in F. D. Horowitz, ed., *Review of Child Development Research,* Vol. IV (Chicago: University of Chicago Press, 1975).

nippleful but without having an object. This behavior subsequently became more frequent. . . . (*Origins of Intelligence, OI,* pp. 25–26)[4]

The observation may at first seem quite pedestrian. But let us review it. Why did Laurent suck between meals? There are several possible interpretations. Sometimes reflex activity may be said to be involved. That is, an "external excitant" or "unconditioned stimulus," like a finger, may automatically set off the reflex of sucking by touching the lips. But in the case of Laurent, a reflex interpretation seems untenable, since no external excitant appears to have been involved. Another explanation might attribute Laurent's sucking to hunger, but this interpretation too seems implausible, since Laurent's sucking sometimes occurred soon after his last feeding (when, presumably, he was not hungry) and not just immediately preceding the next feeding (when he probably was hungry). A third possibility, also rejected by Piaget, involves two steps: (1) We assume that in the past the child's nutritive sucking had been associated with pleasure; that is, when he sucks he gets milk, which reduces his hunger pangs and is therefore pleasurable. (2) Because of this previous association between sucking and pleasure, it gradually occurs that sucking alone in the absence of milk acquires the power to elicit feelings of pleasure in the infant. Consequently, it may be that in the observation cited, Laurent sucked because sucking itself had become rewarding through its past association with pleasure. But this explanation also seems implausible since the extent of the association between pleasure and sucking was limited to such a short period of time.

Since these various explanations—external excitant, hunger, and association with pleasure—do not seem able to account for nonnutritive sucking, Piaget invokes one form of assimilation to explain the results. Recall that in Chapter 1 we defined assimilation as a *functional invariant,* a tendency common to all forms of life. In its most general form assimilation involves the organism's tendency to deal with environmental events in terms of current structures. Piaget has further proposed that assimilation takes three particular forms. In the present instance, the principle of *functional assimilation* applies. (The other two types are *recognitory assimilation* and *generalizing assimilation,* which we will discuss later.) The principle of functional assimilation asserts that when an organism has a structure available, there is a basic tendency to exercise the structure, to make it function. This is particularly true when the structure is not well formed or is incomplete in some way. Also, the principle applies whether the structure is innate, as in the case of the sucking reflex, or learned, as in other instances we will review shortly. When applied to the present observation,

---

[4]In this and subsequent chapters, when a book is frequently cited, we give first an abbreviated title (e.g., *Origins of Intelligence*) followed by brief initials (e.g., *OI*). In later references only the initials are used.

the principle of functional assimilation asserts that Laurent's nonnutritive sucking simply represents the tendency of the sucking reflex to exercise itself or to function. This simple behavioral scheme is not yet well formed and requires exercise to consolidate itself. In other words, Laurent did not suck because he was hungry, or because an external excitant set off the reflex, or because he had associated the sucking with pleasure. He sucked because there is a tendency for available schemes like sucking to function.

A closely related tendency is *generalizing assimilation.* Since schemes need exercise and repetition, they also require objects to be used in satisfying this need. The sucking scheme, therefore, tends to extend itself, to *generalize,* to a variety of objects. While the newborn at first sucks only the nipple, or perhaps a finger that accidentally comes into contact with the lips, the infant later exercises sucking on new objects like a blanket or various toys. Thus, Piaget stresses activity on the part of the infant. The sucking reflex is not simply activated by a series of excitants; rather, the infant, in seeking to exercise this scheme (functional assimilation), actively searches out objects which will allow it to function. The objects serve as nourishment, or "aliments," for the need to suck.

The first two principles—functional and generalizing assimilation—are energetic: they get the newborn's behavior started. In the course of his activities, the newborn has the occasion to learn about the environment. The reflex of sucking becomes "differentiated." Consider this observation concerning Laurent:

> At 0;0(20) [zero years, zero months, and 20 days] he bites the breast which is given him 5 cm. from the nipple. For a moment he sucks the skin which he then lets go in order to move his mouth about 2 cm. As soon as he begins sucking again he stops. . . . When his search subsequently leads him accidently to touch the nipple with the mucosa of the upper lip (his mouth being wide open), he at once adjusts his lips and begins to suck. (*OI,* p. 26)

From this and other similar observations, Piaget concludes that the infant in the first month of life shows a primitive recognition called *recognitory assimilation.* When the infant is not too hungry, he may suck anything—the fingers, the blanket, whatever—to exercise his scheme. But when hunger is strong, the infant shows selectivity or discrimination in choosing objects to suck. While rejecting the skin surrounding the nipple, the infant seizes immediately upon the nipple itself and does this so rapidly that we may reasonably call the behavior a crude form of recognition. One caution here: Piaget does not propose that the infant "recognizes" the nipple in the same sense that an adult does. (We will see later that the infant's concept of objects is immature.) In the present case the infant merely shows that when it is necessary he can perceive the difference between the nipple and other things.

How does the infant learn to recognize the nipple? Learning must be involved since the newborn does not immediately display this kind of recognition; experience is certainly required for it to develop. Piaget's position is that in the course of exercising and generalizing the sucking scheme, the infant comes into contact with a variety of stimulation. Some of the stimulation is visual (the sight of the breast, etc.). Some is tactual-kinesthetic (touches on the lips, the feeling of swallowing milk, etc.). And some stimulation is postural (the infant is generally lying down in a certain position). While accumulating this experience, the infant comes to differentiate among many aspects. He finds that some areas of the breast look different from others; some feel different from others; and that one area yields milk while others do not. The infant comes to make these discriminations through repetitious experience which is the result of functional and generalizing assimilation. Then, when hungry the infant shows evidence of previous perceptual learning[5] by choosing that area which has produced milk in the past and by rejecting other areas. To put the matter in another way, the infant learns about the world in the course of many explorations; when properly motivated, he manifests this learning by the performance of certain distinctive reactions.

Finally, an even more complicated kind of learning occurs during the first stage. The principle of accommodation—of modification of the scheme to suit the demands of the environment—is also operative, and one result is that the infant learns to search for the nipple in an increasingly effective manner. Consider these observations:

At first, when put to the breast, Laurent does not show a particularly systematic search for the nipple. He obviously has not had sufficient experience either to recognize the nipple or locate it. But on

> the third day Laurent makes new progress in his adjustment to the breast. All he needs in order to grope with open mouth toward final success is to have touched the breast or the surrounding teguments with his lips. But he hunts on the wrong side as well as on the right side. . . . As soon as his cheek comes into contact with the breast, Laurent at 0;0(12) applies himself to seeking until he finds drink. His search takes its bearings: immediately from the correct side, that is to say, the side where he experienced contact. . . . At 0;0(26) Laurent . . . feels the nipple in the middle of his right cheek. But as he tries to grasp it, it is withdrawn 10 cm. He then turns his head in the right direction and searches. . . . This time he goes on to touch the nipple,

---

[5]Piaget's "recognitory assimilation" combines several processes usually treated under different rubrics by the theory of perceptual learning. The infant *discriminates* (as when he sees that one area of the breast looks different from another); he *recognizes* (as when he knows that he has made contact with the breast before); and he *identifies* (as when he learns that the nipple gives milk). For a fuller discussion of perceptual learning, see E. J. Gibson, *Principles of Perceptual Learning and Development* (Englewood Cliffs, N.J.: Prentice-Hall, Inc., 1969).

first with his nose and then with the region between his nostrils and lips. . . . He raises his head in order to grasp the nipple. (*OI*, pp. 26, 29)

We quote these observations in some detail to document the extent of the infant's learning during the first month. The infant learns not only to recognize the nipple, but also where to look for it. Thus, in response to the requirements of the situation, he accommodates—he develops new patterns of action, which result in fairly systematic search. How are these patterns of behavior learned? At the outset the child's head movements are "desultory," that is, essentially without order in relation to the nipple. By chance, some of the movements lead to grasping the nipple and some are unsuccessful. As time goes on, the infant learns through this process of trial and error that a turn of the head in the direction of the touch on the cheek provided by the nipple leads to the reward of swallowing milk. With increased experience the infant becomes relatively proficient and flexible in this search and now can proceed not only in a sideways direction toward the cheek, but in an upward or downward direction as well. This last observation is important since some head movements at birth are reflexive. When the infant is touched on the cheek near the mouth, he automatically turns the head in that direction. The sideways movement is the "rooting reflex." Consequently, a learning explanation may not be required for the sideways movement, but does seem necessary for the upward and downward motions.

Such, then, is the first stage. The apparently primitive behavior of the infant in the first month of life in fact involves considerable complexity, and the extent of the learning achieved is not immediately obvious. The result is that the hereditary sucking scheme becomes progressively modified and elaborated as a function of experience. At the end of stage 1, sucking is no longer an automatic pattern of behavior provided by heredity. In accordance with the principle of *organization,* the sucking scheme has become elaborated and has developed into a fairly complex psychological structure which now incorporates the results of the infant's experiences.

While stage 1 involves significant learning, there are also limitations on the infant's accomplishments. Learning is confined to the sphere of the reflexes and does not go far beyond them; the effects of experience are centered on the mechanisms provided by heredity. We shall see how the infant in stage 2 begins to overcome these limitations.

At the time it was proposed, Piaget's view of infancy was novel in several respects. The two most influential theories of the day—Freud's personality psychology and Hull's experimental psychology—both emphasized that the organism seeks *escape* from stimulation and excitation. All motives were seen as analogous to the sexual or hunger drives; when these drives intensify, the organism takes actions to reduce them and to return to a quiescent state. Piaget's emphasis, on the other hand, is that even in the first few days of life the infant often *seeks stimulation*. When capable of activity, he tends to perform it (functional assimilation); when a structure is available, he tends to generalize it to new objects (generalizing assimilation). In Piaget's view, all behavior cannot be explained by the infant's reacting to a noxious state of affairs; instead, the infant sometimes actively *seeks* the stimulation which his behavior provides. It seems fair to say that recent psychological research has shown that the Hullian and Freudian concepts are not fully adequate and that alternative views designed to explain the individual's preference for activity and stimulation must be developed (Hunt, 1961).

STAGE 2: 1 TO 4 MONTHS

In the second stage of sensorimotor development the infant acquires certain habits, which, although fairly simple and centered about his own body, nevertheless surpass the acquisitions of the first stage. Now the historical development of sucking, for example, extends beyond the feeding situation.

Primary Circular Reaction

Piaget's theory involves the notion of *primary circular reaction*. The infant's behavior by chance leads to an advantageous or interesting result; he immediately attempts to reinstate or rediscover the effective behavior and, after a process of trial and error, is successful in doing so. Thereafter, the behavior and the result may be repeated; the sequence has become a "habit." Consider these examples:

> At 0;1(1) Laurent is held by his nurse in an almost vertical position. . . .
> He is very hungry. . . . Twice, when his hand was laid on his right cheek,
> Laurent turned his head and tried to grasp his fingers with his mouth. The
> first time he failed and succeeded the second. But the movements of his arms
> are not coordinated with those of his head: the hand escapes while the mouth
> tries to maintain contact. . . .
> At 0;1(3) . . . after a meal . . . his arms, instead of gesticulating aim-
> lessly, constantly move toward his mouth . . . it has occurred to me several
> times that the chance contact of hand and mouth set in motion the directing
> of the latter toward the former and that then (but only then), the hand tries
> to return to the mouth. . . . [Later, though] it is no longer the mouth that
> seeks the hand, but the hand which reaches for the mouth. Thirteen times in
> succession I have been able to observe the hand go back into the mouth.
> There is no longer any doubt that coordination exists. . . . At 0;1(4) . . . his
> right hand may be seen approaching his mouth. . . . But as only the index
> finger was grasped, the hand fell out again. Shortly after it returned. This
> time the thumb was in the mouth . . . I then remove the hand and place it

near his waist. . . . After a few minutes the lips move and the hand approaches them again. This time there is a series of setbacks. . . . [But finally] the hand enters the mouth, the thumb alone is retained and sucking continues. I again remove the hand. Again lip movements cease, new attempts ensue, success results for the ninth and tenth time, after which the experiment is interrupted. (*OI,* pp. 51–53)

These observations nicely illustrate Piaget's dual role of observer and experimenter. Note how Piaget as patient observer records that the infant spontaneously places the hand in the mouth thirteen times in succession. Then, Piaget as experimenter intervenes in the natural course of events by placing the infant's hand near his waist to determine whether, under these modified conditions, the infant is able to direct the hand to the mouth.

The observations also display the gradual and steady development of thumb-sucking. First, the infant cannot consistently get the hand into the mouth and then slowly learns to do so; next he learns to suck the thumb alone, not the whole hand; and, finally, after a long and continuous process of learning, the infant is able to perform with rapidity the entire sequence of actions.

Piaget's explanation of thumb-sucking again involves principles of assimilation and of accommodation. However, the sequence begins with an unplanned or unintentional occurrence. Recall that another person initially placed Laurent's hand on his cheek; he did not do so himself. After the hand was put there, Laurent took the initiative by attempting to grasp the hand with the mouth. This action was, of course, a previously learned scheme: Laurent had earlier acquired behavior patterns enabling him to search for the nipple. Other observations not described here reveal that in some cases the initial behavior is a chance occurrence, and not caused by the intervention of another person. In either event, the unplanned behavior leads to a result which has value for the infant. In the case of Laurent the hand in the mouth enables the sucking scheme to function. This is rewarding since, according to the principle of functional assimilation, the sucking scheme needs to function. In other words, a fortuitous occurrence has given the infant a chance to exercise one of his previously established schemes, and this activity, in itself, is a satisfying event. But Laurent's movements are not yet fully coordinated; it occurs that the hand falls from the mouth and interrupts the functioning of the sucking scheme. The child then desires to reinstate the pleasurable activity and resume sucking the thumb. This desire, stemming from the interruption, then *directs* the child's behavior. Laurent actively tries to insert the hand in the mouth. In two senses, then, the infant's learning is active: his desire sets in motion the sequence of events, and he initates behavior to fulfill this desire.

The principle of accommodation is now operative. The infant modifies the previously aimless movements of the hand to make them effective in bringing it to the mouth. Initially, Laurent is on the wrong track; he tries to bring the mouth to the hand. It is only after some failure that he reverses the procedure. The learning is slow and seems to involve two factors—muscular adjustments and direction by the proper cues. The infant must learn to make certain new and precise muscular movements and must learn to bring these movements under the direction of the proper cues. When touching the blanket, the hand must be moved in certain ways; when touching the cheek, it must be moved in other ways. The infant learns that particular cues and movements are useful while others are not. The useful ones, of course, are those which lead to placing the hand in the mouth. Thus, success "confirms" some of the movements and cues, while failure eliminates other attempts at accommodation. Yet the observations show that the infant's learning is not complete. He apparently finds it more satisfying to suck the thumb than the other fingers, and through a process of learning similar to that just described becomes able to place the thumb alone in the mouth. Further, the infant's behavior shows the ability to distinguish (recognitory assimilation) the thumb from the rest of the hand. The result of all this learning is finally a smoothly organized and directed series of movements, a new scheme or structure, which can be exercised repeatedly.

In summary, the primary circular reaction involves an action on the part of the infant which fortuitously leads to an event which has value for him and which is centered about his own body. The infant then learns to repeat the behavior to reinstate the event. The culmination of the process is an organized scheme.

Primitive Anticipations

While the newborn in the feeding situation sucks only when his lips are in contact with the breast, the older infant shows a different pattern of behavior. This observation concerns Laurent at the beginning of the second month.

> as soon as he is in a position to eat (in his mother's arms or on the bed, etc.) his hands lose interest, leave his mouth, and it becomes obvious that the child no longer seeks anything but the breast, that is to say, contact with food . . . at the end of the month, Laurent only tries to nurse when he is in his mother's arms and no longer when on the dressing table. (*OI,* p. 58)
> . . . between 0;3(15) and 0;4 . . . [when Laurent] is put in my arms in position for nursing, he looks at me and then searches all around . . . but he does not attempt to nurse. When I place him in his mother's arms without his touching the breast, he looks at her and immediately opens his mouth wide. (*OI,* p. 60)

The infant initially sucks, then, only when the nipple is inserted in his mouth. The nipple is an external excitant which automatically elicits sucking. After a period of experience with feeding, he makes sucking-like movements *before* the external excitant can operate. During the second month, Laurent shows sucking as soon as he is placed in his mother's arms or on the bed. Later, Laurent's sucking-like movements are aroused only by being in the mother's arms. One way of looking at these facts is to say that, while at first only the nipple served as a cue or signal for sucking, later the infant's being in the mother's arms replaced the nipple as a signal for sucking. Another way of phrasing the matter is to maintain that the infant seems to show a primitive *anticipation* of feeding and that this expectancy, as time goes on, is evoked by fewer and more appropriate events than formerly. In either event, the phenomenon is similar to what has been called "classical conditioning," although Piaget's explanation of the facts differs from the traditional one.

Piaget emphasizes that the association between sucking and the various signals (e.g., position in the mother's arms) that precede it is not acquired in a mechanical way. What happens is this: the sucking scheme comes to consist of more than sucking alone. It also involves a set of postural kinesthetic cues. That is, when the infant nurses in the first few months he is almost invariably held in the same position, and the internal body sensations associated with this position become a part of the act of sucking. The body sensations and the movements of the lips form a whole. Then, when the infant is placed in the position for nursing and the postural and kinesthetic sensations are activated, the whole cycle of the sucking act is released. Because the two aspects of the cycle—bodily sensations and lip movements—form a whole, the occurrence of one aspect usually evokes the other. Piaget feels that this process does not involve mere "passive recording" on the part of the child, since the infant himself *enlarges* the initially limited scheme of sucking to include other components such as bodily cues. Furthermore, the association cannot be maintained if it is not consistently "confirmed" by the environment. That is, for postural cues to provoke the child's anticipatory sucking, the sucking must ordinarily be followed by drinking milk. Thus, the association between postural cues and sucking derives its meaning only from a larger set of relationships existing between the scheme of sucking and its satisfaction. The reflex must have a chance to function effectively (to drink milk) before any associations can be formed. Thus, the sequence *bodily cues* ⟶ *sucking* ⟶ *satisfaction of need* forms a whole, and to isolate the first two terms in this sequence and call them a conditioned reflex omits much that is relevant.

Curiosity

In the discussion of the second stage Piaget introduces a motivational principle of great importance. The following is a preliminary observation in connection with the problem of vision:

> Laurent at 0;0(24) watches the back of my hand, which is motionless, with such attention and so marked protrusion of the lips that I expect him to suck it. But it is only visual interest. . . . At 0;0(25) he spends nearly an hour in his cradle without crying, his eyes wide open. . . . He stares at a piece of fringe on his cradle. (*OI*, p. 64)

Why does the infant attend to these mundane features of the environment? He is not rewarded for doing so and is not in any other way encouraged to direct attention to an object like the fringe of the cradle. Again, Piaget invokes the principle of functional assimilation to account for these facts. The eyes are structures, given by specific heredity, and require exercise. In the present instance exercise means looking at thing, and the things looked at are necessary for the functioning of the eyes.

Thus far, the principle of functional assimilation has been applied to the case of vision in much the same way as it was used to explain some features of sucking: both schemes need to function. One result of repetitious looking at things is that they become familiar to the infant. Through a process of perceptual learning, the infant becomes acquainted with the environment and comes to recognize things. These observations are made next:

> At 0;1(15) he systematically explores the hood of his bassinet which I shook slightly. He begins by the edge, then little by little looks backward at the lowest part of the roof. . . . Four days later he resumes this exploration in the opposite direction. . . . Subsequently, he constantly resumes examining the cradle, but, during the third month, he only looks at the toys hanging from the hood or at the hood itself when an unwonted movement excites his curiosity or when he discovers a particular new point (a pleat in the material, etc.). (*OI*, p. 68)

Notice how at first the infant thoroughly examines the cradle until he is apparently familiar with it. Then, during the third month his attention becomes more selective than was previously the case. He no longer seems to explore the cradle and instead directs his attention to novel objects or movements connected with the cradle. For example, he stares at toys hanging from the hood or at a previously unnoticed pleat in the material.

Piaget's explanation of the infant's curiosity involves an extension—really a further specification—of the principle of generalizing assimilation. The infant's looking scheme, according to Piaget, tends to extend the range of objects it "uses." But the infant does not simply look at more and more things. His visual preferences become selective. The infant's attention is directed at events which are *moderately novel:* "one observes that the subject looks neither at what is too familiar, because he is in a way surfeited with it, nor at what is too new because this does not correspond to anything in his [schemes]" (*OI*, p. 68). This motivational principle may appear deceptively simple and trite. In reality, however, it represents a point of view which is radically different from previous (and some current) theories and is only now receiving the attention it deserves. First, like the principle of assimilation, the moderate novelty principle is strongly at odds with theories which stress avoidance of stimulation as the only kind of motivation. On the contrary, according to Piaget's view, the child actively seeks out new stimulation—he is not forced to look at novel objects. Second, the moderate novelty principle is different from other motivational theories in that it is a relativistic concept. That which catches an individual's curiosity is not entirely the physical nature of the event. It is not the object per se that attracts attention; instead, curiosity is a function of the *relation* between the new object and the individual's previous experience. A given toy may elicit interest in one child and boredom in another. Presumably the first child has had experience with toys moderately different from the one in question; the second child may either have had experience with toys *highly* similar to the new one or else may have had no experience with toys, in which case the new object presumably "does not correspond to anything in his [schemes]." In sum, the novelty principle asserts that what determines curiosity is not the physical nature of the object, but rather the degree to which the object is discrepant from what the individual is familiar with, which, of course, depends entirely on the individual's experience.

Imitation

An important aspect of the infant's behavior is imitation. Piaget considers imitation, like all other behaviors, as yet another expression of the infant's endeavors to comprehend reality and interact effectively with the world. Consequently, the development of imitation is seen to progress concurrently with other aspects of the infant's behavior.

During stage 2, as we have seen, the reflexes are modified to become habits or primary circular reactions. This extension of the child's hereditary schemes leads to a rudimentary and sporadic form of imitation. At this stage the child imitates only actions which he has himself previously performed. Since the child's repertory of actions is still restricted, imitation is confined to elementary vocal and visual movements, and to grasping (prehension). Here is an example of the imitation of this stage:

> At 0;1(21), Lucienne spontaneously uttered the sound rra, but did not react at once when I reproduced it. At 0;1(24); however, when I made a prolonged aa, she twice uttered a similar sound, although she had previously been silent for a quarter of an hour.
> At 0;1(25) she was watching me while I said "a ha, ha, rra," etc. I noticed certain movements of her mouth, movements not of suction but of vocalization. She succeeded once or twice in producing some rather vague

sounds, and although there was no imitation in the strict sense, there was obvious vocal contagion.

At 0;3(5) I noted a differentation in the sounds of her laughter. I imitated them. She reacted by reproducing them quite clearly, but only when she had already uttered them immediately before.

At 0;3(24) she imitated aa, and vaguely arr in similar conditions, i.e., when there was mutual imitation. (*Play, Dreams, and Imitation in Childhood, PDI*, p. 10)

The early forms of vocal imitation are characterized by two major features. First, there is the phenomenon of "vocal contagion." A person called a "model" makes a sound, and the infant tries to reproduce it. Limited abilities, however, prevent the infant from perfect reproduction of the sounds. Nevertheless, stimulated by the model's sounds, the infant continues to produce vocalizations of many kinds having little relation to the model's sounds. "Vocal contagion" refers, then, to the model's stimulation of diffuse vocal activity in the infant.

Second, there is "mutual imitation." If the model reproduces a sound which the infant is currently engaged in producing, the child is stimulated to repeat the same sound. If the model again imitates the child, there is set in motion a pattern of alternating imitation by infant and model which continues until one or the other tires or loses interest. This pattern of behavior does *not* occur if the model makes a sound which is new for the infant.

Piaget explains both the contagion and mutual imitation phenomena by reference to the principle of functional assimilation. You may recall that the child has a tendency to repeat schemes which have already been established. In the case of vocal contagion the principle of functional assimilation is applied in the following way. When the model makes a sound the infant does not distinguish it from his own; it is as if the infant had made the sound. Because of the process of functional assimilation, the infant tends to repeat the activity (not distinguished from his own) which has already been set in motion; that is, the infant carries on the activity of making sounds in general.

In the case of mutual imitation a similar explanation is advanced. When the infant produces a sound, the model's imitation merely stimulates the process of functional assimilation. The infant's imitation is in a way illusory; the infant does not so much *reproduce* the model's behavior as merely continue his own. Note that in both cases—contagion and mutual imitation—the infant repeats behavior of which he is already capable. The infant cannot yet reproduce novel activities of a model.

Categories of Reality

Thus far, we have described the inception of several aspects of the infant's behavior. In particular, we have noted the contribution of experience toward the elaboration of the infant's activity, and the ways in which he extends his behavior beyond the feeding situation. As the infant begins to manipulate surrounding objects, he gradually develops a practical "understanding" of external reality. In playing with toys, blankets, his own body, and adults, he learns something about the properties of these things and about the relations among them. And as skills increase in number and scope, the infant acquires an increasingly complex practical knowledge of certain features of the environment.

During the sensorimotor period, the infant elaborates several basic dimensions of reality, especially the primitive notions of the *permanent object, space, time,* and *causality.* At first, these basic dimensions of reality are closely related to the infant's bodily actions, to the movements of his arms, fingers, legs, and eyes. The infant's initial "understanding" of the world is based entirely on what Piaget calls the "plane of action." Only later, after a gradual process of development, does the infant become able to elaborate the categories of reality on the "plane of thought." One of Piaget's central themes is that concrete action precedes and makes possible the use of intellect. Thus, the acquisitions of the sensorimotor period form the foundations of the individual's mental development. We will discuss only one of these categories, the concept of the permanent object. The other notions follow a similar development.

Object Concept (Stages 1 and 2)

To understand the development of what Piaget calls the *object concept,* it is important to keep in mind one essential point. An "object," according to Piaget, is something which the individual conceives of as having a reality of its own, and as extending beyond his immediate perception. For example, a man who has hung his coat in a closet knows several hours later that, in all likelihood, the coat is still there. Although he cannot see or touch the coat, he knows that it remains behind the closet door. The object, therefore, involves more than the direct perception of external reality; the object is conceived to exist independently of a person's perception of it. Strange as it may sound, the infant is at first incapable of this apparently simple notion, and it is only after a long process of development that he elaborates the cognitive skills necessary for a mature object concept.

During stage 1 the infant's reactions are evoked only by immediately present sensory events which may be internal or external. Feeling the pangs of hunger, the infant cries; experiencing a touch on the lips, he sucks. The same holds in the case of visual perception. If the mother's face suddenly appears in the visual field, the infant stares at it. But when the face is just as suddenly withdrawn, the infant immediately stops looking and resumes other activities. It is clear that the infant has no conception that the face continues to exist when he loses visual contact with it. Instead, the infant merely perceives an unrelated series of images or *pictures,* as Piaget calls them, which appear and then disappear.

Certain behavioral patterns which appear in stage 2 are a first step toward the acquisition of the object concept. The infant coordinates various perceptual schemes which, until then, had been used in unrelated ways. Consider the coordination of vision and hearing. In stage 1, if a sound had occurred near a newborn, he would have shown evidence (for example, a startle) of having heard it, but he would have made no effort to bring the source of the sound into sight. In stage 2, however, the infant tries to turn toward the sound he hears to see what produced it. At first these efforts are clumsy, but with practice, they gradually improve and become more successful. Because of this coordination of vision and hearing, external reality is usually experienced through two or more senses simultaneously. The result is that after a time the infant establishes relations between what is heard and seen. He finds that certain sounds, like the voice, usually emanate from certain sources, like the mouth. The infant begins to discover a coherence in the world. Instead of merely perceiving isolated and unrelated aspects of reality, the infant learns that sights and sounds (and other kinds of percepts too) often go together in regular ways. This coordination of basic schemes, since it introduces a measure of coherence to the infant's world, is a vital first step toward acquisition of the object concept.

Another accomplishment of stage 2 concerns *passive expectation.* The clearest example involves vision. At this stage the infant can follow a moving object with his eyes. Or, as Piaget says, the infant accommodates his looking scheme to the moving thing. The interesting observation here is that once the object leaves the visual field, the infant continues to stare at the spot where the thing disappeared. One might almost be tempted to state that he already has the object concept and is hoping for the thing to return. But this interpretation, Piaget feels, is fallacious, since the infant does not actively *search* for the vanished object as he will do in later stages. Instead, the stage 2 infant merely pursues an action (looking) which has been interrupted. If after a short while the thing does not reappear, the infant discontinues passive watching and turns to other elements of his surroundings. But this passive expectation, which does not go beyond the simple repetition of the already-activated looking scheme, is the first step toward the later active search for the missing object and hence toward acquisition of the object concept.

In summary, the first two stages are characterized by a passive attitude toward objects which disappear from the infant's immediate perception. In stage 1, the infant immediately turns attention to those things he can see; in stage 2, he merely repeats earlier actions (looking) which occurred when the object was present. While the second reaction represents an advance over the first, both indicate the lack of the mature object concept.

STAGE 3: 4 TO 10 MONTHS

Secondary Circular Reactions

In stage 2, the primary circular reaction is always centered on the infant's own body. The infant learned, for example, to bring the thumb to his mouth. In stage 3, the infant's horizons expand. He begins to crawl and manipulate things extensively. The circular reactions of this stage are called "secondary," since they now involve events or objects in the external environment. The secondary circular reactions describe the infant's new-found ability to develop schemes to reproduce interesting events which were initially discovered by chance in the external environment. The following excerpt is a lengthy record of such a reaction and illustrates Piaget's skill and caution as an observer:

> Laurent, from the middle of the third month, revealed global reactions of pleasure, while looking at the toys hanging from the hood of his bassinet. . . . He babbles, arches himself, beats the air with his arms, moves his legs, etc. . . . At 0;2(17) I observe that when his movements induce those of the toys, he stops to contemplate them, far from grasping that it is he who produces them. . . . On the other hand at 0;2(24) I made the following experiment. . . . As Laurent was striking his chest and shaking his hands which were bandaged and held by strings attached to the handle of the bassinet (to prevent him from sucking), I had the idea of using the thing, and I attached the strings to the celluloid balls hanging from the hood. Laurent naturally shook the balls by chance and looked at them at once (the rattle made a noise inside them). As the shaking was repeated more and more frequently Laurent arched himself, waved his arms and legs—in short, he revealed increasing pleasure and through this maintained the interesting result. But nothing yet authorizes us to speak of circular reaction. . . .
>
> The next day, at 0;2(25) I connect his right hand to the celluloid balls. . . . The left hand is free. At first the arm movements are inadequate and the rattle does not move. Then the movements become more extensive . . . and the rattle moves. . . . There seems to be conscious coordination but both arms move equally and it is not yet possible to be sure that this is not a mere pleasure reaction. The next day, same reactions.
>
> At 0;2(27), on the other hand, conscious coordination seems definite, for the following four reasons: (1) Laurent was surprised and frightened by the first shake of the rattle which was unexpected. On the other hand, since the second or third shake, he swung his right arm (connected to the rattle) with regularity, whereas the left remained almost motionless. . . . (2) Laurent's

eye blinks beforehand as soon as his hand moves and before the rattle moves, as though the child knew he was going to shake it. (3) When Laurent temporarily gives up the game and joins his hands for a moment, the right hand (connected to the rattle) alone resumes the movement while the left stays motionless. (4) The regular shakes . . . reveal a certain skill; the movement is regular.

At 0;3(10) I attached a string to the left arm after six days of experiments with the right. The first shake is given by chance: fright, curiosity, etc. Then, at once, there is coordinated circular reaction: this time the right arm is outstretched and barely mobile while the left swings. . . . This time it is therefore possible to speak definitely of secondary circular reaction. (*OI*, pp. 160–62)

One interpretation of the infant's behavior is that a secondary circular reaction is involved. The infant, lying in his crib, by chance makes an arm movement which causes the string attached to his hand to move and rattle the toys. Laurent does not, of course, have this goal in mind from the outset. The movement and rattling are interesting to the infant, and he desires to continue them. Over a period of time, he learns the arm movements necessary to reproduce the interesting result. At this point, his behavior is intentional.

But another interpretation is possible, and it is particularly fascinating to observe how Piaget attempts to rule it out. The alternative explanation asserts that the infant's arm movements are not intended to produce the interesting result. Instead, just the reverse is true: the interesting event causes arm movements in the infant. In other words, the infant initially moves his arm by accident. The balls move and make the infant happy. As part of his joy the infant shows physical excitement which again, by accident, produces the shaking of the balls; this in turn starts the cycle over again and is the *cause* of the infant's hand movements.

The observations show that Piaget was quite cautious in his interpretations. He did not accept the first explanation (secondary circular reaction) until the facts made it abundantly clear that the alternative explanation was not plausible. For example, Piaget observed that Laurent seemed to anticipate the result before it occurred; consequently, the result could not be an accident. In fact, the sequence of observations shows why Piaget's observational procedure is not necessarily inferior to the formal experimental method; the advantages of detailed knowledge of the child's history are obvious, and many of the observations perform the same function as control groups in ordinary experiments.

The explanation of the infant's learning of secondary circular reactions involves many of the principles that were invoked earlier. First, the infant's accidental movement produces an external result which is moderately novel and which therefore interests him. Second, the infant perceives that his actions are related to the external result. Piaget asserts that if the infant does not perceive the connection, no further learning is possible. Third, once the interest and the connection between act and result are established, the infant desires to repeat the interesting event. In other words, after the infant looks at and listens to the toys rattling (or, in more technical language, assimilates the interesting event into the visual and auditory schemes), he wants to reinstate the interesting events and assimilate them once again into the schemes of looking and listening. This, of course, is the familiar principle of functional assimilation: once a scheme (in this case viewing and hearing the toys) is able to function, it tends to repeat itself. After this point, the infant's goal of restoring the interesting events motivates and directs actions.

Thus far, the infant has perceived an interesting result, has recognized that it is connected to his actions, and desires to repeat the result. The fourth step involves accommodation; the infant needs to learn the hand movements necessary for consistent reproduction of the result. Part of the process involves rediscovering the movements which were previously effective. While Piaget does not make the matter entirely explicit, it is clear from his observations that a directed trial-and-error process is involved. The infant's behavior is directed in the sense that the desire to reproduce the interesting result guides his actions and in the sense that he attempts only behaviors which are clearly relevant: the infant does not kick his feet, but limits his efforts to arm movements. Within these constraints the process involves trial and error since the infant does not know at first precisely which arm movements are effective. He has to try them out to see which meet with success and which with failure. It is also clear from the observations, and again not explicit in Piaget's explanation, that the infant does not simply rediscover old movements. This may be the original objective and accomplishment, but with practice the infant develops movements which are more precise, skilled, and effective than those which originally and accidentally obtained the goal.

The result of this activity is a secondary circular reaction which is a far more complex structure than anything the infant had developed earlier. Now the infant is interested in the external environment and is able to develop behaviors which serve as a primitive means for obtaining various ends. However, the secondary circular reaction has two deficiencies. First, it is not fully intentional as the infant does not have a goal in mind from the outset; rather, the goal has been discovered by accident, and it is only after this chance event has occurred that the goal guides behavior and gives it thereby a purposive character. A second deficiency is that the behavior is essentially conservative. The infant's aim is to reproduce, to duplicate some behavior which produced interesting results in the past. He does not attempt to invent new behaviors. These two deficiencies lead Piaget to maintain that the secondary circular reaction does not yet constitute *intelligent* behavior.

Primitive Classes

One of the most interesting aspects of Piaget's theory has to do with the infant's formation of classes or meaning. Their development, according to Piaget, begins very early in life. The following observations illustrate the matter:

> At 0;6(12) Lucienne perceives from a distance two celluloid parrots attached to a chandelier and which she had sometimes had in her bassinet. As soon as she sees them, she definitely but briefly shakes her legs without trying to act upon them from a distance. . . . So too, at 0;6(19) it suffices that she catches sight of her dolls from a distance for her to outline the movements of swinging them with her hand.
>
> From 0;7(27) certain too familiar situations no longer set in motion secondary circular reactions, but simply outlines of schemes. Thus when seeing a doll which she has actually swung many times, Lucienne limits herself to opening and closing her hands or shaking her legs, but very briefly and without real effort. (*OI*, pp. 186–87)

In essence, Piaget has observed that when the infant comes into contact with some familiar object he does not apply to it the secondary circular reaction which normally would be employed. Instead, Lucienne exhibits an *abbreviated* form of the behavior and does not seem to intend to produce the usual result. The abbreviated action does not seem mechanical, like a conditioned response. Further, the infant is "perfectly serious" and repeats the action on a number of different occasions.

Piaget's interpretation is that the abbreviated acts are special cases of recognitory assimilation. If you will recall, in earlier stages the infant's overt behavior showed the ability to distinguish between various objects; for example, when hungry he sucked the nipple but rejected a pacifier. Thus, the infant's behavior is said to involve recognitory assimilation when he is selective in applying specific schemes to various aspects of the environment.

The case of abbreviated movements involves a similar selectivity. Lucienne, for example, kicks in response to toys which she has swung, but not in response to other toys. However, the present instance involves more than selectivity. The infant's behavior is abbreviated; she does not choose to display the entire scheme when it would be quite feasible to do so. Piaget interprets the abbreviation as a behavioral precursor of *classification* or *meaning*. Lucienne, of course, does not have an abstract conception of the parrot. She cannot verbalize its properties or identify it as an instance of the class of animal toys. But the abbreviated behavior shows that Lucienne makes a beginning attempt at classification of the object. The brief kicking, for instance, is the first step toward thinking the thought, "That's the parrot; that's something to be swung." Her "understanding" is of course quite primitive and does not yet operate on a mental level. Nevertheless, she has made progress over stages 1 and 2, since she displays behavior which indicates that the initial steps toward internalization of action are occurring. The abbreviated scheme is the first approximation to thought.

Piaget proposes a technical terminology for describing these events. He designates as a *signifier* an object or event that stands for something else; the child's reaction to the object or event is the *signified*. In the present case the signifier is the parrot, and the signified is the child's brief kicking. The signifier is the ''thing,'' and the signified is what it means to the infant. With development, the signifier may be no longer a thing but a word, and the signified may be not a behavior but an act of intellectual understanding.

Primitive Relations

As we shall see later, in Chapter 4, classification is considered a vital aspect of the child's thought and is investigated in great detail. Similarly, we shall see in the same chapter that the notion of *relation* occupies a prominent place in Piaget's theories. And relations, too, have primitive behavioral origins which arise in the course of the first several stages. Here is an example:

> In the evening of 0;3(13) Laurent by chance strikes the chain while sucking his fingers . . . he grasps it and slowly displaces it while looking at the rattles. He then begins to swing it very gently which first produces a slight movement of the hanging rattles and an as yet faint sound inside them. Laurent then definitely increases by degrees his own movements: he shakes the chain more and more vigorously and laughs uproariously at the result obtained.—On seeing the child's expression it is impossible not to deem this gradation intentional. (*OI*, p. 185)

In other words, the infant seems to see the difference between a slight movement on his part and a strong one; similarly, he can discriminate between a loud and a soft rattle. The infant can put two sounds or two movements into relationship with each other. Furthermore, the infant seems to see that the intensity of his movements is directly related to the intensity of sounds made by the rattle. These perceptions of differences in intensity are the origins of quantitative thought. We shall see later how these relationships are developed in stage 4.

Imitation

In stage 3 the infant's attempts at imitation become increasingly systematic. Through the secondary circular reactions the infant acquires increasingly extensive experience of the environment. The infant's schemes increase in number and range, with the result that he is more capable than formerly of behavior which matches that of a model. Since he can now assimilate more models, there is greater opportunity for imitation. It is still the case, however, that the infant continues to imitate only what is familiar—only actions which he already can do—and cannot yet reproduce novel actions. This conservative feature of imitation is analogous to that displayed by the secondary circular reactions.

Object Concept

In stage 2 we saw that the infant made no attempt to search for a vanished object. Stage 3, on the other hand, is characterized by the acquisition of four new behavior patterns which represent considerable progress in the formation of the object concept.

First, there is visual anticipation of the future positions of objects. If, for example, an object drops very quickly and the infant cannot see all the movement, he can nevertheless anticipate the final resting place of the object. At first the infant does this best if he himself has dropped the object. Later, he can anticipate the position of an object dropped by someone else. Consider the following illustration:

> At 0;6(3) Laurent, lying down, holds in his hand a box five centimeters in diameter. When it escapes him he looks for it in the right direction (beside him). I then grasp the box and drop it myself, vertically, and too fast for him to be able to follow the trajectory. His eyes search for it at once on the sofa on which he is lying. I manage to eliminate any sound or shock and I perform the experiment at his right and at his left; the result is always positive. (*The Construction of Reality in the Child, CR,* pp. 14–15)

Here we see that the infant no longer continues passive viewing of the place where he saw the object vanish, as he did in the previous stage, but he now visually searches for it in a new location. This behavior shows that the infant anticipates that the object's movement will continue even though he himself is unable to see it. In this sense the infant confers on the object a preliminary sort of intrinsic permanence which, however, remains subjective since it is closely related to his own actions. He searches for the object chiefly if he himself has caused its disappearance.

A second achievement of this stage is what Piaget calls *interrupted prehension.* This is the tactual equivalent to the above-mentioned behavior of visual accommodation to rapid movements. In other words, if the infant has already set in motion certain movements of the hand or fingers for the purpose of grasping an object and then loses it or does not succeed in grasping it, he will search for the object by continuing the movements.

As in the case of visual accommodation, the infant attributes only a subjective permanence to the object. The object exists only in relation to the action he was performing when it vanished or slipped from his grasp.

The infant originates no new movements to retrieve the lost object, but merely repeats past gestures of holding or attempting to hold the object. Also, if no movements toward the object had been initiated in the first place, the infant makes no active attempt to search for a disappearing object.

Third, we can observe during this stage a behavior which is called *deferred circular reaction*. In this case a circular reaction involving an object is interrupted and resumed spontaneously by the infant at a later time. The resumption of the actions on an object implies that the infant expects it to continue to be available. For example, .

> At 0;8(30) Lucienne is busy scratching a powder box placed next to her on her left, but abandons that game when she sees me appear on her right. She drops the box and plays with me for a moment, babbles, etc. Then she suddenly stops looking at me and turns at once in the correct position to grasp the box; obviously she does not doubt that this will be at her disposal in the very place where she used it before. (*CR*, p. 25)

This is an important step forward, since such behavior is not merely a continuation of previous movements when an object is lost from sight or touch. Here the action has been completely interrupted and replaced by another quite different pattern of behavior. Yet at a later point, not too far removed in time, the infant of his own accord returns to the place where he had been playing and expects what he had been playing with to be there still. This shows that the infant attributes at least some permanence to the object. Despite this accomplishment, the infant's object concept is not yet fully developed. By contrast with advances to be made in the future, the infant's behavior in the present stage is still too closely associated with a practical situation and previous activities, and does not yet involve an entirely mature object concept.

In a fourth reaction typical of the present stage, the infant can now recognize an invisible object even when able to see only certain parts of it. If the infant is shown a toy which (while he watches) is completely covered by a cloth, he makes no attempt to search for the toy. If, however, certain parts are left visible the infant tries to lift the cloth to discover the rest of the toy. But even this ability is curiously limited; he is able to recognize the whole only when some portions are visible. For example, one of Piaget's children was able to recognize his bottle only if either end was visible and the middle hidden. If only the middle portion were shown, he was not able to recognize the bottle and made no attempt to suck on it.

The recognition of partly hidden objects occurs only after the child has acquired sufficient skill in manipulating things. While handling a variety of toys and other objects, the infant explores them visually. By varying the distances and angles of these things, bringing them closer to the eyes, turning them around, and moving them from side to side, the infant will

gradually gain a better knowledge of their shape and their other properties. This sort of knowledge, of course, is necessary for such activity as the
recognition of partly hidden objects and thus contributes toward the development of a genuine object concept.

In brief, we see that the four behaviors of the present stage—(1) visual anticipation of rapid movements, (2) interrupted prehension, (3) deferred circular reactions, and (4) reconstruction of an invisible whole from
a visible fraction—all present similar limitations and shortcomings with
respect to the object concept. These behaviors all indicate that at this stage
the object does not have a fully independent or individual existence but is
closely related to the infant's own action. When the object disappears, the
infant is content to repeat actions that were being performed at the time of
its disappearance. The infant's attempts to rediscover the lost object consist only of a repetition of the past actions associated with the object. No
novel behavior is introduced.

STAGE 4: 10 TO 12 MONTHS

Coordination of Secondary Schemes

The following observations show how after initial failure the child
develops the behavior patterns characteristic of stage 4:

> at 0;6(0) I present Laurent with a matchbox, extending my hand laterally
> to make an obstacle to his prehension. Laurent tries to pass over my hand,
> or to the side, but he does not attempt to displace it. As each time I prevent
> his passage, he ends by storming at the box while waving his hand. . . .
> Same reactions at 0;6(8), 0;6(10), 0;6(21), etc.
> Finally, at 0;7(13) Laurent reacts quite differently almost from the begin-
> ning of the experiment. I present a box of matches above my hand, but
> behind it, so that he cannot reach it without setting the obstacle aside. But
> Laurent, after trying to take no notice of it, suddenly tries to hit my hand as
> though to remove or lower it; I let him do it to me and he grasps the box. I
> recommence to bar his passage, but using as a screen a sufficiently supple
> cushion to keep the impress of the child's gestures. Laurent tries to reach the
> box, and bothered by the obstacles, he at once strikes it, definitely lowering
> it until the way is clear. . . .
> Moreover, one notes that the intermediate act serving as means (remov-
> ing the obstacle) is borrowed from a familiar scheme: the scheme of striking.
> We recall that Laurent from 0;4(7) and above all from 0;4(19) has the habit
> of hitting hanging objects in order to swing them and finally from 0;5(2) of
> striking the objects. . . . Now, this is the usual scheme of which Laurent
> makes use at the present time, no longer in the capacity of an end in itself (of

a final scheme) but as a means (a transitional or mobile scheme). (*OI*, pp. 217–18)

The interpretation of Laurent's behavior utilizes many of the principles discussed in connection with stage 3. There are, however, some important differences. One difference is that Laurent has the goal in mind from the outset. If you will recall, in stage 3 the infant *accidentally* discovers a goal and only then pursues it. In stage 4, on the other hand, Laurent initially perceives the presented object as a familiar goal. The infant has already developed schemes for dealing with the goal and immediately tries to assimilate it into them. Or in simpler language, the infant already knows what to do with the object and wants to do it. The directional force affecting the infant's behavior—his desire to achieve the goal—is, of course, once again a matter of functional assimilation. Once the scheme of the goal—grabbing the matchbox—is activated, it needs to function.

But an obstacle arises (the father's hand or the cushion) which prevents the child from attaining the goal. Now we can see the second feature which distinguishes behavior in stage 4 from that in stage 3. The infant is now required to develop new means for removing the obstacle to achieve his ends. Unlike stage 3, it is not now simply a matter of *rediscovering* some behavior which earlier led (accidentally) to the goal. The infant must show some degree of originality to remove the obstacle. But this originality is of a very limited sort. Instead of *inventing* new means for dealing with the obstacle, Laurent attempts to utilize as means schemes which have been developed in connection with other situations. That is, he generalizes patterns of previously learned behavior to the new problem (generalizing assimilation). In the course of this generalization, the older schemes may be somewhat, but not fundamentally, modified. Also, he may try out several schemes, but in the end retains only the one which works by removing the obstacle. Accommodation is once again dependent on practical success. The result is a coordination of two secondary schemes, each of which had been learned earlier, and each of which is only slightly modified for the present occasion. One scheme serves as the means and the other as the ends. The child's originality rests not in inventing two separate schemes but in combining in a novel way two previously learned patterns of behavior.

Several features of this coordination are emphasized by Piaget. First, it is still essentially conservative. The infant's aim is to treat the goal object in the same way as previously. Once the obstacle is removed, the infant applies a *familiar* scheme. Second, the infant's behavior at this stage is for the first time truly intentional and therefore "intelligent." Piaget's criteria for the existence of intention are three in number: (1) the infant has the goal in mind from the beginning and does not discover it accidentally as was the case in stage 3, (2) an obstacle arises which prevents direct attainment of the goal and necessitates some kind of indirect approach, and (3) to overcome the obstacle, the infant employs a scheme (means) which is different from that employed in the case of the goal (ends).

A third feature of this coordination emphasized by Piaget is that the behavior under discussion is mobile. The novel coordination between two schemes not previously associated is made possible by the infant's relatively new ability to detach his schemes from their usual contents. In other words, the scheme used as means is generalized or transferred from the situation in which it was originally learned. This flexibility in the application of schemes is what constitutes mobility.

Relations

In stage 3 we discussed the very first manifestations of relations in the infant. With the coordination of schemes in stage 4, the infant becomes capable of establishing more complex relationships.

Let us recall, for example, Laurent's coordination of secondary schemes: removing an obstacle to attain a goal. When Laurent does this, it is as if he "understands" that the obstacle stands in a certain relationship to the goal. The obstacle is *in front of* the goal, and it must be removed *before* the goal can be attained. In other words, just as an abbreviated performance of one scheme is a primitive indication of a class, so the *coordination* of two schemes implies a behavioral analogue of the understanding of relations.

Let us take another example:

> at 0;9(17), Laurent lifts a cushion in order to look for a cigar case. When the object is entirely hidden the child lifts the screen with hesitation, but when one end of the case appears Laurent removes the cushion with one hand and with the other tries to extricate the objective. The act of lifting the screen is therefore entirely separate from that of grasping the desired object and constitutes an autonomous "means," no doubt derived from earlier and analogous acts. (*OI*, p. 222)

Thus the sequence is a clear case of secondary circular reaction. Laurent has learned how to get the goal. But has he not also learned something of the relation between obstacle and goal? Laurent's behavior may be interpreted as showing a concrete understanding of certain relations: the cushion is *on top of* the cigar box which in turn is *under* the pillow. We emphasize once again that the child's "understanding" of relations is not abstract like the adult's; instead, it is entirely contained in his means-end behavior.

Perhaps the most remarkable feature of relations is that even in the first few stages, they involve an element of quantity. For example,

At 0;9(4) Laurent imitates the sounds which he knows how to make spontaneously. I say "papa" to him, he replies *papa* or *baba*. When I say "papapapa" he replies *apapa* or *bababa*. When I say "papapapapapapa" he replies *papapapa,* etc. There exists a global evaluation of the number of syllables: the quantity corresponding to 2 is in any case distinguished from 3, 4, or 5. . . .

At 0;10(4) Laurent repeats *pa* when I say "pa," *papa* for "papa" and *papapa* for a number of 4 or more than 4. (*OI,* p. 241)

Thus the infant shows a primitive appreciation of number in the ability to discriminate among different numbers of syllables.

Anticipation

If you will, recall that in connection with the abbreviated schemes of stage 3, we discussed the development of the operations of classification and the relation between the signifier and the signified. For example, when Lucienne briefly shakes her legs at the hanging parrots, the sight of the toys is the signifier and the abbreviated motion is the signified—the primitive meaning of the parrots for the child. In the present stage, the system of meanings is used in the service of anticipation. (This occurs also in stage 3, but in rudimentary form.) Here is an example concerning Jacqueline:

At 0;9(16) . . . she likes the grape juice in a glass, but not the soup in a bowl. She watches her mother's activity. When the spoon comes out of the glass she opens her mouth wide, whereas when it comes from the bowl, her mouth remains closed. . . . At 0;9(18) Jacqueline no longer needs to look at the spoon. She notes by the sound whether the spoonful comes from the glass or from the bowl and obstinately closes her mouth in the latter case. . . .

Lucienne has revealed most of the same reactions. Thus at 0;8(23) she also closes her mouth to the spoonful coming from the bowl (of soup) and opens it to those coming from the glass (of fruit juice). (*OI,* p. 249)

How can we interpret these reactions? First, note that they are *anticipatory.* The infant does not avoid the soup when it is in her mouth, but before it gets there. Apparently the sight of the soup or even its distinctive sound is a signifier, and the signified is the unpleasant taste of the soup. In other words, the infant sees or hears the soup, and its meaning for her is an unpleasant experience. She then closes her mouth, not in response to the actual taste of the soup, but to the meaning that soup has for her before it enters her mouth. Furthermore, the infant in this stage does not form only anticipations which are connected with her own actions. For example, Jacqueline once cried when she saw someone who was sitting next to her get up. Apparently for Jacqueline the sight of the person getting up was a signifier of his expected imminent departure (the signified), and it was to this signified (the expectation of departure) that she reacted.

How do these anticipations develop? Formerly, Jacqueline had observed that the signifier—in this case the person getting up—was followed by another event, his departure. She had consequently perceived a connection between the two events, so that now the signifier gives rise to an anticipation concerning the event to follow.

Imitation

Considerable progress in imitation occurs during stage 4. The infant can now establish relationships between the movements of a model and the corresponding movements of invisible parts of his own body. Also, he begins to imitate new actions of models.

Consider this example of the first case:

> at 0;8(4) Jacqueline began by making a slight noise with her saliva as a result of the friction of her lips against her teeth, and I had imitated this sound at the outset. [On the same day] Jacqueline was moving her lips as she bit her jaws. I did the same thing and she stopped and watched me attentively. When I stopped she began again. I imitated her. She again stopped and so it went on. (*PDI,* pp. 30–31)

Here we see that Jacqueline establishes a connection between what she sees in the model (the movement of his lips) and what she cannot see in herself, but can only feel, namely, her own lip movements. How does she manage to do this? At first with her saliva she makes a sound which is imitated by Piaget. Jacqueline repeats this sound and at the same time carefully watches the movements of the model's mouth. Now while she is reproducing the sound of the saliva and watching Piaget's mouth, she becomes aware of certain tactile-kinesthetic feelings. The sound becomes associated on the one hand with these feelings, and on the other with the sight of the model's lip movements. Thus, the sound is a common denominator linking the visual and kinesthetic cues. Later the sound is no longer necessary, and she becomes able to imitate mouth movements without either the model or herself having to produce the sound first.

The following is an example of the imitation of new actions of a model:

> At 0;9(12) I alternately bent and straightened my finger, and she [Jacqueline] opened and closed her hand. At 0;9(16) she reacted to the same model several times in succession by waving her hand, but as soon as she stopped trying to imitate me she raised her finger correctly. When I resumed she again began to wave goodbye.
>
> At 0;9(19) I tried the same experiment. She imitated me, but used her whole hand which she straightened and bent without taking her eyes off my finger.

. . . Finally at 0;9(22) she succeeded in isolating and imitating correctly the movement of the forefinger. (*PDI,* pp. 46–47)

Here Piaget initiates a new movement in front of the child. Jacqueline, contrary to her reactions of the preceding stage, no longer ignores the new movement, but tries to imitate it. Two restrictions on the initial imitation of novel behavior are apparent in the foregoing example. In the first place, the infant imitates only movements which are similar to those she is already able to perform. For instance, bending and straightening the finger is not too different from bending and straightening the hand. The infant is consequently interested in imitating such behavior since she can assimilate it to some known scheme. Furthermore, imitation is only very approximate at this point. The infant rarely succeeds in reproducing the correct movement on the first trial. She gradually improves her technique with practice and, by a succession of adjustments, accommodates her schemes to the novel movement.

Object Concept

The behavior of the stage 4 infant toward objects shows a marked progress in comparison with that of the previous stage and is a result of the infant's improved manipulatory skills. Since the infant is now better able to coordinate hand and eye movements, he can explore objects more adequately than before. By holding an object while he brings it closer to or further from the eyes, or by turning it around in the hand, he becomes aware that the object remains the same even though many visual changes have taken place. This discovery leads to the attribution of qualities of permanence and substance to objects. As a result, when an object vanishes the infant tries to find it again by active search. He no longer attempts to rediscover the object by merely prolonging or repeating the actions already underway when the object disappeared. Instead, the infant now initiates new movements and actions which indicate that the object has become detached from its previous subjective relationship with the infant's own activity.

In certain conditions, however, the object concept continues to retain some of its subjective qualities. This phenomenon may be seen clearly from the following observation:

At 0;10(18) Jacqueline is seated on a mattress without anything to disturb or distract her (no coverlets, etc.). I take her parrot from her hands and hide it twice in succession under the mattress, on her left, in A. Both times Jacqueline looks for the object immediately and grabs it. Then I take it from her hands and move it very slowly before her eyes to the corresponding place on her right, under the mattress, in B. Jacqueline watches this movement but at the moment when the parrot disappears in B she turns to her left and looks where it was before, in A. (*CR,* p. 51)

Jacqueline presents the reaction typical of this stage. In certain situations the infant is unable to take into account the number or complexity of the movements of an object, and attempts to look for the object in the place where she had previously succeeded in discovering it. In other words, if the situation is too complex, she tends to attribute to the object a sort of absolute or privileged position which is that associated with previously successful discoveries. If, on the other hand, the object simply disappears in one spot, the infant searches for it in the right place.

In stage 4, then, the infant sometimes attributes to the object qualities of substance and permanence. In straightforward situations the object is detached from the infant's actions and is an objective entity. Should its movements become too complicated for the infant to follow, however, the object once again takes on certain subjective properties and becomes related to the infant's past actions, especially those which had previously proven successful in discovering the object.

STAGE 5: 12 TO 18 MONTHS

Tertiary Circular Reaction

In stage 5 behavior loses its conservative emphasis, and the child, who has now begun to walk, begins to search for novelty. Here is an observation on Laurent:

> at 0;10(2) Laurent discovered in "exploring" a case of soap, the possibility of throwing this object and letting it fall. Now, what interested him at first was not the objective phenomenon of the fall—that is to say the object's trajectory—but the very act of letting go. He therefore limited himself, at the beginning, merely to reproducing the result observed fortuitously.
>
> . . . at 0;10(10) . . . Laurent manipulates a small piece of bread. . . . Now, in contradistinction to what has happened on the preceding days, he pays no attention to the act of letting go whereas he watches with great interest the body in motion . . . [the falling bread].
>
> At 0;10(11) Laurent is lying on his back. . . . He grasps in succession a celluloid swan, a box, etc., stretches out his arm and lets them fall. He distinctly varies the positions of the fall. Sometimes he stretches out his arm vertically, sometimes he holds it obliquely, in front or behind his eyes, etc. When the object falls in a new position (for example, on his pillow), he lets it fall two or three more times on the same place, as though to study the spatial relation; then he modifies the situation. At a certain moment the swan falls near his mouth; now he does not suck it (even though this object habitually serves this purpose), but drops it three times more while merely making the gesture of opening his mouth. (*OI,* pp. 268–69)

The striking thing about these observations is Laurent's curiosity about the objects in his world. Laurent does not focus interest on himself or on those properties of an object which aid in attaining some goal; instead, he seems curious about the object as an object, and he seems desirous of learning all he can about its nature. This interest in novelty for its own sake is called a *tertiary circular reaction.*

Piaget's explanation begins with noting that the infant often discovers the initial result by chance. For example, in the process of playing with his soap dish Laurent accidentally dropped it and observed the fall. Moreover, the initial chance event interests the infant, and this interest can be explained in terms of the moderate novelty principle described earlier. The infant, of course, desires to *reproduce* the interesting event, and this behavior involves the principle of functional assimilation. Consequently, Laurent repeats the original act and drops the case of soap several times in succession.

Thus far the infant's behavior is no different from that of stage 3: an interesting result accidentally occurs, and the infant attempts to find a means by which to conserve it. However, at this point two distinctive features of the tertiary reaction manifest themselves. First, instead of continuing simple and rigid repetition of the interesting event, Laurent initiates behavioral changes which produce variations in the event itself. Laurent drops the bread and then the toys from different heights or from different positions. Second, he acts as if he now has interest in the new actions of the objects themselves and searches for novelties—for the unexpected. He seems to treat the unanticipated trajectories of the toys as something to be understood.

The explanation of the tertiary circular reaction involves several steps:

1. At first the infant tries to assimilate the new objects into his usual scheme of dropping. He finds, however, that the habitual scheme does not work very well as he meets with resistance. That is, the infant tries to drop the piece of bread in the same way he dropped the soap case; then he tries to drop the swan in the same way he dropped the bread. Since all these objects do not fall in the same way, he meets with a resistance which is imposed by the reality of the objects themselves. Laurent finds that his available scheme of dropping does not apply in the same way to all of the objects. Each object has properties of its own which must be taken into account.

2. The infant becomes interested in these resistances. Piaget points out that at this stage of development the infant is more capable than before of appreciating novelty. If you will recall, the "interesting" was defined as that which is moderately different from what the infant recognizes as familiar. Consequently, the more things the infant is familiar with and the more schemes he has, the more objects and events he is able to recognize

as novel and interesting. The newborn's world is largely restricted to sucking; events outside the oral sphere (as most events are) cannot be interesting because of the lack of schemes relevant to them. But the infant at stage 5 has developed skills which permit contact with increasingly larger segments of the world; consequently, there is much that he will find interesting. In summary, the more complex the system of schemes, the more the infant will be attracted to novelty. He will then be interested in the resistances encountered by applying old schemes to new events.

3. The infant is interested in the properties of objects from another point of view, too. At this stage the infant has begun to attribute permanence to objects and recognizes that they have an existence independent of his own. In fact, objects are even "centers of forces," with powers and properties of their own. This new objectification of the world also contributes to the infant's desire to explore.

Once the infant recognizes and has interest in the potential novelties of a situation, he begins to accommodate, by "groping" or using a kind of trial-and-error procedure to discover the properties of the objects. The infant's groping does not involve completely random responses; rather each of his explorations guides the next. The results of one "experiment" lead to new experiments. For instance, Laurent may release the swan from points which are increasingly high above his head and observe the extent to which the swan bounces when it hits the bed. The infant, of course, does not know beforehand what will happen; he modifies his behavior to find out. By exploring the object and accommodating his own behavior to it, the infant may eventually become able to master the object—to assimilate it without difficulty into his (modified) schemes. In this way he begins to explore and understand novel aspects of the world.

Discovery of New Means

The infant's tendency toward experimentation permits the discovery of new means for attaining a goal. Consider the following observation on Lucienne at 1;0(5). Piaget presents her with this problem. On a table is a large box turned upside down. The box is so arranged that it moves only by pivoting around its center point. On the box, away from the infant's reach, is an attractive toy, a bottle.

> Lucienne at first tries to grasp the box, but she goes about it as though the handkerchief were still involved. [Pulling a handkerchief was a scheme which Piaget had previously observed in the child.] She tries to pinch it between two fingers, in the center, and tries this for a moment without being able to grasp it. Then, with a rapid and unhesitating movement she pushes it at a point on its right edge. . . . She then notes the sliding of the box and makes it pivot without trying to lift it; as the box revolves, she succeeds in grasping the bottle. (*OI*, p. 287)

To get the object, Lucienne at first attempted to apply an already available scheme; pinching the box like a handkerchief. Then, however, she "groped" and accommodated her behavior in a trial-and-error sort of way. The result was discovery of a new means. Lucienne struck the box, and this action was successful in bringing the toy close. But while her behavior was to some extent characterized by groping, or trial and error, her actions were nevertheless *directed* in two senses. First, her accommodations were directed by the goal: Lucienne wanted to get the bottle and was trying out various means for this purpose. The means were hardly selected in a random fashion; she did not, for instance, try to obtain the toy by taking off her socks. Second, Lucienne interpreted the groping by means of her already available schemes. That is, after Lucienne by chance hit the box and saw it move, she was able, through her past experience, to "understand" the meaning of her action. She interpreted the hitting as another method for displacing objects. Thus the child's groping is directed both by the goal and by earlier schemes which enable her to understand what is happening. Therefore, learning is not explained solely by contact with the environment, that is, by experience with a world that simply forces the infant's behavior to take certain forms. The infant herself also makes an important contribution as she interprets and gives meaning to the data of experience.

Imitation

At stage 5 the child becomes capable of the systematic imitation of new models. In the previous stage, the infant had begun to imitate new models which were not too different from his own spontaneous actions, but he was rarely correct on the first trial. In the present stage the infant becomes more systematic in his techniques of imitation. Here is an example:

> At 0;11(20) she [Jacqueline] watched me with interest when I touched my forehead with my forefinger. She then put her right forefinger on her left eye, moved it over her eyebrow, then rubbed the left side of her forehead with the back of her hand, but as if she were looking for something else. She reached her ear, but came back toward her eye. . . .
> At 0;11(28) J., confronted with the same model, continued merely to rub her eye and eyebrows. But afterwards, when I seized a lock of my hair and moved it about on my temple, she succeeded for the first time in imitating me. She suddenly took her hand from her eyebrow, which she was touching, felt above it, found her hair and took hold of it, quite deliberately.
> At 0;11(30) she at once pulled her hair when I pulled mine. She also touched her head when I did so, but when I rubbed my forehead she gave up. . . . It is noteworthy that when she pulled her hair she sometimes turned her head suddenly in an attempt to see it. This movement is a clear

indication of an effort to discover the connection betwen tactual and visual perception. . . .

At 1;0(16), J. discovered her forehead. When I touched the middle of mine, she first rubbed her eye, then felt above it and touched her hair, after which she brought her hand down a little and finally put her finger on her forehead. On the following day she at once succeeded in imitating this gesture, and even found approximately the right spots indicated by the model. (*PDI,* pp. 55–56)

Two points are of interest concerning these examples. First, they clearly show that the infant is more adept than she formerly was at the immediate imitation of new actions of models. The infant tries to control her movements in a systematic way. For example, Jacqueline tries to look at her hair when she pulls it. Second, the examples illustrate some general processes of imitation. The chief aim of imitation is to reproduce the act of a model. When the model's actions are new, as in the present case, accommodation is required. That is, the infant must modify her movements to make them like the model's. Thus, accommodation has priority over assimilation. In the case of intelligent behavior, on the other hand, the processes of assimilation and accommodation are in balance. The infant attempts both to modify her behavior in response to the demands of the environment (accommodation) and to understand this environment in terms of her own schemes (assimilation).

Object Concept

In stage 5 the infant is finally able to follow correctly a visible sequence of an object's movements. He now understands positional relationships between the object and other elements of the environment. Therefore, even if the object disappears successively in a number of places the infant will search for it in the place where it was last seen. The infant does not, as in stage 4, look for the object in the place where it had previously been discovered. Thus, the object is no longer connected with a practical situation (the infant's past successes), but has acquired a permanence of its own. At this stage, though, the infant can understand only visible movements of the object. If he is unable to see all the displacements and must therefore infer that some are invisible, the infant reverts to an earlier reaction—looking for the object where he had been successful in finding it in the past. The reason for the failure is that when invisible movements of the object are involved, the infant must *infer* relationships of position but is not yet capable of inference. Consider the following illustration:

At 1;1(18) Lucienne is seated on a bed, between shawl A and cloth B. I hide a safety pin in my hand and my hand under the shawl. I remove my hand closed and empty. Lucienne opens it at once and looks for the pin. Not finding it, she searches under the shawl and finds it. . . .

But with a béret, things become complicated. I put my watch in the beret and the beret under pillow A (on the right); Lucienne lifts the pillow, takes the beret, and removes the watch from it. Then I place the beret, again containing the watch, under cushion B on the left; Lucienne looks for it in B but, as it is hidden too far down for her to find it at once, she returns to A.

Then, twice, I raise cushion B so that Lucienne sees the beret obviously containing the object; both times she resumes looking in B but, not finding the watch right away, returns to A! She searches even longer in A than in B after having seen the object in B! (*CR,* pp. 76–77)

Here we see that the object seems to be endowed with a dual nature. On the one hand, if the infant is able to follow the object's movements perceptually, she believes in its permanence and continued existence. If, however, she cannot follow the movements visually but must imagine them, the infant no longer endows the object with the property of permanence. The object reverts to its earlier status of being associated with a previously successful scheme.

STAGE 6: 18 MONTHS TO 2 YEARS

Beginning of Thought

In the course of his five stages of development, the infant has most certainly made great progress. The newborn displays simple patterns of learning which are limited to the sphere of hereditary mechanisms; the infant in stage 5 has a genuine interest in the things of the environment, explores them, and even has the ability to *invent* new ways of dealing with the world. But the infant's achievement to this point is as nothing compared with the next development. Before stage 6 the infant was not capable of thought or language and so was largely limited to the immediate data of experience. Stage 6, however, forms the transition to the next period of development in which the infant is able to use mental symbols and words to refer to absent objects. This period of symbolic thought begins to free the infant from the concrete here and now and introduces him to the world of possibilities. In Chapter 3 we shall discuss symbolic thought in detail; at present we will limit ourselves to a brief description of its beginnings, as illustrated by these observations:

Piaget is playing with Lucienne, at 1;4(0) and hides an attractive watch chain inside an empty match box.

I put the chain back into the box and reduce the opening to 3 mm. It is understood that Lucienne is not aware of the functioning of the opening and closing of the match box and has not seen me prepare the experiment. She only possesses two preceding schemes: turning the box over in order to empty it of its contents, and sliding her fingers into the slit to make the chain come out. It is of course this last procedure that she tries first: she puts her finger inside and gropes to reach the chain, but fails completely. A pause follows during which Lucienne manifests a very curious reaction. . . .

She looks at the slit with great attention; then, several times in succession, she opens and shuts her mouth, at first slightly, then wider and wider!

[Then] . . . Lucienne unhesitatingly puts her finger in the slit, and instead of trying as before to reach the chain, she pulls so as to enlarge the opening. She succeeds and grasps the chain. (*OI*, pp. 337–38)

This observation reveals an important advance in the child's capabilities. Lucienne was confronted with a situation for which a new solution was required. To get the chain out of the box she tried methods which had in the past been successful in similar situations. But these schemes were not adequate for the new problem. What would the stage 5 infant do in these circumstances? He would experiment with various new means until one of the inventions was successful. His behavior would show groping.

But Lucienne does not do this. Instead, she pauses and looks at the box intensely. Her chief overt behavior at this time is only an opening and closing of the mouth. After this delay, she immediately solves the problem. What does the opening and closing of the mouth signify? Piaget interprets it as showing that she tries to think about ways of solving the problem. Lucienne is not yet proficient at thought; she is not yet capable of representing the situation to herself fully in mental terms. Consequently, she "thinks out" the problem partly by way of movements of the mouth. Even though her thought is not yet fully internalized, it involves a considerable short cut over the groping of stage 5. Now Lucienne need not act out her attempted solution, for she is at least partially able to employ a more economical procedure: to *think*. Thus, Lucienne is on the threshold of a new period of intellectual development in which the acquisition of the symbolic function permits the growth of true mental activity.

Imitation

The notable achievement of stage 6 is the appearance of the capacity to represent mentally an object or action which is not perceptually present. The capacity for such *representation* has repercussions for the progress of imitation and contributes to the appearance of two new reactions during stage 6. In the first place, when faced with new models, the infant no longer needs to perform overtly trial attempts at imitation; instead, he now tries out the various movements mentally. Having made the necessary mental adjustments, the infant can then perform the correct action. Since the process is largely mental, the stage 6 infant can imitate more quickly than the one who must first try out all the movements. The internalization of the trial-and-error process consequently leads to what appears to be an immediate imitation of models.

Another feature of the present stage is that the infant becomes capable of imitating for the first time a model which is no longer present. This *deferred imitation* is due to the fact that the infant can imagine the model even though it is absent. That is, the infant is capable of evoking (representing) the absent model in some internal symbolic form, for example, by means of a visual image. Consider the following example of deferred imitation:

> At 1;4(3) Jacqueline had a visit from a little boy of 1;6 whom she used to see from time to time, and who, in the course of the afternoon, got into a terrible temper. He screamed as he tried to get out of a playpen and pushed it backward, stamping his feet. Jacqueline stood watching him in amazement, never having witnessed such a scene before. The next day, she herself screamed in her playpen and tried to move it, stamping her foot lightly several times in succession. (*PDI*, p. 63)

The internalization of the action is quite clear. The infant does not reproduce the scene at the time of its occurrence, but at some later period. Therefore, representation was required for the child to preserve the original scene for it to be evoked at a later time.

Object Concept

Finally, at stage 6 the concept of the permanent object is fully elaborated. The infant not only takes into account visible displacements of the object, but can also reconstruct correctly a series of invisible displacements. For example,

> At 1;7(23) Jacqueline is seated opposite three object-screens, A, B and C (a beret, a handkerchief, and her jacket) aligned equidistant from each other. I hide a small pencil in my hand saying, "Coucou, the pencil." [The child had previously found it under A.] I hold out my closed hand to her, put it under A, then under B, then under C (leaving the pencil under C); at each step I again extend my closed hand, repeating, "Coucou, the pencil." Jacqueline then searches for the pencil directly in C, finds it and laughs. (*CR*, pp. 79–80)

Jacqueline has seen the pencil disappear only once and into Piaget's hand. She does not, however, look into his hand to find the pencil, but under the last object where he had placed his hand. This reaction indicates that she believes that the pencil continued to exist within the hand during the whole sequence of displacements, and that she has inferred that the invisible object was displaced from A to B to C. In other words, Jacqueline has formed a mental image of the pencil and can follow the image through a series of complex displacements.

SUMMARY AND CONCLUSIONS

The infant's development in the sensorimotor period is a truly remarkable achievement. In stage 1, the newborn depends heavily on reflexes for interaction with the environment. The environment, however, does not simply turn on and off these tools provided by heredity. The infant, even in the first month of life, profits from experience and actively modifies the reflex schemes. He learns, for example, to recognize the nipple and to search for it.

In stage 2, the infant shows behavior patterns which are removed from the feeding situation. (1) He develops the primary circular reactions, for example, the motor coordinations necessary for bringing the hand to the mouth. (2) The infant learns in a primitive way to anticipate future events. When placed in the appropriate position, the infant anticipates nursing by initiating sucking movements. (2) The first signs of curiosity appear. The infant shows an interest in moderately novel events. (4) The infant sometimes repeats the behavior of models. This is a very primitive kind of imitation, since it occurs only when the model performs an action highly similar to a scheme available to the infant. It is as if the infant did not distinguish the model's acts from his own; therefore, the apparent imitation is merely the infant's repetition of behavior no different from his own. (5) The infant lacks a mature object concept, but develops several patterns of behavior which are preliminary steps in the right direction. He coordinates the previously independent schemes of looking and hearing, among others, and shows passive expectancy by watching for a brief time the spot where an object has disappeared.

In stage 3, the infant's behavior and interest extend beyond his own body and makes more extensive, but still immature, contact with the external environment. (1) The infant develops secondary circular reactions. By chance, he discovers an interesting environmental event and attempts to reproduce the actions which caused it. (2) The infant shows preliminary indications of classification or meaning. Presented with a familiar object, he sometimes reacts by showing mere abbreviations of the actions it usually elicits. This behavior appears to be a precursor of mental recognition and understanding of the object. (3) The infant's imitation is now more systematic and precise. He is fairly successful at imitation of models, but only when familiar patterns of behavior are involved. (4) The infant makes considerable progress toward attainment of the object concept. If he himself has caused an object's disappearance, the infant attempts a visual or tactual search. This search only involves continuation of behavior (like looking or grasping) which is already under way. To this extent the object concept remains subjective—intimately bound to the infant's own behavior.

In stage 4, the infant's behavior is increasingly systematic and well organized. (1) He is able to coordinate secondary schemes. He has a goal in mind from the outset and uses one scheme as a means for attaining the goal and a second scheme for dealing with the goal. This behavior is purposive and therefore intelligent. (2) By interacting with the environment, the infant learns something about relations among objects. In removing an obstacle to a goal, for instance, the child achieves a preliminary and concrete understanding of the fact that the obstacle is *in front of* the goal and must be removed *before* the goal can be attained. (3) The infant's increasing understanding of the environment is apparent in the ability to anticipate events which do not depend on his own actions. At this period the infant expects people to act in certain ways; he begins to recognize that they are "centers of forces" independent of himself. (4) The infant begins to imitate the novel behavior of models, but is not yet strikingly successful. Also he imitates actions—like sticking out the tongue—which he cannot see himself perform. (5) The infant's object concept is almost fully developed. He employs a variety of behavior to search for vanished objects. He clearly attributes to things a degree of substance and permanence and begins to conceive of objects as autonomous and as independent of his own subjective state. Nevertheless, he is not yet successful at following a complex series of displacements of an object.

Stage 5 is the climax of the sensorimotor period. (1) The infant shows an active interest in producing new behavior and novel events. Before this stage, the infant's behavior was essentially conservative. He tried to rediscover old actions which happened to lead to interesting results. (2) When confronted with an obstacle the infant attempts to develop new means for dealing with it and does not rely solely on schemes which were successful previously. (3) The infant is now increasingly adept at imitating new actions of models. The infant attempts, for instance, to produce sounds he has never uttered before. (4) The infant has reached a further stage in the sensorimotor development of the object concept and can now comprehend a complex series of displacements and search for the object in the proper place.

Stage 6 forms the transition to symbolic thought. (1) In our preliminary overview we saw that the infant attempted to *think* about a problem, to develop solutions on a mental rather than a physical level. (2) Similarly, the infant can now imitate a model even though the latter may not be present. It is apparent that after observing a model, the infant forms a mental representation of it, so that the later imitation is based not on a physically present model, but on its mental surrogate. (3) The infant now can reconstruct a series of invisible displacements of an object because of these new abilities in representation.

In the most general sense, development reveals a process of *decentration*. The infant begins life in an undifferentiated state, not separating self from environment or wish from reality. He is *centered* about the self. For example, we have seen how the infant in the first few stages does not have a mature object concept. A thing ceases to exist when it passes outside his immediate perception. Furthermore, for the infant the world is merely a series of unstable and unconnected "pictures." Neither self nor external environment exist as autonomous entities. In the course of development the infant advances from this "adualistic" or undifferentiated state to one of greater separation of self and environment. He *decenters* from the self. In the case of the object concept, for example, the infant now conceives of things existing independently. Objects now are centers of forces and have properties which do not depend on his will. This greater understanding of the external world is at the same time an increased comprehension of the self. The realization of the separateness of things necessarily involves the simultaneous apprehension of the existence of self. In other words, the person who believes that his wishes influence the movements of things does not understand either self or things; the person who believes that the two are separate has a greater understanding of both.

Piaget stresses several points concerning development in the sensori-motor period. First, the age norms are only approximate. As we noted earlier it is impossible to give precise age norms because only three infants provide the data for study. More important, Piaget fully recognizes that the timing of the stages depends on a host of factors which vary among children. Development is a function of complex interaction among many factors, among which may be the nature of the social environment, the infant's rate of physical maturation, and so on. Given these complexities, it is clear that infants' progress through the stages will show many individual differences. For instance, Piaget cites the example of Jacqueline who was born in the winter. Because she was bundled up in the carriage to protect her against the cold, she did not have as much opportunity as did the other children, born in warmer weather, to develop coordination between hand and eye. From findings like these, Piaget concluded that the sensorimotor stages do not appear at precisely defined ages in the infant's life.

Second, Piaget insists, however, that the ordering of the stages is invariant. A child must pass through stage 3 before stage 4, and the reverse cannot occur. Also, a child cannot skip a stage entirely. The reasons for Piaget's assertion are both empirical and theoretical. First, Piaget's observations showed that his three children followed the sequence of development in the order described. Second, each stage is both a culmination of the one preceding and a preparation for the one to follow. Since each stage lays the groundwork for the following stage, it is hard to see, on rational grounds alone, how the order of any two stages can be reversed.

Third, Piaget emphasizes that development is a gradual and continuous process. One does not find sudden transformations in an infant's behavior so that one day he is characterized by stage 3 and the next by stage 4 activities. Development takes time, and because of this one seldom sees "pure" examples of the behaviors which Piaget uses to describe a stage. Piaget's stages are, in fact, ideal types which are abstracted from the continuum of the infant's development. While these abstractions are very useful and convenient, Piaget is careful to remind us that in the normal course of events the infant's behavior takes many forms intermediary between those described by the stages. Also, development is not always consistent across all spheres of behavior. The "stage 4 infant" is again only an abstraction. In fact, one sees infants whose object concept may be characterized by stage 4, while at the same time their level of imitation is stage 3, and so on.

Fourth, Piaget stresses that the behaviors characteristic of a given stage do not disappear when the infant attains the next stage. Instead, even as new abilities are added the infant retains many of the old ones. For example, the stage 5 infant, confronted with an obstacle and trying to remove it, may first apply schemes which have been successful in other situations (stage 4 behavior), and only then may he attempt to invent new means (stage 5 behavior).

In conclusion, we would like to make a few general comments about Piaget's theory of infancy and clarify some aspects that are often misunderstood. First, Piaget's position on the role of the environment is subtle, and consequently often misinterpreted. He feels that it is obvious that the environment exerts effects on the infant, but acceptance of this proposition hardly solves any problems. The task then becomes to discover *how* the environment operates. Piaget feels that the environment does not mold behavior by simply imposing itself on a passive subject, evoking the infant's response and rewarding it. Instead, Piaget's central theme is that the infant is *active;* that is, the infant seeks contact with the environment. His curiosity does not permit waiting for environmental events to happen; rather he searches them out and seeks increased levels of stimulation and excitation. When some environmental event occurs, the infant does not register it passively, but instead interprets it. It is this interpretation, not the event itself, which affects behavior. Suppose we have two infants, one who is capable of anticipations concerning adults and one who is not. Both witness an adult who rises and puts on a coat. One infant cries and the other remains calm. "Experience"—seeing the adult get up and put on the coat—has affected the infants differently. The explanation is that one infant expected him to leave and the other did not. The infants interpreted the events in different ways. We might even say that there existed two different "realities," each one constructed by an infant. The infants assimilated the perceived event into their differing expectations concerning adult behavior. This assimilation or interpretation gave the event meaning and produced the subsequent behaviors. So the infants did not passively register a mere "copy" of reality; instead, they interpreted, constructed, and assimilated, or, in short, gave meaning to the events.

Experience, then, does not exert effects *on* an infant, but instead, exerts effects *with* an infant. The child modifies raw experience as much as it changes him.

Second, Piaget is sometimes misunderstood concerning his views of the roles of maturation and learning. It should be abundantly clear that Piaget is not a simple maturationist. He does not believe that the infant's development unfolds solely as a result of some kind of physical maturation. Piaget's position is that maturation plays a role in development, but it certainly is not the only factor. As we have seen, he believes that the effects of the environment are quite important, and to this extent Piaget is in agreement with the environmentalists. But, as has been noted, Piaget's account of learning is quite subtle and is in many ways at variance with other theories of learning. For example, he introduces novel motivational principles, such as assimilation and the moderate novelty principle, and emphasizes the infant's interpretation of the raw data of sensory experience. In short, Piaget is neither a maturationist nor an environmentalist, at least not in the dominant behaviorist tradition. His position incorporates elements of both traditions, and, in addition, elaborates on them in highly original ways. He thinks of himself as an "interactionist," for his theory stresses that intellectual development results from an interplay between internal and external factors.

As we shall see in Chapter 6, Piaget has elaborated and supplemented his account of experience and maturation since his writing of the books on infancy. The later theory of "equilibration" expands on the role of experience and, in addition, introduces the concept of internal cognitive conflict.

Third, the nature of Piaget's stages is occasionally misunderstood. Piaget is sometimes compared with Gesell, who offered an account of infancy in terms of stages of development. Gesell's stages were merely listings of specific *behaviors* which occurred at different ages. For example, the infant is found to crawl at such and such an age, to walk at another, to run at another, and so on. While such information may be valuable, it is clear that Gesell's stages merely list the empirical phenomena and have no theoretical content whatsoever. By contrast, Piaget's stages are a theoretical taxonomy. Take, for example, stage 4, which is concerned with the coordination of secondary schemes. Piaget's theory proposes that in this stage the infant can coordinate two previously disparate patterns of behavior to attain a preconceived goal. This statement—the theory of this stage—is an abstraction which transcends the details of any specific behaviors that merely illustrate the stage. The statement is intended to allow us to understand what the infant does *regardless* of the particular behaviors involved. Piaget's stages are therefore theoretical or explanatory, and as such are radically different from Gesell's.

3

The Years 2 through 11:
The Semiotic Function
and Piaget's Early Work

The present chapter covers two broad topics. The first to be considered is the development of cognitive processes in the child of approximately 2 to 4 years. At this time some very important advances occur in the child's thought. One such advance is the onset of the semiotic function. We will concentrate on the young child's use of mental symbols and words, and on symbolic play. The second topic to be considered is the development of certain characteristics of thought in the child from 4 to 11 years. We shall review Piaget's early work on this topic and cover such matters as egocentrism, communication, and moral judgment.

THE SEMIOTIC FUNCTION

The sensorimotor period involves a rapid and remarkable development of behavioral schemes. The newborn entered the world with only a limited repertory of automatic behavior patterns provided by heredity. Yet after a period of only about two years, the infant can interact quite effectively with the immediate world of things and of people. He possesses schemes enabling him to manipulate objects and use them as means for the attainment of his goals. The infant also experiments with things to achieve a practical understanding of their properties. But all of these abilities, although useful, are nevertheless concrete, that is, limited to immediately present objects. For example, while the infant may be able to use a stick to bring an object within reach, he cannot conceive of relationships between objects that are not within his immediate scope of vision. The infant is able to act only on things which are perceived directly. Toward the end of the second year, the child begins to develop novel *cognitive*, or mental, processes.

One important aspect of cognitive development is the appearance of the *semiotic function.* This refers to the fact that from 2 to 4 years the child begins to develop the ability to make something—a mental symbol, a word, or an object—stand for or represent something else which is not present. For example, the child can use a mental "picture" of a bicycle, or the word "bicycle," or a small schematic toy to stand for the real bicycle when it is not in immediate view. The ability to represent in this way makes it possible for the child to operate on new levels. At this stage the child is not restricted to acting on things in the immediate environment because the semiotic function allows the evocation of the past. For example, his mental symbol of the bicycle permits the recollection of previous experience with this toy.

The semiotic function manifests itself in several ways. During the period from 2 to 4 years the child begins to employ mental symbols, to engage in symbolic play, and to use words. Let us review each of these activities in turn.

Mental Symbols

One example of the use of mental symbols involves deferred imitation. Let us recall the example of the temper tantrum:

> At 1;4(3) [Jacqueline] had a visit from a little boy of 1;6, whom she used to see from time to time, and who, in the course of the afternoon, got into a terrible temper. He screamed as he tried to get out of a playpen and pushed it backward, stamping his feet. J. stood watching him in amazement, never having witnessed such a scene before. The next day, she herself screamed in her playpen and tried to move it, stamping her foot lightly several times in succession. (*Play, Dreams, and Imitation, PDI,* p. 63)

The important feature of the observation is that Jacqueline's imitation was deferred: it occurred some time after she had originally seen the boy throwing the tantrum. Her behavior therefore did not simply copy an immediately observable model. If she could not see the tantrum, on what was her behavior based? How can we explain delayed imitation? One interpretation is that when Piaget observed her, Jacqueline happened to throw a tantrum for the first time, quite independently of anything the boy had done. But the explanation is quite implausible, because her behavior was so much like that of the boy. Consequently, we are forced to postulate a more complicated explanation that involves mental symbolism. The reasoning is as follows. We know that in throwing the tantrum Jacqueline did not simply copy an immediately present model. Nevertheless, her behavior was clearly similar to the boy's. Consequently, we assume that Jacqueline must have formed a mental symbol of the tantrum and then based her behavior on this symbol. In other words, Jacqueline must have had available a mental event which stood for or represented the boy's real action. The ability to symbolize in this way allowed her to copy the boy's behavior at a later time.

What is the nature of mental symbols? It is difficult to answer this question since we have no method which permits a direct "look" at the child's thought. One possibility, however, is that the child's mental symbols are, at least in part, comprised of visual images. Perhaps Jacqueline "pictured" the tantrum to herself. While visual imagery does indeed occur (and may or may not have been used by Jacqueline), Piaget reminds us that mental symbols may take other forms as well. Although sometimes a person may use visual imagery, he may at other times represent objects by their sounds, or even by an abbreviated form of their movements. Piaget also proposes that the individual may not even be conscious of these mental symbols. A child may display imitative behavior without realizing that it is based on the actions of another person. Surely, after Freud's work, it should come as no surprise that many of our thought processes are unconscious.

We have seen, then, that the mental symbol may or may not be conscious and may or may not involve visual imagery. Does the mental symbol involve language? Was Jacqueline able to imitate the tantrum because she carried in her head the *words,* "He is lifting his arms, he is shouting," and so on? Although this sort of interpretation—a verbal mediation approach—has its adherents, Piaget rejects it. He cites two major reasons. First, certain experiments with animals show that chimpanzees, for instance, have mental symbols which of course could not be based on language. If nonverbal symbolism is possible in animals, then why not in the human too? Second, observation of the child shows that behavior like deferred imitation occurs while language skills are still very primitive. It is quite unlikely that Jacqueline was at that time capable of a reasonably full verbal description of the boy's temper tantrum. Yet, her imitation was quite accurate. Since a mental symbol based on the child's crude language could not have provided a basis for such accurate imitation, the linguistic explanation must be ruled out. Thus, to explain Jacqueline's deferred imitation, we must postulate her use of mental symbols. These symbols probably do not involve language to a significant degree, but we cannot confidently specify their exact nature.

A second example of mental symbolism can be seen in the child's reaction to hidden objects. If you will recall, in stage 6 of the sensorimotor period, the child could reconstruct a series of invisible displacements of an object. In an observation described in Chapter 2, Piaget hid a small pencil in his hand and then placed the hand consecutively under a beret, under a handkerchief, and finally under a jacket where he left the pencil. Jacqueline did not look for the pencil in her father's hand, which was the last place she had seen it, and which is where the younger child searches; instead, she immediately reached under the jacket and found the pencil.

How can we explain Jacqueline's behavior? It was not random, since she acted in essentially the same way on many occasions. Piaget assumes that Jacqueline formed a mental symbol of the pencil. When Piaget covered the pencil in his hand, Jacqueline believed in its continued existence. When the hand was placed under a succession of objects, the use of the mental symbol enabled her to follow mentally the invisible displacements. The availability of a mental symbol is thus necessary for a mature object concept.

Thus far, we have seen two kinds of behavior—deferred imitation and search—which may be interpreted as demonstrating the existence of mental symbolism in the child. We may now explore the development of mental symbols.

The Formation of Mental Symbols

How does the child form mental symbols? There seem to be at least two possible answers to this difficult question. One explanation is that the ability to symbolize is an entirely new function which suddenly makes its appearance when the child is about 2 years of age. Another possibility is that symbolism has precursors in the sensorimotor period. Emphasizing continuity in intellectual development, Piaget adopts the second alternative. He postulates that the semiotic function is derived from imitation. Consider the following observation from the sensorimotor period:

> At 1;3(8) J. [Jacqueline] was playing with a clown with long feet and happened to catch the feet in the low neck of her dress. She had difficulty in getting them out, but as soon as she had done so, she tried to put them back in the same position. . . . As she did not succeed, she put her hand in front of her, bent her forefinger at a right angle to reproduce the shape of the clown's feet, described exactly the same trajectory as the clown and thus succeeded in putting her finger into the neck of her dress. She looked at the motionless finger for a moment, then pulled at her dress, without of course being able to see what she was doing. Then, satisfied, she removed her finger and went on to something else. (*PDI,* p. 65)

Here we have a case of imitation put to the service of understanding an unusual phenomenon. In the course of playing with a familiar toy, Jacqueline discovered that the clown did something unexpected and initially unexplainable. Its feet caught her dress in a way that had not occurred before. Jacqueline immediately tried to understand the cause of the unexpected event. Her method of doing so was through imitative action: she formed her finger into the shape of the clown's foot, placed the finger in her dress, and then pulled to see what would happen. She discovered that the finger got caught and therefore prevented free movement of her arm. In this way she came to understand that the shape of the clown's foot similarly restricted its removal. Another way of looking at the observation is to say that it involves a special kind of imitation: Jacqueline used her own body to represent or stand for the clown's movements. Her actions symbolized those of the clown. This is not an isolated observation; Piaget finds that the child often imitates things. For example, he noted that Lucienne, upon observing that her father's bicycle could be made to move back and forth, performed the same motions herself. She swayed to and fro at about the speed of the bicycle.

Piaget argues that such imitation of things is the sensorimotor *forerunner* of mental symbolism. The infant's swaying back and forth is the behavioral equivalent of the older child's mental symbol of the bicycle. In other words, for the infant the action of swaying signifies a bicycle, whereas for the older child a mental symbol performs the same function. Toward the end of the sensorimotor period, the child's imitation ''goes underground,'' figuratively speaking. Instead of imitating things on the level of overt behavior, the older child does so internally. For instance, in place of actually swaying back and forth, the older child might imitate the bicycle by making very slight and almost imperceptible movements of his muscles. Or, instead of forming the finger in the shape of the clown's foot, the older child might tense his finger muscles so slightly that an observer would not notice. Moreover, this internal imitation is no mere oddity. The child's internal and almost undetectable movements *constitute* the mental symbol. The child's muscles perform an abbreviated imitation of swaying, and these bodily sensations symbolize for him the bicycle. When the child's finger tenses ever so slightly, this internal imitation, which is not necessarily a visual image, signifies the clown.

We have seen, then, that the sensorimotor child represents things by acting like them. The older child, on the other hand, performs such imitation internally, and these abbreviated body movements constitute the mental symbol. Eventually the child becomes so proficient at internal imitation that the movements are extremely abbreviated and, therefore, almost impossible to detect.

Several interesting points can be made concerning the formation of the mental symbol. First, Piaget's theory gives us additional insight into the nature of the child's mental symbols. We said earlier that they might involve a visual component and that they probably do not consist of linguistic features. Now we know that mental symbols initially involve the child's actions in an important way. The mental symbol of the bicycle consists not only of a visual image, but it also may involve bodily sensations corresponding to the bicycle's movements.

Second, in referring to the symbol as consisting of internal imitation, Piaget uses the term imitation in a very broad sense to account for visual imagery. Consider this hypothetical example. When a person sees a table, his perception accommodates to it. His eyes must follow the table's outline, detect its color, focus to localize the table in space, and so on. In these ways, the person establishes a number of relationships concerning the table (space, color, etc.) which together form his perception of it. In other words, the environment does not simply impose on him the perception of the table. Instead, the perception is derived from his own activity—from a series of intricate movements of his eyes and from complex activity in the brain and nervous system. Visual perception is an activity, just as the child's swaying is an activity. Next we see the role of imitation. At a later time when the table is no longer present, the person may repeat in an abbreviated form the movements involved in his initial perception of the table. That is, his eyes may again move as they did when they traced the table's contour, adjusted to its distance, and so on. This internal and abbreviated imitation of the perceptual activity *constitutes* the visual image of the table. Since an image of an object is seldom as rich or as detailed as the original perception, the image merely represents or symbolizes the actual object. In brief, the mental symbol may involve visual imagery, and the latter may be considered the internal imitation of the originally perceived object.

Third, Piaget introduces a technical vocabulary for dealing with representations. As Figure 1 shows, the *semiotic* or *representational function* involves signifiers—mental events, words, or things which stand for something else—and the signified, to be described shortly. Signifiers signify or represent something to the individual. One type of signifier is the *symbol,* which may be *personal* and *idiosyncratic,* and resembles the thing it stands for. For one child, a toy may symbolize the bicycle; for another child, the visual image (resembling the bicycle's appearance) may suffice. Consequently, one person's symbol may not transmit to another person any information at all about the action or object that is represented. *Abbreviated movements,* as in swaying like a bicycle, seem to be the developmental forerunners of symbolism. Symbols may be *mental* or *concrete.* Concrete symbols, which we shall review shortly, may involve using one object (e.g., a handkerchief) to stand for another (e.g., a blanket). Mental symbols take several forms. We have already seen that one type of symbol is the *visual image;* other types include *auditory images.* The symbol involves a predominance of *accommodation.* This is so because the symbol consists of internal imitation, and imitation involves modifying one's behavior to fit that of a

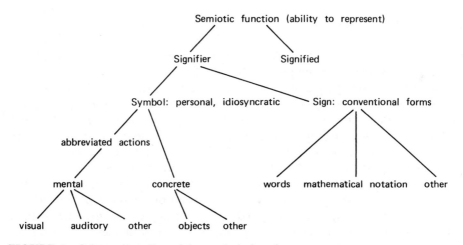

FIGURE 1 Schematic outline of the semiotic function.

model, or in broader terms, to meet the demands imposed by the social or physical environment. Another type of signifier is the *sign,* which typically refers to a *word* used in conventional language. (The sign could also refer to other conventions like mathematical notation, football diagrams, etc.) A *word* is social, not personal, and is arbitrarily related to the thing it stands for. "Bicycle," for example, is not an idiosyncratic term: most of us agree that "bicycle" stands for the same object, and therefore use of the term transmits considerable information. Also, the word "bicycle" bears no resemblance to the real thing; if our linguistic community so decreed, we could legitimately substitute "elephant" for "bicycle." In summary, signifiers involve various types of symbols and signs.

The complexity of Piaget's terminology should not obscure the fact that the ability to form mental representations is an achievement of great magnitude. In the sensorimotor period this capacity was lacking. If you will recall, the only signifiers were concrete attributes of things. For example, the mother's voice or footsteps signified to the infant that she would soon arrive. However, this primitive signifier, or "index," was linked to the infant's actually hearing the voice or footsteps. He had no mental representation for these events; therefore, the signifier had meaning for the infant only when the events actually occurred. By contrast, the older child can use mental representations to stand for absent events or things. Things no longer need to be present for the child to act on them. In this sense, the ability to represent eventually liberates the child from the immediate present. He can imagine things that are both spatially and temporally separate from himself. It may therefore be said that the use of mental representations permits the child to transcend the constraints of space and time.

Meaning

Having reviewed Piaget's theory of the formation of mental symbols, we shall now deal with the process by which they acquire meaning. Let us consider an apparently simple question: To what does the child's mental symbol, like swaying back and forth, refer? We may pose the same question with regard to the word: What does "bicycle" designate? Our first response to this question is to say that both the mental symbol and the word obviously refer to the real bicycle. But according to Piaget, the matter is more complicated than that. The "signified" (what the symbol or word stands for, or its meaning) is not the real object, but rather the child's understanding or intellectual construction of the real object. To put it differently, symbols or words do not refer to things, but instead stand for one's knowledge of things. Suppose one child uses the word "bicycle." For him, a bicycle has two wheels, a seat, and handlebars. A bicycle is something that goes delightfully fast, and, also, it is one kind of vehicle. For another child, however, the signified may be somewhat different. This child agrees that a bicycle has two wheels, a seat, and handlebars, but having often fallen from bicycles, he therefore feels that they are frightening and dangerous. Further, he has no conception of the bicycle as a vehicle. Note that for both these children the word "bicycle" evokes some common meaning: two wheels, handlebars, and so on. Both children can therefore easily identify what a bicycle is and what it is not. In this "denotative" sense, the word does refer to the real object. But the children also disagree as to the word's meaning; for one, a bicycle is delightful and for the other it is frightening. Also, for one child it is a member of the class of bicycles which in turn is included in the larger class of vehicles. The other child, on the other hand, employs no such class hierarchy. In Piaget's terms, each child has assimilated the word "bicycle" into a different set of schemes (the signified or the meaning). Therefore, the word "bicycle," or the children's personal mental symbols for it, does not refer to the real thing but to their understanding of it.

To summarize, internal imitation (accommodation) provides the child with symbols. The child then endows these symbols and words too with meaning, assimilating them into his mental schemes. Therefore, what the symbol or word refers to (the signified) is always personal, if not idiosyncratic, although in the case of words there is a sufficient amount of common signification for communication among individuals to occur.

Symbolic Play

A further example of an activity implying use of the symbolic function is symbolic play. Here is an observation.

[At 1;3(12) Jacqueline] . . . saw a cloth whose fringed edges vaguely recalled those of her pillow; she seized it, held a fold of it in her right hand, sucked the thumb of the same hand and lay down on her side, laughing hard. She kept her eyes open, but blinked from time to time as if she were alluding to closed eyes. (*PDI*, p. 96)

The observation involves several interesting features. First, Jacqueline acted toward the cloth in roughly the same way as she behaved toward a pillow. She put her head on it, sucked her thumb, and so on. Second, Jacqueline's behavior revealed a certain playfulness; that is, she laughed at what she was doing. Apparently, she thought her actions were quite funny.

One simple interpretation of this behavior is that the child merely confused the cloth with the pillow. But this explanation is not very plausible because it fails to explain why the child laughed. After all, Jacqueline did not ordinarily giggle upon going to bed.

Piaget interprets the behavior as a case of the playful use of concrete (not mental) symbols. It is clear from Jacqueline's laughter and from her attitude of pretense that she knew perfectly well that the cloth was not really a pillow. Her playfulness indicates that she realized that the cloth was a substitute for another thing. In other words, the cloth was a symbol or signifier, and what it signified was the pillow. The cloth, of course, was a concrete object and not a mental symbol.

How did this assignment of meaning to the cloth come about? Piaget's interpretation is that meaning is achieved in terms of assimilation. While in the past Jacqueline had performed the actions of lying down, closing the eyes, and so on only in connection with the pillow, she now extends these schemes to an object which she knows is not a pillow. We can therefore say that Jacqueline assimilated the cloth into schemes previously applied only to the pillow. It is the process of assimilation to schemes (the signified), then, which provides the meaning for the symbol. Moreover, Jacqueline is aware of the make-believe character of her acts. Her playfulness should not make us underestimate the seriousness and importance of her accomplishment: she has achieved a primitive comprehension of the nature of symbols. Indeed, we often find that the child's ''play'' involves significant intellectual activity.

It is interesting to note that Piaget feels that symbolic games play an important role in the child's emotional life as well. The child from 2 to 4 years is in a very vulnerable stage of development in the sense that he is beginning to acquire a new set of ways of dealing with the world around him. The child also finds that he must conform to a set of social rules, not the least of which is language. The child must accept the fact that words stand for things without any apparent justification. His capacity for self-expression via language is extremely limited and rudimentary and the words available frequently are inadequate to express needs and feelings. The child must obey commands whose purpose he cannot understand. The child's natural spontaneity is being compressed into the social mould of his culture, and he is generally powerless to resist.

These feelings of inadequacy lead to frustration for the child and, subsequently, to conflict with surrounding persons. Symbolic play, which forms a large part of the child's activity in this stage, is an appropriate means of providing an adjustment to reality. With this form of interaction the child can assimilate the external world almost directly into his own desires and needs with scarcely any accommodation. He can therefore shape reality to his own requirements. Furthermore, in symbolic play, the child can act out the conflictual situations of real life in such a way as to ensure a successful conclusion in which he comes out the winner, and not, as is sometimes the case in real life, the loser. In brief, symbolic play serves a necessary cathartic purpose and is essential for the child's emotional stability and adjustment to reality. Indeed, symbolic play often serves as the basis for psychotherapy with young children.

Language

We have now seen two different manifestations of the semiotic function: the use of mental symbols and symbolic play. We will turn now to a third aspect of the semiotic function and see how the child uses language and gives it meaning.

In the sixth stage of sensorimotor development, the child's first use of words is not representational in the sense of referring to absent objects. Instead it is intimately related to his ongoing actions. Consider this example concerning Laurent:

> at 1;5(19) *"no more"* meant going away, then throwing something on the ground, and was then used for something that was overturned (without disappearing). He thus said *"no more"* to his blocks. Later *"no more"* merely meant that something was at a distance from him (outside his field of prehension), and then it referred to the game of holding out an object for someone to throw back to him. At 1;6(23) he even said *"no more"* when he wanted something someone was holding. Finally, at 1;7 *"no more"* became synonymous with "begin again." (*PDI*, p. 218)

Note that Laurent did not use *"no more"* in a representational way. He did not make the words stand for an absent thing or event as in the sentence, "There is no more water in the garden." Instead, Laurent's use of "no more" was concrete in two senses. First, he employed the words in connection with objects that were immediately present like the overturned blocks. Second, the words were used to express his immediate desires, as when he wanted something a person was holding. In addition to being tied to concrete things or actions, the child's first words are very unstable. The phrase "no more" was used to refer to going away, to something over-turned, to something at a distance, and so on. The meaning of words is not constant for a young child. In fact, for him, words have little socially agreed upon meaning; instead, they are quite personal, and in this respect they resemble idiosyncratic mental symbols.

The next step in the development of language involves the use of words in a representational way. At about 2 years of age, the child gradu-ally begins to use words to stand for absent things or events. For example, at 1;11(11) after returning from a trip, Jacqueline told her father about it. She said, "Robert cry, duck swim in lake, gone away" (*PDI*, p. 222). These events had occurred some time previously, and Jacqueline was able to remember them. Moreover, she was capable of using words to stand for past events. Thus, through a gradual evolution, words are no longer used by the child to refer solely to ongoing actions, desires, or immediately present events.

Now that words have generally assumed a representational character and refer to absent things, we may ask whether the child uses them in the same way as the adult. For example, we saw that Jacqueline used the words "duck swim in lake" to refer to events in the past. Despite the fact that the words are representational, does the child give them the same meaning that an adult does? Another way of putting the question is to ask whether the child's *concept* of duck, or the meaning assigned to the word "duck," is the same as the adult's. The mere fact that the child uses the word does not necessarily imply that he gives it what we consider its ordi-nary meaning. Here are some observations which may clarify the issue:

> at 2;7(12), seeing L. [Lucienne] in a new bathing suit, with a cap, J. [Jacqueline] asked: *"What's the baby's name?"* Her mother explained that it was a bathing costume, but J. pointed to L. herself and said: *"But what's the name of that?"* (indicating L's face) and repeated the question several times. But as soon as L. had her dress on again, J. exclaimed very seriously: *"It's Lucienne again,"* as if her sister had changed her identity in changing her clothes. (*PDI*, p. 224)

The observation shows that Jacqueline's concept of her sister, and the use of the word "Lucienne," are quite different from the adult's. Jac-queline's thinking attributes little individuality to her sister. There is not one Lucienne who is the same person regardless of superficial changes; instead, as a result of wearing different clothing, the real Lucienne is seen as two different little girls. The child at this age fails to recognize that a person or thing remains the same, or conserves its identity, when it under-goes minor variations in appearance.

In addition to perceiving insufficient individuality, the child also shows other unusual uses of words. Once Jacqueline was in the garden and walked on the landlord's flowers. She remarked *"Me spoil Uncle Al-*

fred's garden'' (*PDI*, p. 224). She had had earlier contact with her uncle's garden, and in the present case used the phrase ''Uncle Alfred's garden'' to refer to the landlord's. In other words, she used one phrase to refer to two different things. All gardens are ''Uncle Alfred's garden.'' In the case of her sister, Jacqueline saw the same individual under different guises as different individuals; in the present instance she saw different ''individuals'' (gardens) as the same ''individual.'' Clearly, in neither case did Jacqueline's use of words correspond to an adult's. The concepts or meanings evoked by ''Lucienne'' or ''Uncle Alfred's garden'' were quite primitive. In a sense, the child's early words resemble *symbols*—they are personal and idiosyncratic.

Reasoning

During the years 2 to 4, the child shows three different kinds of reasoning. In one type, the child is faced with a simple situation which has been experienced before. The child then ''reasons'' about the situation very concretely in terms of what had occurred in the past. For example, at 2;4(16) Jacqueline called her father who did not answer. She concluded from this: *''Daddy didn't hear.''* At about the same time Jacqueline saw her father getting hot water and reasoned: *''Daddy's getting hot water, so he's going to shave''* (*PDI*, p. 231). In both cases, Jacqueline had had previous experience with her father in similar situations. Her ''reasoning'' about them was limited merely to simple memory of what had occurred in these situations in the past. Piaget feels that this type of reasoning is simply an application of previous experience to a current situation and is not to be confused with the genuinely deductive reasoning of the mature person.

In a second kind of reasoning, the child's desires distort thinking. For example, at 2;10(8) Jacqueline wanted to eat oranges. Her parents explained that this was impossible because the oranges were still green and not yet ripe. Jacqueline ''seemed to accept this, but a moment later, as she was drinking her camomile tea, she said: *'Camomile isn't green, it's yellow already . . . Give me some oranges!'''* (*PDI*, p. 231). Apparently Jacqueline, having a strong desire for oranges, reasoned that if the tea were yellow then the oranges must be yellow too, and therefore she could have them to eat. At this stage, the child attempts to reason to achieve some goal, but thought distorts reality in accordance with desire. This is similar to Freud's notion of wish fulfillment. (As will be evident shortly, the tea observation is also an example of transduction.)

A third type of reasoning is what Piaget calls ''transductive.'' In logic a distinction is sometimes made between deduction and induction. Deduction is usually characterized as a process of reasoning from the general to the particular. For instance, if we assume that all men have hearts of gold, and if we are then shown a particular man, we deduce that he has a heart of gold. Induction is usually considered a method for reasoning from the particular to the general to establish general principles from examination of particular cases. For instance, if we have met a large number of men all of whom have hearts of gold, we might conclude that all men have hearts of gold. According to Piaget, the young child's reasoning lies in between induction and deduction. The child does not go from the general to the particular (deduction), or from the particular to the general (induction), but rather from the particular to the particular without touching on the general. Transductive reasoning sees a relationship between two or more concrete (particular) items when there is none. For example, on an afternoon when Lucienne did not take a nap, she said: *"I haven't had my nap so it isn't afternoon"* (*PDI*, p. 232). In this case, Lucienne's thought proceeded from the nap (one particular) to the afternoon (the second particular) and concluded that the afternoon depended on the nap, when of course the relationship was of a different type.

Summary and Conclusions

In the period from 2 to 4 years the child achieves the capacity to form mental representations which stand for absent things or events. To deal with things, the child no longer requires that they be immediately present; instead, the child is able to create a mental substitute for the real thing. This ability frees the child from the immediate here and now. Instead of having to manipulate things, he works with their substitutes. The child forms mental symbols through imitation. The child looks at things, handles them, and acts like them, and in these ways incorporates a great deal of information about them. These actions of the child lay the foundation for mental symbolism. In fact, imitation may be considered to bridge the gap between sensorimotor and later intelligence. During the sensorimotor period the infant develops abilities in imitative behavior. When the child is proficient at imitation at a later age, he begins to imitate internally, and thereby forms the mental symbol. In Piaget's terminology mental symbols are *signifiers*. The symbol is personal and resembles what it refers to. For example, Lucienne swayed back and forth to represent a bicycle. Once mental symbols are formed, the child gives them meaning through the process of assimilation. He assimilates them into the schemes which are already available. Therefore, what the symbol refers to (the signified) is always personal and intimately related to the child's experience. A good example of the relation between the symbol and its meaning is the child's playful use of symbols. In a make-believe fashion, the child makes some things (symbols) stand for others. The child playfully assimilates some objects into schemes appropriate for others. Another type of signifier is the sign or word which is also used to refer to something else. The word, however, usually does not resemble its referent, but has a conventionally agreed-upon meaning to facilitate communication.

During this period the child uses words in several ways. After a preliminary stage in which words are closely related to ongoing actions and desires, the child uses language to refer to absent things and events. The child, however, does not use words in the same way that an adult does; the meaning assigned to words, or the concept associated with them, is still quite primitive. The child's concepts are in fact only *preconcepts:* they are sometimes too general and sometimes too specific. The child also shows signs of an initial reasoning. Sometimes it is successful, but only when it does not go far beyond mere memory for past events. At other times the reasoning may be faulty. This is either due to the tendency for wishes to distort thought or to the transductive nature of the child's thought: he reasons from the particular to the particular.

These, then, are the beginnings of symbolic activity in the young child. His initial efforts are imperfect, and from the adult point of view involve many "errors." A long evolution is necessary before the child can achieve maturity in thought; logical thinking does not emerge fully formed in the child of 2 years.

Piaget argues that language plays a limited but not negligible role in the formation of the child's thought. Clearly, language does not fully shape the child's mental activities. Despite his new ability at language, the child often thinks nonverbally. He forms mental symbols which are based on imitation of things and not on their names. Language does, however, make a contribution. For example, when an adult uses a word which refers to a *class* of things, the child is given a glimpse at one facet of adult reasoning. An adult's language forces the child, to some degree, to consider the world from a new perspective. Nevertheless, it is probably fair to say that the child's thought depends less on his language than the child's language does on his thought. As we saw earlier, the child interprets words in terms of his own personal system of meanings, and the child's meaning is not necessarily the same as the adult's. Although the culture provides the child with language, the latter does not immediately socialize the child's thought. In other words, language does not completely impose on the child the culturally desirable ways of thinking. Instead, the child distorts the language to fit his own mental structure. The child achieves mature thought only after a long process of development in which the role of language is but one contributing factor.

THE CHILD FROM 4 TO 11 YEARS
(PIAGET'S EARLY WORK)

We have now reviewed the infant's accomplishments in the sensorimotor period (0–2 years) and the child's acquisition of the semiotic function (2–4 years). It is hard to emphasize sufficiently the magnitude of these achievements. In the space of only a few years, the child has transformed himself from an organism almost totally dependent on reflex and other hereditary equipment to a person capable of symbolic thought. During the years to follow (after the age of 4), neither sensorimotor nor symbolic activities disappear. The child older than 4 years continues to develop sensorimotor schemes applicable to a wide range of objects, to improve skills in language, and to acquire mental representations for increasingly large portions of the surrounding world. But at the same time the child's development extends into a number of new areas.

The present section offers an account of intellectual growth in the child from about 4 to 11 years. Recall that Piaget's first five books cover this age span and present preliminary and tentative conceptualizations. Later works offer more elaborate and mature theorizing on the same age range. We will describe here Piaget's early views on the child from 4 to 11 years; Chapter 4 reviews the later work. As we shall see, Piaget's early work, although preliminary, is still quite fascinating and, according to some criteria, rates among his finest accomplishments.

The Use of Language

Piaget's early work begins with a consideration of children's use of language. At the outset he poses a fundamental question: What is the function of the child's language? Our first response is probably that the purpose of language is communication. The child, like the adult, most likely uses language to express thoughts to others, and to transmit information. But a little reflection should suffice to convince us that even in the adult, language is not entirely communicative. When alone, adults often talk to themselves on a mental level. Occasionally, they even speak aloud when no one else is present. Therefore, our initial hypothesis about the communicative nature of language is not always true.

If this is so, then several questions immediately arise. How much of language—particularly children's language—is communicative and how much is not? What is the noncommunicative variety like? And when it is not communicative, what purpose does children's language serve? To answer these and other questions, Piaget carried out a series of investigations. He began by observing two 6-year-old boys for about a month in their class at school. The children, who were from the poorer sections of Geneva, attended a progressive class. The students could draw or make what they liked, could work individually at "games" of mathematics and reading, had the freedom to talk or play together, and could go without permission from one room to another. As the two boys pursued their activities, Piaget and another observer took down in full detail the children's speech as well as the context in which it occurred. Piaget attempted to avoid interfering with the children's activities and tried not to influence their behavior in any way. The intention, of course, was to obtain a full record of the child's use of language in his natural school environment. If you will recall, Piaget used such naturalistic observation in his studies of infancy and the period from 2 to 4 years. Several of the advantages and disadvantages of this method have already been discussed in Chapter 2. One question that was not considered is whether or not Piaget is correct in assuming that the children's behavior is not affected by the presence of an observer. Do children act and speak differently when watched by an adult? Unfortunately, there is little empirical evidence on this issue. At the moment we can only use our informal experience in similar situations to hazard a guess that after a short period of time young children generally learn to ignore adult observers and seem to behave quite naturally.

After recording the two children's speech, Piaget attempted to categorize each sentence spoken by each child. He discovered several varieties of both communicative and noncommunicative language. Noncommunicative or "egocentric" speech may be divided into three types. One type is *repetition*, which involves the child's mimicking something she has just heard; for example, "Jac says to Ez: *'Look, Ez, your pants are showing.'* Pie, who is in another part of the room [and was one of the two children Piaget observed], immediately repeats: *'Look, my pants are showing, and my shirt too.'*" (*Language and Thought, LT,* p. 35). The statement clearly involved copying another's speech since Pie was in fact quite properly dressed. Thus Pie's utterance was a clear case of repetition and did not serve a communicative function. Very often too the child is not aware that he is merely repeating what another person has said, but believes that his statement is an original one. According to Piaget's records, repetition made up about 1 or 2 percent of the total number of statements.

A second kind of egocentric speech is the *individual monologue*. This type occurs when the child is alone and yet talks aloud, often at great length. For example, "Lev sits down at his table alone: *'I want to do that drawing there . . . I want to draw something, I do. I shall need a big piece of paper to do that'*" (*LT,* p. 37). Since no one else was present apart from the observer, who by this time presumably no longer disturbed the child, Lev's statement clearly did not involve communication. In the case of Pie, monologue constituted 5 percent of his speech, and for Lev the figure was 15 percent.

Perhaps the most interesting kind of egocentric speech is the *collective* monologue. This occurs when two or more children are together and one of them speaks a soliloquy to which the others do not listen. The speaker may intend to interest the others in his remarks and may in fact believe that the others are listening. But the egocentric nature of the monologue prevents the others from understanding him even if they wanted to. Despite the fact that the speaker is in a group, his statements are not communicative; he is merely talking to himself aloud. For example, when sitting with some other children and apparently playing with toys or drawing, Lev said, *"I say, I've got a gun to kill him with. I say, I am the captain on horseback. I say, I've got a horse and a gun as well"* (*LT,* p. 41). Note that Lev's continual use of the phrase "I say" seems to indicate that he wanted the others to listen to him and that he intended to transmit information. But at the same time, Lev's statement is unclear: we do not know whom he intended to kill with the gun, who was the captain on horseback, and so on. Moreover, Lev's remarks were unrelated to anyone else's and did not succeed in making the other children listen. In fact, each child, although apparently working with and speaking to the others, offered soliloquies like Lev's. There was no "give and take" among members of the group or any continuity in the discussion; each child spoke about what interested him at the moment, and this involved mostly his own activities. The collective monologue is therefore neither truly social nor communicative as it is merely the simultaneous occurrence of at least two monologues. According to Piaget's calculations, the collective monologue involved 23 percent of Lev's speech and 30 percent of Pie's. Egocentric speech as a whole—repetition, monologue, and collective monologue—represents 39 percent of Lev's and 37 percent of Pie's total number of sentences.

The remainder of the children's speech is communicative or "socialized." In this case the child takes into consideration the point of view of the listener and attempts to transmit information to him. For example, he tells another child certain simple facts, for example, how to operate a toy. Or he criticizes another child, or asks him questions, or in other ways interacts with him. While serving a communicative function, such speech nevertheless shows certain deficiencies. Young children do not attempt to explain events to one another, and they do not speak in terms of the causes of events. Also, young children do not try to give proof or logical justification for what they have proposed. One reason is that they do not consider the possibility that the listener may have a contrary opinion.

After establishing these facts in the case of Lev and Pie, Piaget then went on to study a larger group of twenty children varying in age from 4 to 7 years. Again, the method was naturalistic and involved the recording of the children's spontaneous remarks. In general, the findings replicated the data on Lev and Pie. A significant proportion of speech was egocentric, and this proportion was especially large in the speech of the youngest children, at about age 4.

These, then, are the results of Piaget's naturalistic observations. There seems to be a decline in egocentrism and an increase in communication as the child gets older. The child's language, especially in the early portion of the years from 4 to 5 or 6 years, does not entirely serve the function of communication. Often, the child does not assume the point of view of the listener; he talks of himself, to himself, and by himself.

How can we explain the noncommunicative nature of the child's speech? What purposes does it serve? Piaget offers a number of interesting hypotheses which he regarded as tentative, and not conclusive. First, consider verbal repetition, where the child simply mimics what others say or repeats phrases of his own. Piaget's interpretation is that repetition is "simply the joy of repeating for its own sake . . . the pleasure of using words . . . for the sake of playing with them" (*LT,* p. 35). You will no doubt observe that this explanation is another version of the principle of functional assimilation—the tendency to repeat schemes and to exercise them. In the present case the child mimics both his own words and those of others, just as earlier in the sensorimotor period he repeated patterns of behavior. Consequently, repetition is not motivated by the desire to communicate, but by the need to exercise verbal schemes.

But repetition comprises only a small portion of the child's speech. Let us now turn to the individual monologue which involves a substantial proportion of the total number of statements. To explain the monologue, Piaget offers two hypotheses which are not mutually exclusive. One hypothesis is that the individual monologue serves the purpose of wish fulfillment. When the child's actions are not successful in producing an intended result, he uses words to achieve his goal. If, for example, he would like to move a box but cannot because it is too heavy, the child might *tell* the box to move, thus using words to bring about what his activities cannot accomplish. The child's language, therefore, is in part a kind of fantasy, a word magic. A second explanation of individual monologue is that words and actions, for the child, are not yet fully differentiated. When beginning to learn language, the 2- or 3-year-old child often calls an immediately present object by its name or uses a word to describe ongoing actions. Consequently, in his initial experience with language, the thing (or action) and the word for it are simultaneously present, and the two are seen as a whole. The word is in a sense part of the thing, and vice versa. It takes a long time for the child to disassociate fully the word from its referent; he must learn that the word bears a totally arbitrary relation to that to which it refers and that the word is not a part of it. Even in the period under discussion (4 to 7 years), the child has not fully grasped the relation between word and thing. Consequently, when he acts—plays with toys, draws, and so on—he tends to say the words associated with his behavior. Thus, the monologue is in a sense a part of the child's action and is not designed for the purpose of communication.

In the case of the collective monologue, similar explanations can be employed. Sometimes the child in a group merely repeats what another says because of functional assimilation; sometimes his remarks are magically intended to produce results which he otherwise cannot achieve; and, finally, his utterances often merely accompany activities in which he is engaged.

All three types of speech—repetition, individual monologue, and collective monologue—may be characterized as *egocentric*. Piaget does not use the term in the sense of selfish or self-serving. The young child is characterized as egocentric not because of conceit or because of an attempt to satisfy desires at the expense of other people, but because he is centered about himself (or his own ego in the general sense) and fails to take into account the other's point of view. When delivering a monologue in a group, the desires of the egocentric child do not necessarily clash with those of other children; rather he is insensitive to what the others need to hear. To communicate, one must consider what information the listener does and does not have and what he is and is not interested in, and this the young child does not do.

One may criticize the naturalistic study of the child's language in several ways. Perhaps Piaget found the use of noncommunicative language to be extensive only because of the liberal atmosphere of the school where the emphasis was on individual rather than group activity. If you will recall, the children were allowed to do what they liked, and the situation was so devised that the children learned from individual play. Under these circumstances, it might be the case that the children felt no real need for communication, and consequently they did not display these abilities.

We may, however, cite as evidence against this argument an experiment by Piaget on verbal communication. Briefly, the task involved an experimenter's giving some information to one child (the speaker) who was then supposed to transmit it to another child (the listener). Piaget made clear to the speaker that the task was to communicate. These instructions presumably oriented the child toward the goal of communication rather than that of play. Therefore, the experiment might give insight into the child's ability to transmit information when he felt the need to do so. The experiment was also used to obtain information about the listener's ability to understand the speaker. Even if the speaker were communicative, did the listener comprehend what was said? However, since the methods used to assess the listener's understanding were rather poor, we will not concentrate on this aspect of the study.

Let us now describe the experiment in greater detail. In one portion, pairs of children were used as subjects. There were thirty children at ages 7 to 8 years and twenty at ages 6 to 7 years. The experimenter sent one of the pair out of the room and told the other a story. This child, to be referred to as the speaker, was instructed to listen carefully since he would have to tell the same story to the other child, whom we will call the listener. Then the experimenter read a story, repeated the difficult parts, and tried to make the speaker attend carefully. Several different stories, varying from six to nine sentences in length, were used, although at any one time the speaker was required to tell only one story to the listener. Next, the listener was brought into the room, and the speaker told him the story.

The experimenter took down everything that was said and, in addition, questioned both the speaker and the listener to determine the degree to which they understood. After the experiment with stories, the same pairs of children were used to investigate communication concerning mechanical objects. This time, the examiner explained to the speaker how a faucet or a syringe works. Diagrams were used to make the matter clear, and the speaker was permitted to make use of the diagram in explaining the mechanical process to the listener. Again, the experimenter recorded everything that the speaker said.

While the experiment yielded many results, we shall focus on the verbalizations of the speaker. Did children in the experiment succeed in producing communicative speech, and if not, what was their language like? In general, the experiment on communication replicated the results of Piaget's earlier naturalistic observations; that is, in both cases a substantial proportion of speech was noncommunicative or egocentric. For example, the experiment on communication showed that young children often use pronouns and demonstrative adjectives—such as *he, she, it, that, this*—without indicating clearly to what they are referring. In the midst of an explanation of the faucet, the speaker might say "If you move it with that other thing, then it will go." This child fails to consider that the listener might not know what "it" and "that other thing" designate. This tendency is carried so far that often the speaker completely fails to name the objects involved in a mechanical explanation. The child is also poor at expressing the order of events. One child explaining how a faucet works began by telling how the water falls into the basin, and only later did he bother to say how the water goes through the pipe. Or, in telling a story, the child might begin with the end and end with the beginning.

A young child may also express causal relations poorly, and seldom connect the cause with its effect. For example, in telling a story in which a fairy turned certain children into swans, one child said, *"There was a fairy, a wicked fairy. They turned themselves into swans"* (*LT*, pp. 126–27). Note how the child did not express the central causal relation; it was the fairy who caused the children to become swans. The child merely mentioned the two events without indicating their connection. The second sentence also illustrates the tendency to use pronouns without describing their referents. To whom does "they" refer?

Often the child may also omit large parts of the explanation or story. Even though he understands and remembers these portions (as shown by Piaget's later questioning), the child may fail to mention them. In effect he assumes that the listener already knows parts of the story or explanation. Omissions of this kind clearly reveal a lack of sensitivity to the needs of the listener.

Another aspect of egocentric speech is manifested in the observation that the child's story or explanation does not form a coherent and integrated whole. The account is fragmentary; it is merely composed of a large number of specific and unrelated items which are juxtaposed one upon the other. For example, here is one child's account of how a faucet works:

> The handle is turned on and then the water runs, the little pipe is open and the water runs. There, there is no water running, there the handle is turned off, and then there is no water running, and here the water is running. There, there is no water running, and here there is water running. (*LT,* p. 130)

Clearly this explanation involves a mere collection of individual statements which are not integrated into a reasonable whole. One aspect of such juxtaposition is a tendency already described: the inability to state causal relations.

In summary, the preceding five properties of the young child's speech—the faulty use of pronouns and demonstrative adjectives, the incorrect ordering of events, the poor expression of causality, the tendency to omit important features, and finally, juxtaposition—all are concrete manifestations of the child's egocentrism—the inability to take into consideration the other person's point of view. With development these egocentric manifestations decrease and speech becomes more communicative. The speaker becomes aware of the views of others and adapts his speech accordingly.

Piaget's experiment on verbal communication also studies the understanding of the listener. Although the methodology was questionable, several of Piaget's impressions are of interest. The results showed that, in general, the listener does not understand the speaker very well. Part of the listener's inability to understand is clearly due to the speaker's faulty presentation. Few people could comprehend the explanation of the faucet just described. But Piaget feels that part of the listener's difficulty is due to his own patterns of thought and not to the speaker's egocentric speech. Even when the speaker is relatively clear, the listener distorts his utterances in several ways. One, the listener almost always thinks that he understands what the speaker says, even when it is very obscure. The listener very seldom asks questions to clarify a point or to obtain additional information. The listener feels confident that he has understood when in fact he has not. Two, the speaker's remarks evoke in the listener a kind of free association. In Piaget's terms, the listener assimilates the remarks into his own schemes which often bear little relation to what the speaker is attempting to communicate. For example, after listening to the story in which the bad fairy turned several children into swans, one 6-year-old child distorted the account in important ways. Instead of saying that the children were turned into swans, he maintained that they were dressed in white clothes. Then he elaborated on this proposition until the end of the story was no longer recognizable. He transformed one part of the story and, giving free rein to his imagination, went on from there to construct a new tale of his own. In brief, while the speaker fails to take account of the needs of the listener, the listener also distorts what he hears, elaborates on it, and is satisfied that he has understood, whereas, in actual fact he has not.

It is easy to see that Piaget's experiment on communication is deficient in several ways. Piaget does not make clear the methods used to assess either the speaker's or the listener's understanding of the story or explanation. The measurement of comprehension is a difficult and delicate matter that requires more attention than Piaget has given to it. Piaget also may not have fully eliminated the possibility that faulty memory, and not egocentrism, may sometimes underlie the speaker's lack of ability to communicate. Perhaps the young child is not able to tell a lengthy story simply because of the failure to remember large parts of it. Despite Piaget's attempts to control for the memory factor by questioning, it is not altogether clear to what extent he was successful.

Another factor to be considered is that Piaget's subjects were poor children. Is it not possible that lower-class children have different verbal abilities from middle-class children? If so, Piaget is too quick to generalize his findings to children in general. While these and other criticisms may be raised and seem to have validity, one must remember that Piaget's first studies were intended as exploratory. Their aim was to uncover interesting issues for investigation, to propose preliminary hypotheses, and not to reach firm conclusions. Piaget's studies on communication seem to have fulfilled his original goals. His research raises interesting questions. For example, is it true that the young child cannot express cause-and-effect relations, or that the listener so extensively distorts what the speaker says? Despite its deficiencies, Piaget's research is of great historical significance: it was one of the first attempts in child psychology to deal with the crucial issue of the functions of human language.

Thus far we have seen that the young child from about 4 to 7 years displays a significant amount of egocentric speech and that the older child after about 7 years is increasingly proficient at verbal communication. Why does egocentric speech decrease as the child gets older? Piaget proposes an interesting hypothesis to explain the waning of egocentrism. When the child is young, particularly in infancy, adults take great pains to understand his thoughts and desires. The mother must know which toy the infant wants or what bothers him and is not able to rely exclusively on words to understand him. Consequently, the young child does not need to communicate clearly; even if his speech is unclear, adults will make every effort to understand. As the child grows older, however, he is thrown more and more into the company of older children who are not as solicitous as adults. Other children do not try so hard to penetrate the obscurities of his language. Moreover, they argue with him; they challenge what he says and force the child to defend himself. It is under social pressures of these kinds that the child is gradually forced to adopt better modes of communication. In the attempt to express himself and to justify his arguments, the child eventually learns to take into account the other's point of view. Not to do so is to be misunderstood and to lose the argument. In this way, then, does egocentrism diminish.

Clinical Method

Piaget's early work was in part concerned with the contents of the child's thought. He attempted to discover the spontaneous ideas of the child at different stages of his development. What is the child's conception of the nature of dreams, or what is his explanation of the fact that boats float on water? The study of content is particularly difficult, because as we have seen in the previous section, young children have great difficulty in communicating their thoughts. It is therefore crucial for the investigator of content to employ sensitive and accurate methods. Piaget has devoted careful consideration to the choice of a proper method. He has rejected the testing approach, assigned a limited role to naturalistic investigation, and adopted the clinical procedure. Let us consider each of these decisions in turn.

The essential feature of the testing method is a series of questions which are posed in the same way to all who take the test. If we are investigating the origin of the sun, for instance, we might ask all children, "Where did the sun come from?" It is important that the question be put in precisely the same way to all children. In fact, the reading of the question (the intonation, stress, and so on) should be as consistent as possible. If a child does not seem to understand, the examiner may repeat the question. But this is usually the maximum of flexibility permitted: the examiner may not rephrase the question or otherwise alter it. The purpose of a standardized administration is to guarantee that all subjects are faced with the same problems. Then if 4-year-olds generally give one type of answer and 8-year-olds another, the examiner may reasonably conclude that there is a real difference between the age groups. If, on the other hand, the form of the questioning varied across age groups, the examiner would not know whether the difference in answers is genuinely related to age or is due simply to the difference in questions. While the testing method has important psychological uses, Piaget feels that it is not suitable for his task—the discovery of content (or the discovery of structure, a problem to which Piaget also applies the clinical method).

The testing method has the disadvantage of inflexibility. If a child gives an interesting response, the examiner cannot pursue it. If a child misunderstands the question, the examiner cannot clarify it. If the child's answer suggests an additional topic for investigation, the examiner must leave the matter unexplored. In addition, the test procedure may be suggestive. If the child is asked, "Where did the sun come from?" the question implies that the sun did have an origin, and this idea may not have occurred to the child before. Consequently, his answer may not reveal the contents of his spontaneous thought, but may be merely a hastily considered response to a question encountered for the first time. And, finally, the test method does not usually allow the examiner to establish the stability of the child's response. If a child is asked what the sum of 2 and 2 is, and says "4," his answer may be tentative or firm. If he is unsure, further questioning may induce the child to change his mind. If his belief is firm, nothing will sway him. In the testing procedure the child gives an answer and that is the end of it: a tentative "4" is as good as a sure one. For these reasons, then, Piaget rejects the testing approach.

Another method for the investigation of spontaneous content is the naturalistic procedure as used in Piaget's study of infancy or language. In a sense, this is an ideal method. Suppose we observe that a child spontaneously asks the question: "Who made the sun?" The statement gives a clear insight into the content of his thought. It is immediately obvious that he believes that some agent, perhaps a person or perhaps God, intervened to create the sun, and that it did not evolve naturally. Surely this spontaneous question is far more valuable than a response to a standardized question.

The naturalistic method, however, is subject to a number of drawbacks. One may observe a child for a very long time before he will say anything of interest. Suppose we are interested in the child's conception of the origin of the sun; it is extremely unlikely that he will ask the relevant question while being observed. Consequently, the naturalistic method, despite its clear utility, cannot be used as the chief instrument of research. At best, naturalistic observation can serve only a subsidiary role in two ways. It can suggest questions for intensive clinical examination. If, for example, we hear a child ask, "Who made the sun?" then we can interview a large number of children to test the generality of the assumption underlying his question. Second, the naturalistic observation can serve as a check on the results of clinical questioning. If interviewing suggests that children believe that clouds are alive, then patient, naturalistic observation may furnish data to support or refute this hypothesis.

Piaget feels that the clinical method avoids the deficiencies of the testing and naturalistic procedures, and in addition offers a number of attractive features. The clinical method is hard to describe since it is so flexible and provides a general framework for questioning the child rather than a set or standardized form. This account is therefore intended only as an outline of the clinical method. The basic aim of the method is to follow the child's thought without deforming it by suggestions or by imposing the adult's views on the child. One important feature is that the experimenter tries to adopt the language of the child and keep the level of questions accessible to the child. Terms which are beyond his reach are avoided and replaced as much as possible by those which the child has spontaneously emitted. The examiner usually begins by asking a nondirective question. Instead of saying, "Who made the sun?" or "How did the sun evolve?" the examiner might ask, "How did the sun come about?" If the child does not understand, the examiner is free to rephrase the question by asking, for example, "How did the sun get there?" After the child answers, the experimenter forms an hypothesis concerning the nature of the child's beliefs. For example, if the child first answered, "It was put there," the examiner might guess that the child believes that a person created the sun. Subsequent questions are used to test this hypothesis. The examiner might then ask: "Can you tell me how it was put there?" If the child says, "God put it there," then the examiner might follow up aspects of this response. Does the child really believe in divine intervention, or is this just a superficial mimicry of what he has been taught in Sunday school? To answer this question, the examiner may challenge the child's belief to see how firmly he holds to it. Or the examiner may wonder whether the child means to say that the sun already existed before God "put it there" or that God created it too. Further questions must be asked to decide between the two alternatives. Of course, if the examiner's hypothesis is not confirmed, he must allow the child's answers to lead him to the correct interpretation. It is easy to see that no two clinical examiners, even if they are testing the same child, will pursue the same line of questioning. It is also clear that clinical questioning is very delicate and subject to several kinds of errors. The examiner may talk too much and thereby suggest answers to the child. Or the examiner may not talk enough and fail to pose the questions necessary for determining the child's meaning. Piaget feels that at least a year of daily practice is necessary before the examiner can achieve proficiency at clinical questioning.

We may raise a number of criticisms of the clinical method. How do we know that Piaget is a good clinical examiner? His books give only portions of selected clinical interviews. It is possible that the published interviews are exceptional—from the point of view of method and support for Piaget's theory—and that the unpublished protocols are poorly done. Perhaps in the latter case the examiner suggested answers to the child, asked the wrong questions, and so on. Also, we may wonder whether Piaget's diagnoses—the judgments derived from the interview—are reliable. That is, would other persons agree with the interpretations, or are Piaget's diagnoses quite idiosyncratic? It is also true that since the clinical interviews are unstandardized, it is very difficult for independent investigators to test Piaget's work. If another psychologist attempted to repeat Piaget's research and obtained different results, the Piagetian criticism could always be that he failed to use the clinical method properly. Another criticism that is raised is that Piaget usually commits a large number of methodological sins unrelated to the clinical method. For example, he does not usually report the number of subjects seen in an investigation, or their exact ages, or their social backgrounds. In describing the results he presents only fragments of interviews and fails to give a statistical summary of the children's reactions. To summarize, the clinical method is deficient. Perhaps the chief objection is that it requires us to take a lot on faith: that Piaget conducts the interview without suggestion, that he interprets the results properly, and so on. As we well know, scientists prefer to take as little on faith as possible.

The deficiencies in Piaget's research are real. Yet we must be careful not to exaggerate them; we must evaluate the clinical method in the overall context of Piaget's work. Piaget felt that the early portion of his research was essentially exploratory. His goal was to open up new areas for investigation and to propose preliminary hypotheses for further examination. The early work was not intended to prove a theory or to present definitive views on intelligence, and Piaget felt that methods should be as flexible as possible at the preliminary stages of research. It seemed premature to him to introduce rigorous procedures when almost nothing was known about the subject matter, and when it was by no means clear what the proper methods should be. If Piaget had attempted to establish every point with the maximum of certainty, then he probably would not have advanced beyond the study of children's verbal communication (one of his first research topics). Once the pioneering research has been done, then it is always possible to check the results by more standardized methods and revise the tentative hypotheses.

The Content of Thought

Piaget's early investigations of content are extensive. His two books on the subject are *The Child's Conception of the World (CCW)* and *The Child's Conception of Physical Causality (CCPC)*. They cover a large number of topics which include the child's beliefs concerning dreams, meteorology, the origin of trees, the nature of shadows, the explanation of the steam engine, and so on. To illustrate this work we shall describe only one topic: the origins of the sun and moon.

According to Piaget's findings there are three stages in the child's concept of the sun and moon. The stages occur in sequence somewhere between about 3 and 12 years. Piaget does not attempt to specify precise age norms because there are large variations in responses. Here is an example of a stage 1 protocol, a 6-year-old's beliefs:

How did the sun begin?—*It was when life began.*—Has there always been a sun?—*No.*—How did it begin?—*Because it knew that life had begun.*—What is it made of?—*Of fire.*—But how?—*Because there was fire up there.*—Where did the fire come from?—*From the sky.*—How was the fire made in the sky?—*It was lighted with a match.*—Where did it come from, this match?—*God threw it away.* . . . How did the moon begin?—*Because we began to be alive.*—What did that do?—*It made the moon get bigger.*—Is the moon alive?—*No . . . Yes.*—Why?—*Because we are alive.* (*CCW,* pp. 258–59)

The protocol illustrates three kinds of beliefs common to children in the first stage of development. The first belief is *animism.* The child believes that the sun and moon are alive in the same sense that people are alive; that is, the sun is credited with *knowing* that life had begun. The second belief is *artificialism.* The child asserts that the sun resulted from the actions of an outside agent. It was not a natural process that formed the sun, but an act of intervention on the part of God. The third belief illustrated by the protocol contains the idea of *participation.* The child perceives some continuing connection, or some participation, between human activities and those of things. His belief is that the moon began because people began to be alive. Note that this explanation is not artificialism, since the child does not assert that people created the moon. His conception is vague, and he merely assumes a dim relation between people and the planets; he believes that there is some sort of influence or participation between them.

The second stage of the child's concept of the sun and moon is transitionary. The child continues to believe in artificialism and animism, but less blatantly than before. The following excerpt involves an 8-year-old child:

How did the sun begin?—*It was a big cloud that made it.*—Where did the cloud come from?—*From the smoke.*—And where did the smoke come from?—*From houses.* . . .—How did the clouds make the sun shine?—*It's a light which makes it shine.*—What light?—*A big light, it is someone in Heaven who has set fire to it.* (*CCW,* p. 274)

Note that at the beginning of the protocol the child invoked only natural phenomena to explain the sun's origin. The sun was formed by clouds which in turn derived from smoke. However, when asked where the smoke came from, the child proposed an artificialist explanation. The smoke came from houses and, by implication, from fires which people created. Artificialism is even more apparent in the second part of the protocol where the child maintains that someone in Heaven has created a light that makes the sun shine.

In the third stage, the child gives up notions of artificialism, animism, and participation. While his explanations are often crude and incorrect, he attributes the sun's formation to natural processes in which human or divine agents have no role. Sometimes, of course, the child's accounts are based on what he has been told in school. Yet sometimes they are not, and even then the child proposes explanations invoking physical processes of the planet's origins.

Moral Judgment and Behavior

Piaget's early work covered a wide range of topics including verbal communication, concepts of physical causality, and moral judgment and behavior. This last topic will be considered now. Piaget begins his study of moral behavior and judgment with a detailed consideration of children's games of marbles. He describes how children conceive of the game and follow its rules. At first glance it may seem quite unusual to study morality by means of the apparently trivial game of marbles. Our intuitive definition of morality probably relates to such matters as lying and stealing, and not to mere games. But according to Piaget the essential aspect of morality is the tendency to accept and follow a system of rules which usually regulate interpersonal behavior. Our society has gradually developed norms which control how an individual treats others, behaves toward property, and so on, and these regulations, supplemented by the individual's own conceptions, constitute the moral system. On closer inspection it would seem as if the rules governing the game of marbles fulfill all the definiing conditions of a moral system. The rules control how individuals behave toward one another in terms of the actions which comprise the game, they determine individual and property rights, and they are a cultural product which has been passed down from generation to generation. The game of marbles also has a unique advantage from the point of view of child psychology. The rules have been developed largely by children, and the game is played almost exclusively by children. Therefore, the child's conception of the game and his playing of it reflect the workings of his own mind and is subject to little adult influence. Unlike rules dealing with lying or stealing, the game of marbles is the child's creation, not the adult's. If we question the child about the game, his answers do not simply parrot the teachings of adults, but give a genuine indication of his own thought. But is not the game just play, something that is not at all taken seriously, and that therefore bears no relation to morality, which is a grave matter? We may answer this criticism by pointing out that the child does take the game seriously. While a game has its "fun" aspects, if one observes children playing, one realizes that they are deeply engrossed in their activities, consider the other players' actions of some importance, and are not entirely disinterested in the outcomes. Is the adult who "plays" the stock market very different?

To study children's behavior in the game of marbles, Piaget first acquired a thorough knowledge of the rules of the game. Then he asked about twenty boys, ranging from 4 to 12 or 13 years of age, to show him how to play. (In Switzerland the game of marbles is played exclusively by boys.) In the course of his game with the child, Piaget tried to appear as ignorant as possible about the rules so that the child would feel that he had to explain them. In this way Piaget was able to determine both whether the child understood the rules, and, if so, whether he followed them. Sometimes Piaget observed pairs of children, particularly younger ones, play the game without him. Piaget also questioned the child about the nature of the rules. He was interested, for example, in whether the child believed that the rules might be changed and in the child's conception of the origin of rules.

Let us consider the practice of rules, or moral behavior. From about ages 4 to 7 years, an *egocentric* stage occurs where children do not know or follow the rules, but they insist that they do. As an example of this stage, let us examine the following:

Piaget separately examined two boys who were in the same class at school, who lived in the same house and often played marbles with one another. The first boy described and played by a set of rules which was highly unusual and idiosyncratic. The second boy did not understand the first boy's rules and moreover proposed an unusual system of his own. Thus, each of the boys, who often played "together," in fact followed his own system of rules which bore little relation to the other child's. There was little notion of "winning," in the adult sense, and little genuine competition between the two players. For the young child, "winning" means "having a good time," and it was, therefore, quite possible for all players to win in this particular game. Each child was merely playing an individual game and did not really need the other. At the same time, the children believed that they were playing like other children and that they knew and followed the rules quite well.

The behavior at marbles is similar to the speech of children of the same age and is, therefore, called egocentric. In both cases the child is centered about himself and fails to take into account another person's point of view. In the game of marbles the young child plays for himself and not with someone else. He has his own set of rules and is relatively uninfluenced by what the other does. In the case of speech, the child talks by himself and not with someone else. He speaks for his own purposes, and his monologue is relatively unaffected by the other's comments. Egocentrism is therefore a tendency common to both speech and moral behavior.

The next stage, that of *incipient cooperation,* lasts from about 7 to 10 or 11 years. The game begins to acquire a genuinely social character, and the child has a much firmer grasp of the rules. While his knowledge of the game is not perfect, he has mastered the basic rules and attempts to learn the rest. The child of this stage both cooperates and competes with his partner. There is cooperation in the sense that the child agrees with his partner on a common set of rules which are then followed. (Cooperation does not mean here that the two or more children assist each other to attain a common goal.) There is competition in the sense that each child tries to win for himself, while at the same time he adheres to the mutually agreed-upon framework. Nevertheless, play is not yet fully mature. Since the child has not yet mastered all of the rules, the game does not proceed smoothly, and there are difficulties and conflicts. Again, there is a parallel between play and speech. In both instances, the child of about 7 years of age begins to take into account an external point of view. In marbles he allows a set of rules to govern his behavior, and he interacts with the partner. In speech he tries to anticipate what the listener needs to know, and he accepts linguistic conventions which facilitate real interaction.

The final stage of moral behavior is that of *genuine cooperation* which begins at about 11 or 12 years of age. Now the child acquires a thorough mastery of the rules. As before, he agrees with the others on the way to play the game, and it is within this common framework that he tries to win. In addition, however, the older child shows a kind of legalistic fascination with the rules. He enjoys settling differences of opinion concerning the rules, inventing new rules, and elaborating on them. He even tries to anticipate all the possible contingencies that may arise.

Piaget tells a delightful anecdote about the legalistic tendencies of this stage. He observed a group of boys aged 10 and 11 who were preparing to have a snowball fight. Before getting on with it, they devoted a considerable amount of time to dividing themselves into teams, electing officers, devising an elaborate set of rules to regulate the throwing of snowballs, and deciding on a system of punishments for transgressors. Before they had actually settled on all these legalistic aspects of the game, it was time to return home, and no snowball game had been played. Yet, all the players seemed content with their afternoon.

We may summarize by stating, then, that there are three major stages of the practice of rules: *egocentrism,* where each child does not know the rules or how to apply them but thinks he does; *incipient cooperation,* where mastery of the rules has improved and children begin to share them to compete; and finally, the stage of *genuine cooperation,* where children know the rules well and enjoy elaborating upon them.

After establishing the child's knowledge and practice of rules, Piaget went on to question the child about their inviolability. He asked the child whether the rules might be changed, whether they always existed in their present form, and how they originated. In determining the child's conception of the rules, Piaget of course used the clinical method (as he did in establishing knowledge of the rules). He found that there are two major stages in notions concerning the inviolability of rules. The first stage, which is in turn divided into two parts, lasts from about 4 or 5 years to about 9 or 10 years. Thus it overlaps the first two stages of the practice of rules (egocentrism and incipient cooperation). In the first part of the first stage, which we shall call the *absolutistic* stage, the child believes that some authority originated the rules of marbles and that no one ever played the game before that authority played it. Moreover, the authority conveys on the rules a sacred, unchangeable character: they are absolute and cannot be altered. Here is part of a protocol of a 5-year-old illustrating some of these beliefs:

> How did you get to know the rules?—*When I was quite little my brother showed me. My Daddy showed my brother.*—And how did your daddy know?—*My Daddy just knew. No one told him. . . .*—Tell me who was born first, your daddy or your granddad?—*My Daddy was born before my granddad.*—Who invented the game of marbles?—*My Daddy did. (Moral Judgment,* MJ, p. 55)

We see that the child believes that the rules emerged, fully formed, from his father, who is so prestigious that he was born before his own father.

While believing in the sanctity of rules, the young child from about 4 to 6 years in the first part of stage 1 is also willing to accept changes in the rules. He agrees to place the marbles in a circle, whereas a square is the usual convention. This seems paradoxical: the child thinks that the rules are sacred but easily consents to their modification. Piaget feels that the child's acceptance of changes is only apparent. He has such a poor grasp of what the rules are that he believes the changes to be merely alternative and quite legitimate versions of the rules. In other words, the child consents to alterations only because he does not know that they really are alterations.

In the latter part of the first stage (from about 6 to 10 years), the child's knowledge of the rules increases, and he is consequently able to recognize a real change in the rules when it is proposed. Now he refuses to accept these alterations and asserts that the rules are immutable. For example, Piaget asked one boy of 6 years to invent a new game, and he refused, saying "I've never invented games." Then, after Piaget suggested a new game of marbles to him, the boy played it for a time. But when asked, "Could this game ever become a fair game?" the boy responded "No, because it's not the same [as the usual game of marbles]" (*MJ*, p. 60).

If you will recall, many of the children who are in stage 1 of the conception of rules are simultaneously in stage 1 of the practice of rules (egocentrism). This means that at the same time that the child believes the rules to be sacred and immutable, he also does not know them too well and does not follow them. Again we seem to be faced with a paradox: how can he place so much faith in the same rules that he consistently breaks? To understand this apparent contradiction, we must consider the child's acquisition of rules. Usually he learns them from an older child whom he considers similar to adults, and whom he therefore imbues with the same respect and authority that he gives to adults. In Piaget's terms, there is a relationship of *constraint* or *unilateral respect* between older and younger children; the former's authority is unconditionally accepted so that the younger child assigns to the rules the same authority that he considers the older child to have. Since the adult and the older child are considered infallible, so are the rules which they propagate. In addition, the young child is egocentric. As we saw in the case of language, he cannot take the point of view of others. Since he is wrapped up in his own concerns, he cannot understand the value of rules which protect the interests of others. It is not so much that he is selfish; rather he does not perceive the legitimate needs that other persons have. Since this is so, he does not understand the purpose of rules. For him they are merely external things which cannot be changed.

We can say, then, that the young child imbues rules with absolute respect since they derive from a prestigious person and that he sees the rules as external objects which cannot be changed because his egocentrism prevents him from understanding the purpose of rules.

Piaget then notes that all of the factors mentioned—the relation of unilateral respect, egocentrism, the conception of the rules as authoritative and external—prevent the young child from participation in the formation of rules. Since the young child cannot assume the older child's point of view, how can he cooperate in developing fair rules? Because the young child does not participate in making the rules, they remain quite external to him. The rules are not really his; they are a kind of foreign body imposed on him. It should come as no surprise that they do not effectively transform his behavior. In other words, because the child has not cooperated in devising the rules, he does not understand them and, therefore, is not able to follow them.

In the second stage of the conception of rules, beginning at about 10 or 11 years, the child believes that the rules can be changed, that they originated through human invention, and that they are maintained only by mutual consent among equals. Consequently, the child will agree to a modification of the game so long as all of the other players agree, and so long as the change is a fair one. Since he himself participates as an equal in the invention of new rules, he feels obligated to follow them and does so.

To explain the shift from the absolutistic morality of the younger child to the flexibility of the older child, Piaget proposes a social learning theory. He begins by noting that as the child in Western society grows older, he becomes progressively free of parental and other adult supervision. During the first five years or so of life, the child is very closely tied to his parents. After that point he goes to school, spends an increasing amount of time with peers, and generally assumes greater responsibility for his own life. As these events take place, the child gradually learns to make decisions for himself and does not necessarily accept as authoritative the views of other persons who are now considered his equals. In other words, the child escapes from the attitude of unilateral respect toward elders and begins to adopt a position of mutual respect. As a result of this development he does not unquestioningly accept rules as binding and immutable. Because he now sees himself as the equal of others, he desires to assist in the formation and modification of the moral code.

Another and related factor influencing the decline of the absolutistic concept of rules is the child's increasing contact with divergent points of view. As the child widens his sphere of contacts beyond the immediate family, he discovers that there are diverse and conflicting opinions and customs. He finds that not everyone accepts the views promulgated by his parents. This conflict between what he has been taught and what other people believe forces the child to reassess his own position and to resolve the differences in opinion. In attempting to do so, the child reasons about rules and comes to the conclusion that they must, to some extent, be arbitrary and, therefore, changeable.

To summarize, as he grows older the child evolves from a position of submission to adults to one of equality. He also is confronted with beliefs contradictory to those he has been taught. Both these experiences influence the child to see rules as having a human, and hence fallible, origin, and to agree to participate in their formation and alteration. Since the child now has a hand in the formation of rules, they no longer exist as a foreign entity imposed on his conscience; they no longer exist as a code which may be unquestionably respected, occasionally obeyed, and seldom understood. The child now chooses to follow rules which are his own or at least freely agreed upon.

Piaget goes on to examine the development of judgments concerning explicitly moral situations. To study this he told children stories which posed a moral dilemma and asked them to resolve it. For example, if a child stole some apples, what would his punishment be? In this way Piaget attempted to discover the child's conception of justice, punishment, lying, and similar matters. To illustrate these investigations, we will focus on the conception of goodness and naughtiness.

Piaget presented his subjects with a series of stories of two types. In one story, the central character performed an act which unintentionally resulted in considerable damage; in the other, he caused a negligible amount of damage as a result of a deliberately improper act. The subject's task was to decide who was good and who was naughty.

Here is an example of the first type:

> A little boy who was called Augustus once noticed that his father's inkpot was empty. One day that his father was away he thought of filling the inkpot

so as to help his father, and so that he should find it full when he came home. But while he was opening the inkbottle he made a big blot on the table cloth. (*MJ*, p. 122)

The corresponding story involving negligible damage is as follows:

There was a little boy called Julian. His father had gone out and Julian thought it would be fun to play with his father's inkpot. First he played with the pen, and then he made a little blot on the tablecloth. (*MJ*, p. 122)

After telling each pair of stories, Piaget asked whether the two children were equally guilty, or which of the two was the naughtier and why. He used the clinical method to probe the child's responses. The results were that until the age of 10, children give two kinds of answers. One of the answers maintains that the character's guilt is determined by the nature of his motives. The boy who wanted to help his father but caused a great deal of damage is less guilty than the boy who engaged in an improper act which resulted in negligible damage. Piaget calls this a "subjective" conception of responsibility since the child takes into account the motives (the subjective state) of the character in the story. The second type of judgment found in this stage (and found, moreover, in many of the same children who sometimes give a subjective answer) is less mature. This answer maintains that the character's guilt is determined not by his motives, but by the sheer amount of damage he has caused. The boy who wanted to help his father is nevertheless guilty because he made a large stain, whereas the boy playing with the pen is not guilty since his stain was so small. Consider this protocol, from a girl of 7 years:

Which is the most naughty?—*The one who made the big blot.*—Why?—*Because it was big.*—Why did he make a big blot?—*To be helpful.*—And why did the other one make a little blot?—*Because he was always touching things. He made a little blot.*—Then which of them is the naughtiest?—*The one who made a big blot.* (*MJ*, p. 126)

It is evident from the protocol that the child was perfectly aware of each character's intentions, and yet ignored them. What determines guilt is not intention but quantity of damage. Piaget characterizes such a response as a case of *moral realism*. The judgment is "realistic" in the sense that the criterion of guilt is not subjective (the intention) but material or "real" (the amount of damage). The child considers only the facts of damage, not the subjective state of motive. Also, the child's judgment observes the letter and not the spirit of the law. The rule (in this case, "Thou shalt not spill ink") is an absolute, so that any action which conforms to it is good, and any which does not is bad.

Piaget finds that the young child's moral realism is pervasive. Consider the definition of a lie. One 6-year-old gave a typical response in saying: "It's when you say naughty words" (*MJ*, p. 141). He went on to agree that "fool" is a lie because it is a word you should not say. We see then that the child's definition is "realistic": a lie is a bad thing and does not at all refer to the intention to deceive. A second example concerns young children's comparison of the magnitude of lies. To study this sort of judgment Piaget read the children two stories. In one story a boy was frightened by a dog and told his mother that the dog was "as big as a cow." In a second story a boy deliberately deceived his mother about his school grades. Young children often maintained that the story about the dog was a greater lie than the story about the grades. The reason was that seeing a dog the size of a cow was a less probable event than getting good grades. In the case of the dog there is a much greater discrepancy between actual facts (the real size of the dog) and the lie (the dog being as large as a cow) than in the case of grades, where the lie (a good grade) seems almost as likely as the fact (a bad grade). In other words, seeing a dog as large as a cow is far less likely to occur than having good grades and, therefore, appears to be a bigger lie. Intention to deceive is irrelevant, and the important criterion has to do with the probability of occurrence of the events. Thus the young child's judgment of lies is as "realistic" as his decision concerning goodness and naughtiness. It focuses on the external or material aspect of the question and fails to take into account the intentional or subjective aspect.

Why does a significant proportion of the young child's responses involve moral realism? Part of the reason is probably that parents are sometimes "realistic" themselves. Some adults punish the child more for breaking fifteen cups unintentionally than for purposely destroying one cup. But this is not the whole story. Parents punish a statement intended to deceive (a real lie) more than a mere exaggeration (for example, the dog as big as a cow). The child, however, thinks that the exaggeration is naughtier than the intention to deceive, so it seems that the child's judgment does not simply reflect the punishments which he has actually received from adults. It is apparent, then, that two additional factors are involved. One factor is the relation of unilateral respect. Since the parent is respected, so are his rules. If the parent forbids the breaking of cups, then the act of doing so is bad regardless of intention. Another factor is the child's egocentric patterns of thought. Since he cannot assume points of view different from his own, he cannot see the other's need for truth, and consequently, he is not aware of the fact that his "lies," in which he himself often appears to believe, are deceiving the listener. Unilateral respect and egocentrism, then, contribute to moral realism just as they do to the concept of rules as inviolable and sacred.

The child gradually abandons moral realism in favor of a more "subjective" approach. In judgments of goodness and naughtiness he focuses on motivation, not extent of damage. In judgments of lying he considers the intention to deceive, not just the likelihood that the event could have occurred. As was the case in the conception of rules, the child's progress is due largely to his new independence from the family, to his increased interaction with others, to his contact with divergent views, and to similar factors.

We may make several comments concerning moral behavior and judgment. First, Piaget emphasizes that the various stages overlap, that the same child may be in both stages simultaneously depending upon the content of a particular situation, and that primitive forms of moral judgment are often characteristic of adults as well as children. Neither the stages nor the course of their development are clear-cut, and Piaget does not wish to give an impression of orderliness where little is to be found. Second, Piaget's social learning theory—that primitive moral judgment derives in fact from unilateral respect and mature conceptions from cooperation and similar factors—is speculative because there is no direct evidence linking adult constraint with moral realism. Nevertheless, the theory points in interesting directions. The effect of the social environment on intellectual processes has hardly been considered. Undoubtedly the theory will require clarification and elaboration, particularly with regard to the reciprocal effect which seems to exist between cooperation and the diminution of egocentrism. Does the child take the other's point of view mainly because the two persons interact, or do they interact mainly because they can each take the other's point of view? Or, as seems more plausible, could it be that there is a complex relationship between cooperation and the passing of egocentrism?

A third comment is that Piaget's theory, like Freud's, is somewhat pessimistic. According to Freud it is inevitable for both social and biological reasons that the child will experience an Oedipal conflict, which will result in the adoption of a harsh and authoritarian superego or conscience. For Piaget, too, it seems inevitable that the young child will display egocentric thought and that he will stand in a relation of unilateral respect to the adult. Egocentrism defines certain properties of thought observed in young children which appear to be unavoidable and which must be overcome before the child can reach a more mature level of cognitive functioning. Unilateral respect is inevitable too; even if the parent tries, he cannot create a total atmosphere of mutual respect. The parent must arbitrarily impose upon the child some regulations because the child cannot understand their complex rationale. Since egocentrism and unilateral respect are inevitable, so is their product, moral realism.

A fourth comment is that Piaget has not yet fully demonstrated that the moral judgments elicited by his questioning on stories correspond to moral judgments in "real life." Piaget's arguments may be convincing—for example, that children take the game of marbles seriously—but no amount of argument can resolve the issue. What is required is naturalistic study. We need to see whether moral realism, for example, is indeed found in children's moral judgments in the natural situation.

A fifth comment concerning moral behavior and judgment is that Piaget's work has certainly fulfilled its original purpose: to stimulate further experimentation and theorizing. Moral judgment has been a popular topic for research, and in the main, independent investigators' findings have been consonant with those of Piaget.[1]

Reasoning

Piaget's early work touched upon the child's reasoning, too. The research again was preliminary, and as we shall see in Chapter 4, he later intensively elaborated upon the same topics. At this point we will consider several types of reasoning: syncretism, juxtaposition, and ordinal and part-whole relations.

In one of his studies Piaget presented thirty-five 9-year-old boys and girls with a series of proverbs and a collection of explanatory sentences. The child's task was to connect each proverb with the proper explanatory sentence. For example, one proverb is, "Drunken once will get drunk again." The sentence which expressed the same idea is, "It is difficult to break old habits," and not, "Some people are continually drunk." Piaget also questioned each child concerning the reasons for his choice.

One 8-year-old child said that the sentence corresponding to "When the cat's away the mice can play" is "Some people get very excited but never do anything." When Piaget asked his justification, he responded:

> Because the words are about the same. . . . It means that some people get very excited, but afterwards they do nothing, they are too tired. There are some people who get excited. It's like when cats run after hens or chicks. They come and rest in the shade and go to sleep. There are lots of people who run about a great deal, who get too excited. Then afterwards they are worn out and go to bed. (*LT,* p. 149)

The child's process of reasoning is certainly very confused. One way we may characterize it is in terms of *syncretism,* a tendency to connect a series of separate ideas into one confused whole. In the present case the child tries to tie together an absent cat with excited people. The child assigns to disparate things a similarity which is almost unfathomable to the adult. How does the tendency toward syncretism work? According to Piaget, when the child reads the proverb he constructs an interpretation of it. This interpretation may be only loosely related to the real meaning of the proverb because the child, in effect, free associates when he hears the words.

---

[1]For a review of this literature, see T. Lickona, ed., *Moral Development and Behavior* (New York: Holt, Rinehart and Winston, 1976).

In the case of the subject whose protocol was just described, subsequent questioning revealed that he interpreted the proverb as meaning "The cat runs after the mice." The child then searched among the alternative sentences to find the one corresponding to the proverb. His interpretation or understanding guided this process, so that he viewed the sentences in terms of his interpretation of the original proverb. In Piaget's terminology, the child assimilates the sentences into the scheme which originally contributed toward his understanding. The subject cited thus perceived a similarity between his understanding of, "The cat runs after the mice," and the sentence, "People get excited." Then, after the child has interpreted a proverb and seen a relation between the interpretation and a sentence, he says that the sentence and the proverb have the same meaning. By means of an intermediary—the scheme which enabled him to understand in the first place—he has conglomerated two apparently disparate items. In a sense, syncretism is a case of assimilation gone wild. The child does not accommodate to the real meaning of the proverb; rather, he assimilates it into his own scheme, and then he goes on in the same way to assimilate the sentence into this scheme too.

Now we will consider the phenomenon of *juxtaposition*. If you will recall, in his study of verbal communication Piaget found that young children seldom express causal relations. In describing some mechanical device, the child merely says that *a* and *b* occurred; he does not say that *a* caused *b*. Instead of being related one to the other, the two events are merely juxtaposed, that is, placed one after the other. To investigate this matter more directly, Piaget performed an experiment on forty children from about 6 to 10 years of age. He gave each child an incomplete sentence ending with the word "because," and asked him to complete it. For example, he might ask, "Water gets hot because . . .". If the child answered, "the fire was turned on," then Piaget might continue by asking, "And the fire was turned on because . . .". In this way, he attempted to determine if children could use the notion of causality when they are almost directly asked to do so. The responses to the sentences and to clinical questioning revealed a frequent inability to express causal relations. Here are some examples:[2]

> the man fell from his bicycle, because *he broke his arm.* . . . I had a bath, because *afterwards I was clean.* . . . I've lost my pen because *I'm not writing.* . . . He fell off his bike, because *he fell and then he hurt himself.* (*Judgment and Reasoning, JR,* pp. 17–18)

At least two explanations of the chid's responses are possible. According to one explanation, the child's answers express sophisticated relationships. The sentence "I had a bath, because *afterwards I was clean*"

[2]The sentence to be completed is in roman type, and the child's answer is in italic.

means "We can tell that I had a bath because afterwards I was clean" or "My cleanliness implies that I had taken a bath." A second interpretation of the same sentence is that the child has a poor understanding of causality: he reverses cause and effect and merely juxtaposes one event after the other. Which explanation is correct? A number of factors seem to support the second interpretation, juxtaposition. In his natural speech the child seldom uses the word "because" or other similar words to express relations, causal or otherwise, between events. Also, some of the answers to Piaget's test do not reveal sophisticated relationships of the type proposed by the first hypothesis. An example is, "He fell off his bike, because *he fell and then he hurt himself.*" This statement does not directly connect falling with injury; the two events are merely juxtaposed. The more accurate interpretation of the child's responses seems to be that they reveal a failure to perceive causality (let alone more sophisticated relations) and indicate a tendency merely to place events one after the other without specifying the relations among them.

Juxtaposition can also be seen in another and different context, namely, the child's drawing. In depicting a bicycle, for instance, the child draws many of the parts but does not synthesize them into a proper whole. He may draw the chain but not connect it to the wheel; he may draw the seat but not attach it to the frame. We see that the child considers only isolated events and ignores the relations between them.

Since syncretism and juxtaposition seem to be opposites, their simultaneous existence in the young child poses a paradox. How can the same child both ignore the parts in favor of the whole (syncretism) and ignore the whole in favor of the parts (juxtaposition)? Piaget attempts to resolve the paradox by arguing that both juxtaposition and syncretism are expressions of a common mode of thought—the inability to think about several aspects of a situation simultaneously. Juxtaposition involves failing to see any relation among the parts of a whole, and the result is that they are seen as discrete and unrelated to each other. The child is thus unable to think simultaneously about the parts as separate things *and* about the relations which unite them. Similarly, in the use of syncretism, the child perceives a whole or the common relationships, but fails to recognize the differences within the whole. He also has focused on one aspect of the situation at the expense of the other. In other words, since the child cannot focus simultaneously both on the differences among things and on their common relationships, he is apt to see either a succession of unrelated events (juxtaposition) or a conglomerated whole (syncretism). Both types of distortions result from the same deficiency in thought.

In yet another investigation Piaget studied relational thinking. He presented a number of children with this problem: "Edith is fairer (or has fairer hair) than Suzanne; Edith is darker than Lili. Which is the darkest, Edith, Suzanne, or Lili?" (*JR,* p. 87). The problem in effect involves what Piaget was later to call *ordinal relationships*. Suppose we know that b is a smaller number than c and that b is a larger number than a. Which is the largest number? The answer, of course, is c. If we substitute Lili for a, Edith for b, and Suzanne for c, and "has lighter hair than" for "is a smaller number than," then we have the same problem in the two cases: both deal with the understanding of relations of ordering, whether these be in terms of lightness of color, size of number, and so on. Both problems present the child with partial information concerning the ordering (e.g., that $b < c$ and $b > a$) and ask him to deduce the entire ordering (that $a < b < c$). Piaget found that children even as old as 13 years found the problem to be very difficult. For example, a 9-year-old said: "You can't tell, because it says that Edith is the fairest and the darkest" (*JR*, p. 88). Piaget again explains their difficulty in terms of an inability to consider several aspects of a situation simultaneously. It is because the child cannot at the same time focus on $b < c$ and $b > a$ that he fails to deduce $a < b < c$ or that Suzanne is the darkest of the lot.

Another investigation yielded remarkably similar results. The study dealt explicitly with the relations of the part to the whole. The aim was to discover whether the child believed that the part was *included in* the whole. The questions were phrased in terms of the relations between cities (the parts) and countries (the whole). Here is an example:

> Stu (7;8) says that *"Geneva is in Switzerland"* and that *"Switzerland is bigger* [than Geneva]*."* But Genevans are not Swiss. "Then where must you come from to be Swiss?"—*"From Switzerland."* We draw a circle representing Switzerland, and ask Stu to put the cantons in their places. . . . Stu inscribes within the circle three or four smaller ones—Geneva, Vaud, etc., but he still maintains that Genevans are not Swiss people. The Swiss are the inhabitants of the big circle. (*JR*, p. 123)

Note that at the outset the child seems to maintain that the city is part of a larger whole (*"Geneva is in Switzerland"*). But when he is questioned about the matter, he denies that Genevans are Swiss or that the part is in fact included in the whole. The child again sees part and whole separately: they are unrelated entities.

We see in summarizing that Piaget's studies of reasoning find that the child has a tendency to group together various different events into a loose and confused whole (syncretism), that he sometimes fails to see the relations among separate events (juxtaposition), that he fails to understand ordinal relations, and that he cannot deal with the relations between a part and the whole of which it is a member. All these types of reasoning reveal a common deficiency: an inability to think simultaneously about several aspects of a situation.

Piaget makes an extremely interesting general comment about his investigations. He postulates that his findings, since they are the results of questioning children, hold true on the "plane of verbal thought" but not on the "plane of action." That is, while children may fail a problem when its solution requires verbal expression, they may be quite able to deal with the same dilemma on a practical, behavioral level. While the child first solves problems on the plane of action, he then must relearn his solutions on the plane of verbal thought. In a sense, action is more advanced than verbal thought (for the child from 7 to 11 years); the latter lags behind the former. Piaget terms the lag a *vertical décalage*. The verticality refers to an ascending age scale: what the child learns at age 7 on the plane of action, he must restructure at age 11 on the plane of verbal thought. "Décalage" refers to the gap or lag.

GENERAL SUMMARY AND CONCLUSIONS

Piaget's early work is greatly varied. The first studies deal with the child's use of language. Naturalistic observation reveals that children younger than the age of 7 years often fail to use speech as a vehicle for transmitting information to one another, and instead frequently repeat another's remarks or engage in individual or collective monologues. An experiment confirms these findings: when young children are given the explicit task of conveying information to another child, they fail to communicate. They do not consider the informational needs of the listener. Moreover, the listener distorts what the speaker says by giving it idiosyncratic interpretations.

In other investigations Piaget uses the clinical method. He rejects the testing approach because of its rigidity and rejects the naturalistic approach because of its failure to yield a sufficient amount of relevant information. The clinical approach, he feels, is more flexible and, therefore, is especially well suited to the exploratory aims of initial stages of research. He uses the clinical method to investigate the child's conception of the world, and finds that the child exhibits several primitive thought patterns. *Animism* is the tendency to consider natural events to be alive in the same sense as human beings are. *Artificialism* is the tendency to believe that some agent—human or divine—created natural events. *Participation* is the vague idea that human actions and natural processes interact and are related.

A further study, again using the clinical method in part, deals with moral judgment and behavior. Children below the age of 7 years fail to follow the rules of a game while at the same time believe that the rules are sacred and inviolable. Older children display both a greater tendency to follow the rules and to believe that they can be changed. In explicitly moral situations, young children believe that guilt and moral responsibility are determined not by intention but by the amount of damage produced. These "realistic" moral tendencies are seen in the case of lying as well, and decline with age.

In studies of reasoning, Piaget finds that the young child's thought is characterized by *syncretism,* the tendency to group together into a confused whole several apparently unrelated things or events, and by *juxtaposition,* the failure to see the real connections among several things or events, and the failure to understand either part-whole or ordinal relations. All these tendencies reflect a common pattern of thought: the inability to consider several aspects of a situation simultaneously.

Piaget employs a social learning theory to explain the child's development particularly in the areas of language and moral judgment. He postulates, for example, that the child's primitive moral judgment is the result of egocentric thought tendencies and the relation of unilateral respect toward the adult. The child's moral judgment becomes more mature when he adopts a position of mutual respect toward adults and comes into contact with new social institutions and points of view.

There are several comments we may make concerning Piaget's early research. First, what are the relations among the various findings? The young child is egocentric in communication, has an absolutistic concept of rules, is realistic in his moral judgment, and in his reasoning displays syncretism and juxtaposition. These varied terms at first may seem to refer to different and unrelated phenomena. One might think that moral realism and syncretism, for instance, refer to different patterns of thought, and that there is no commonality between them. But Piaget feels that such a view is mistaken: there is indeed a strong similarity among many of the young child's reactions to the problems posed by the various investigations.

The common pattern underlying these apparently diverse reactions is the inability to deal with several aspects of a situation simultaneously. This is due to the egocentric nature of the child's thought or the incapacity to shift attention from one to another aspect of a situation. In the case of speech, the young child cannot consider *both* the other's point of view and his own at once, and therefore centers solely on his own point of view. In the case of rules, the young child fails to consider both his own interests and the needs of others. Consequently, he often breaks the rules. He sees the origin of rules from a limited perspective, too. Emanating from a person whom he regards as prestigious, they must likewise be prestigious. The child fails to consider both the parent's prestige and his reasons for devising the rules. In the case of moral judgment, the child cannot consider both degree of damage and intention, and he bases his judgment entirely on the former. As far as reasoning is concerned, we have already seen how both syncretism and juxtaposition are expressions of a single tendency, namely, that of focusing on a limited aspect of the problem. The same may be said of the understanding of ordinal and part-whole relations. In the former, the child considers only certain parts of relations but not others; in the latter, he focuses on the part but not the whole, or vice versa.

As the child grows older and comes into contact with opposing points of view and varied social institutions, his thought goes through a process of decentration. In speech, he considers both what he wants to express and the listener's needs. In games, he considers the other's interests as well as his own and is, therefore, willing to follow and modify the rules. In moral judgment, he considers both the outcomes of a person's behavior and its intent. And in reasoning, he tries to consider the complexities of problems—both the differences and similarities among the same set of events. Thus, the child decenters his thought just as in the sensorimotor period the infant decentered his behavior. The newborn *acts* as if the world is centered about himself and must learn to behave in more adaptive ways. Similarly, the young child *thinks* from a limited perspective and must widen it. Both infant and young child must decenter—the former, his action and the latter, his thought.

In addition to characterizing the young child's thought in terms of centration, Piaget occasionally described it in Freudian terms. Freud described several primitive mental operations usually found in certain kinds of mental illness and in the deepest layers of the normal person's unconscious. Freud felt that this type of thinking, called "autistic thought," displays certain regularities. For instance, it shows a tendency to fuse disparate things into one image. Thus, in a dream we may perceive a character who is a "condensation" of two distinct persons. In his early work Piaget proposed that the thought of the child is intermediate between autistic and adult thinking. For example, the child's syncretism is similar to, but more mature than, the tendency toward condensation. While at the beginning of his career Piaget borrowed a few ideas from psychoanalysis, he was never a disciple of Freud but always an independent investigator. As time went on, his limited dependence on Freud diminished further with the result that Piaget's later work is totally devoid of Freudian concepts.

Piaget not only abandoned Freudian ideas, but became dissatisfied with the clinical method as administered at that time. He came to feel that it relied too heavily on language. The child thinks in nonverbal ways too, and the exclusively verbal clinical method was not always effective in tapping these thought processes. Consequently, he turned to somewhat different methods which we will describe in the next chapter.

Despite their methodological deficiencies, Piaget's early investigations may be considered among the most interesting of his achievements. The major part of the early studies dealt with *socially and practically relevant* phenomena: the child's ability to communicate information, to follow rules, and to make moral judgments. All these matters are obviously important for the child's practical success in the world and for his interactions with others.

By contrast, Piaget's later work deals, as we shall see, with more abstract phenomena: the child's understanding of number or classification. These have less obvious relevance to the child's ordinary activities. Probably, his ability to understand the cardinality of number makes less of a difference to his daily life than his ability to communicate to other children. Also, in his early books, Piaget showed a strong interest in the role of social factors in development. Later research, as we shall see, convinced Piaget that other factors of equal importance were involved. With time his interests have tended to focus on these factors rather than on the social environment.

Finally, we may note that the explanatory concepts which evolved from Piaget's early work are vague. They are stated in ordinary language and are often not entirely clear. Much confusion, for example, has arisen over the concept of egocentrism. But as we have stated repeatedly, Piaget fully recognized that his early concepts were only preliminary and tentative, not final and conclusive. He hoped that his early work would stimulate research by others, and that he himself could clarify his concepts at a later time. The first of his expectations has been fulfilled: there has been much research on moral judgment, for example. We will see in the next chapter how Piaget elaborated and even formalized some of his early and tentative notions, including ordinal and part-whole relations.

4

The Years 2 through 11: Piaget's Later Work

This chapter deals with aspects of Piaget's later work (from approximately 1940 onward) on the child from about 2 to 11 years. As was shown in Chapter 1, this portion of Piaget's research and theory is voluminous and covers such matters as the child's conception of chance, space, geometry, movement, number, and other topics. Since we cannot review all the later work here, we shall focus on what we consider to be basic issues and concepts which reappear in and apply to almost all of Piaget's recent writings. We will consider (1) the revised clinical method, (2) the child's classification of objects or events, (3) the ability to place them in ordinal relations, (4) the concept of number (particularly its conservation over transformations), (5) the nature of mental imagery, (6) the development of memory and consciousness, and (7) some general characteristics of thought.

THE REVISED CLINICAL METHOD

We saw in Chapter 3 that Piaget's original clinical method was highly dependent on verbalizations. The examiner posed the questions in words, and the child was required to give the answers in the same way. The examiner's questions usually did not refer to things or events that were immediately present, and the problems did not always involve concrete objects which the child could manipulate or even see. For example, the examiner might depict a child who had unwittingly broken some cups and might then ask the subject being questioned for a judgment concerning the child's naughtiness and the punishment to be meted out. In such a situation as this, the subject is required to do several things. He must interpret the examiner's description so as to picture the scene to himself; he must make a special effort to comprehend certain crucial aspects of the question, like the word "naughty"; and he must express his judgment in words.

After some experience with this method, Piaget came to feel that it was inadequate because it relied too heavily on language. The child might not understand everything said to him, particularly if the words did not always refer to concrete objects. Even if the child did understand, perhaps he could not adequately express in words the full extent of his knowledge. Consequently, Piaget modified his procedures, and the result is what we shall call "the revised clinical method" (sometimes called the "method of critical exploration"). The new method involves several features. First, the examiner's questions refer to concrete objects or events which the child has before him. No longer must the child imagine these things merely on the basis of a verbal description. Second, an effort is made to let the child express his answer by manipulating the objects, and not solely express himself through language.

For example, let us suppose that the examiner wishes to know whether the child can form two distinct classes. To investigate the matter he might present the child with an array of circles and squares all mixed together in no order, and ask him to put together the ones that belong together, or sort out two distinct piles. What the child *does* with the objects—what sort of piles he makes—and not what he says about them, constitutes the primary data of the study. If after encouragement a child still cannot form a pile of circles separate from a pile of squares, then the examiner might conclude that he does not have the classification skills under investigation. While completely nonverbal tests are desirable, it is often hard to invent them. This is especially true for Piaget, since he usually investigates the child's understanding of abstract concepts that are not easily manifested in the behavioral manipulation of concrete materials. The revised clinical method, therefore, must often depend for its data on the child's verbal responses. But even when this is necessary, the child's answers refer to a problem stated in terms of concrete materials which are present.

Third, Piaget introduced the use of *counterarguments* or *countersuggestions*. These involve presenting the child with a point of view that contradicts his own, and asking him what he thinks of the opposing view. The purpose of these counterarguments is to determine the stability and authenticity of the child's thinking. Children who have mastered a concept will resist the countersuggestion; those who have not tend to be swayed by the contradictory argument.

A fourth feature of the revised clinical method is not new: the examiner's questioning is flexible. Rather than employ a standardized list of questions, he modifies them or adds new ones as the situation demands. As before, Piaget still feels that there is no point either in asking a child a question that he does not understand or in failing to clarify an answer.

To summarize, the revised clinical method involves posing questions concerning concrete materials; allowing the child to "answer" by manipulating the materials, if this is at all possible; introducing counterarguments; and, as in the earlier clinical method, stating questions and pursuing answers in a flexible and unstandardized way. Whether or not the revised clinical procedure gives an accurate assessment of the child's abilities is a matter for debate. In general, most psychologists (outside of Geneva) do not use this method in research, mainly on the grounds that it is not sufficiently standardized. We think that this attitude is mistaken, especially since there are very good reasons for avoiding standardization.[1] In any event, the revised clinical method is less exclusively verbal than Piaget's earlier procedure and attempts to give an accurate assessment of the child's thought processes which in large measure may be nonverbal.

CLASSIFICATION

Piaget has used the revised clinical method to study classification in the child. The preceding chapters have already touched on this and related matters, and it may be useful to review some of the material here. We saw that there is a primitive sort of motor classification in the sensorimotor period (0 to about 2 years) when the infant applies to objects in the environment abbreviations of familiar schemes. For example, Lucienne saw a toy parrot hanging above her crib and kicked her feet very slightly. This was an abbreviation of a scheme which she could quite easily have applied to the present situation. It seemed as if her action classified the parrot as a "thing to be swung." Moreover, the abbreviation shows that the behavior was becoming internalized. Eventually it could be replaced by the thought: "That's the parrot; that's something I can swing." But the abbreviated schemes are not yet instances of legitimate classification. One reason is that the schemes apply to individual objects over a period of time and not to a collection of objects. For example, Lucienne kicked from time to time whenever she saw parrots and thus indicated recognition. But this

---

[1]See H. P. Ginsburg, "The Clinical Interview in Psychological Research: Aims, Rationales, Techniques," *For the Learning of Mathematics,* Vol. 3 (1981), pp. 4–11, and S. Opper, "Piaget's Clinical Method," *Journal of Children's Mathematical Behavior,* Vol. 1 (1977), pp. 90–107.

recognition does not imply that she considered the parrots to belong to a class. Mature classification, on the other hand, involves the conception of a collection of things, whether they are immediately present or imagined. A second reason why it is not possible to credit Lucienne with classification has to do with *inclusion relations,* which will be expanded on shortly. Briefly, this refers to the ability to construct a hierarchical classification, such that toy parrots are a subclass of a larger, more inclusive class like toys in general.

From about 2 to 4 years the child begins to classify collections of objects in a way that is quite primitive. He uses the preconcept. Sometimes he fails to see that one individual member of a class remains the same individual despite slight perceptual changes, and sometimes he thinks that two different members of the same class are the same individual. Between 5 and 10 years, the child's classification is still faulty in several ways. There is the phenomenon of juxtaposition, the inability to see that several objects are indeed members of the same class. There is also syncretism, the tendency to group together a number of disparate events into an ill-defined and illogical whole.

As was pointed out, Piaget's investigations of the preconcept, syncretism, and juxtaposition, conducted in the 1920s and 1930s were preliminary and tentative. First, there existed methodological defects: the data were almost exclusively verbal so that Piaget's interpretation was based largely on what the child said. Second, Piaget's concepts—syncretism, juxtaposition, the preconcept—were somewhat vague and needed elaboration. In the 1950s Piaget returned to the study of classification in the child from about 2 to 12 years. These investigations make use of the revised clinical method; they also modify the notions of preconcept, syncretism, and juxtaposition and suggest new ways of conceptualizing the child's classificatory activities.

Some Properties of a Class

Before examining Piaget's research into classification, we must clearly understand what he means by a class. Suppose we have before us a number of objects all mixed together. The array contains a large red triangle, a small blue circle, a large pink circle, and a small black triangle. All the objects are discriminably different one from the other. That is, there is no difficulty in perceiving that any one object is different from any of the others. For example, the large red triangle is very obviously larger and redder than the small black triangle. Suppose, too, that we wish to place these objects into two different classes. One way of doing this is to put in one separate pile the large red triangle and the small black triangle. In the second pile would go the small blue circle and the large pink circle. If the original array contained additional triangular objects, regardless of their size or color, they would of course go in the first pile. Similarly all other circular objects would go in the second pile. The two piles each represent a class. Of course, we might classify the objects in another way. We could put in one pile the two small objects (regardless of their color or shape) and in the second pile the two large objects. There are usually many different classes that one may form from a given array of objects.

Piaget makes a number of points about the classes formed from the original array (for purposes of illustration consider just our first example, the class of triangles and the class of circles):

1. No object is a member of both classes simultaneously. For example, the large red triangle is in the class of triangles and not also in the class of circles. Thus, the classes are mutually exclusive or disjoint. This holds even if there are more than two classes formed. (For example, we might divide some animal pictures into the classes of lions, tigers, and elephants, all of which are disjoint.)

2. All members of a class share some similarity. For example, the small blue circle and the large pink circle both share the property of circularity. Circularity is the defining property, the crucial attribute, of the class; that is, we include in the class of circles any object which is circular. Another way of putting it is to say that circularity is the *intension* of the class. The defining property or intension of the other class is triangularity.

3. Each class may be described in terms of a list of its members. Instead of describing a class in terms of its defining property or intension (for example, the class of triangular objects), we may simply list the objects in the class (for example, large red triangle and small black triangle). Such a list is the *extension* of the class. Note that the list may involve concrete objects (like large, blue circles) or abstract ideas, events, actions, and so on (like the list of the parts of speech).

4. The defining property of a class determines what objects are placed in it. Another way of stating this is that intension defines extension, or the "field of application" of a concept. For example, if we know that one class is to be formed on the basis of triangularity and another on the basis of circularity, we can predict the content of the list of objects in each class.

These are some fundamental properties of classes, as Piaget defines them. (There are other crucial attributes too, like inclusion relations, which we will discuss later.) Piaget then asks whether the child classifies objects in accordance with these properties. When asked to group objects, does the child form mutually exclusive classes? Do his classes have defining properties which determine the list of objects in each class?

Piaget discovers three stages of development. The first two—both of which we may call *preoperational*—occur roughly during the years 2 to 7. The third stage—that of *concrete operations*—occurs roughly from the years 7 to 11.

Stage 1

To investigate classification, Piaget performed a number of experiments which used the revised clinical method. In one study, he tested a number of children from about 2 to 5 years of age. They were presented with flat geometric shapes of wood and of plastic. The shapes included squares, triangles, rings, and half-rings, all of which were in several colors. The shapes were mixed together and the child was told: "Put together things that are alike." Sometimes additional instructions were given: "Put them so that they're all the same" or "Put them here if they're the same, and then over there if they're different from this one but the same as each other" (*Early Growth of Logic, EGL,* p. 21).

The children displayed several methods of grouping the objects. One method is called the *small partial alignment*. With this method the child uses only *some* of the objects in the original array and puts them together in several ways apparently without any overall guiding plan. For example, one child began by putting six half-rings (semicircles) of various colors in a straight line; then she put a yellow triangle on top of a blue square; later she put a red square in between two blue triangles; then put squares and triangles in no particular order, in a straight line. There are several points to note about this performance. Sometimes similarities among objects determine the collection. For example, the subject whose performance was just described began with a line of half-rings. At other times the same child grouped things on the basis of no detectable similarity; that is, she put a yellow triangle on a blue square, or a red square between two blue triangles. In both of these cases, there is no similarity of either color or form.

It is clear that small partial alignments are not true classes for several reasons. One of them is that intension does not define extension; that is, no consistent defining property determined which geometric forms were put in various collections. The child does not operate under an overall guiding plan like a system of rules (defining properties) which organize the way in which he arranges the objects.

Other children of this age use the geometric figures to construct an interesting form or picture. One child arranged a number of circles and squares to represent a long vertical object and then proclaimed it to be the Eiffel Tower; another child placed a number of half-rings in between several squares, all in a horizontal line, and described the result as a bridge. Piaget calls these productions *complex objects*. It is obvious that like the small partial alignments, and like some other types of collections not described here, the complex object is not a true class. Figures are not placed in the complex object because they share some defining property; rather, extension is determined solely by the requirements of the picture under construction.

In another investigation, Piaget presented children of the same age with nongeometric figures for classification—little toys which included people, houses, animals, and so on. Once again, the results showed an inability to form classes. One child put two dolls in a cradle, then two wheelbarrows together, then a horse. When the examiner asked the child for all the objects like a horse, she gave him all the animals and then a baby and two trees. This example illustrates the fact that although the young child may perceive similarities among the objects, these do not fully determine what objects go into the collection. That is, the child saw that all animals were in some respect similar and gave them to the examiner when asked for objects like the horse. If the child had stopped there, she might have formed a class which was based on the defining property of "animal-ness." However, she went on to throw in the baby and two trees. The similarity (intension) that she first perceived did not fully determine which objects were to be grouped together (extension). It is as if the child forgot about the initial defining property (animalness) and then switched to some other.

We may make several comments on these investigations. First, they make clear the nature of the revised clinical method. The examiner gives the child concrete objects to work with. The task instructions and questions are still verbal, of course, but they refer to real things that the child can manipulate. The child is required to say very little. Most of his responses are not verbal but behavioral. He does not have to say that all of the animals do or do not go together; rather, he can put them together or fail to do so.

Second, although the revised clinical method is an improvement over what was used before, we wonder whether the task was entirely clear to the child. The instructions (e.g., "Put together things that are alike") seem rather vague and susceptible to many interpretations. We suspect that different methods of presenting the task to the child might produce entirely different results. Piaget considered this objection and tried an essentially nonverbal method. He began to classify the objects himself and asked the child to do the same thing. The result again was not true classification, but "complex objects," and so on. While this method was not successful, it does not exhaust the possibilities. Other investigators have explored different procedures, with some success.[2]

Stage 2

Children from about 5 to 7 years produce collections that seem to be real classes. When presented with the situation described earlier, one child produced two large collections, one which contained all the polygons and

[2]See, for example, R. Gelman and C. R. Gallistel, *The Young Child's Understanding of Number* (Cambridge, Mass.: Harvard University, Press, 1978), Chap. 3.

FIGURE 2   Classification of geometric objects.

the other the curvilinear forms. Moreover, each of these collections was subdivided further. The polygons, for instance, contained separate piles of squares, triangles, and so on, and the curvilinear forms involved separate collections of circles, half-rings, and so on. Thus, the child not only seems to form classes, but arranges them hierarchically, as in Figure 2. There are two general collections (polygons and curvilinear forms) at the top of the hierarchy, and these both branch out into several subcollections below (squares, triangles, etc.). The child's activities may be characterized in several additional ways. (1) He places in the appropriate collection *all* of the objects which were in the initial array. The younger child did not do this; he left some objects unclassified. (2) Intension fully defines extension. That is, if the child defines a collection on the basis of the defining property of circularity, *all* circles go into that pile, and *none* is placed in any other pile. (3) At a given level of the hierarchy, similar defining properties are used to determine collections. For example, at the lower level of the hierarchy in Figure 2, all the collections are defined in terms of geometric form—squares, triangles, and so on. It is not the case that some collections are defined by form and some by color. To summarize, it would seem that the child from about 5 to 7 years produces rather elaborate hierarchical collections which deserve to be called true classes.

Piaget feels, however, that the child of this stage fails to comprehend one crucial aspect of the hierarchy he has constructed. The child does not understand key relations among the different levels of the hierarchy. This is the problem of *class inclusion* which we will now illustrate. Suppose we are given a randomly organized array of blue and red squares and black and white circles. We construct an arrangement (see Figure 3) such that there are two major collections (squares versus circles) and within each of these there are two further subdivisions (blue versus red squares and black versus white circles). Thus, there is a hierarchy whose higher level is defined by shape and whose lower level is defined by color. Consider for the moment only one-half of the hierarchy, namely, the squares which are divided into blue and red. If we understand inclusion relations, then we can make statements of this sort: (1) *All* of the squares are either blue or

FIGURE 3   Classification of squares and circles.

red. (2) There are more squares than there are blue squares. (3) There are more squares than there are red squares. (4) If the red squares are taken away from the squares, then the blue ones are left. (5) If the blue squares are taken away from the squares, then the red ones are left. (6) All the blues are squares, but only some of the squares are blue. These, then, are some of the possible statements about inclusion relations—the relations of the parts to the whole, of the whole to the parts, and the parts to the parts. They may seem very obvious, but so do many other principles which children fail to understand.

Piaget investigated the understanding of inclusion relations in children of various ages. Let us consider now the child from about 5 to 7 years. Piaget presented each of his subjects with a number of pictures of flowers and other things. The child was first required to group the pictures in any way he wished, and then he was asked a number of questions concerning inclusion relations. The results concerning spontaneous classification replicated what was found earlier: the child from 5 to 7 years constructs collections which seem to involve a hierarchy. One child formed two large collections: flowers versus other things; then he further subdivided the flowers into primulas versus other kinds of flowers. In terms of Figure 4, the child seemed to have constructed the top two levels of the hierarchy. (He did not make a further subdivision in terms of yellow versus other primulas.) It would seem that the construction of such a hierarchy implies the understanding of inclusion relations. If the subject divided the flowers into primulas versus other kinds, must he not understand that there are more flowers than there are primulas? The results of Piaget's questioning, however, point to different conclusions. Consider this protocol of a child aged 6 years 2 months:

A little girl takes all the yellow primulas and makes a bunch of them, or else she makes a bunch of all the primulas. Which way does she have the bigger bunch?—*The one with the yellow primulas will be bigger.* [He then counted the yellow primulas and the other primulas and found that there were four of each kind] *Oh no, it's the same thing. . . .*—And which will be

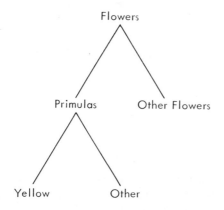

FIGURE 4   Classification of flowers and other things.

bigger: a bunch made up of the primulas or one of all the flowers?—*They're both the same.* (*EGL,* p. 102)

Although this child had earlier constructed a hierarchical arrangement of the materials, he maintained that the yellow primulas did not form a smaller collection than the primulas as a whole and that the primulas did not form a smaller collection than the flowers as a whole. Both of these answers, of course, are quite wrong. In both cases, the part is smaller than the whole from which it derives.

What is the explanation for the child's inability to comprehend inclusion relations? Piaget postulates that once the child has divided a whole into two subgroupings, he cannot then think simultaneously in terms of the larger collection and the subdivisions which he has constructed from it. For example, suppose a child divides a collection of flowers (the whole) into primulas versus other flowers (subdivisions of the whole). When he is asked "Are there more primulas or more flowers?" he must consider both the original collection (flowers) and one of his subdivisions (primulas) at the same time. He must compare the "size" of one against that of the other. Under these conditions, he focuses or *centers* on the collection he can see (the primulas) and ignores the original collection (all of the flowers), which is no longer present in its initial state (a collection of the primulas and other flowers all mixed together). And since he centers on the part, ignoring the whole, his answers to inclusion questions are often wrong.

Stage 3

Children from about 7 to 11 years of age are both capable of constructing hierarchical classifications and of comprehending inclusion. For example, after constructing a hierarchy, one child of 9 years and 2 months was asked:

> Which would make a bigger bunch: one of all the primulas or one of all the yellow primulas?—*All the primulas, of course, You'd be taking the yellow ones as well.*—And all the primulas or all the flowers?—*If you take all the flowers, you take the primulas too.* (*EGL*, p. 109)

This protocol makes quite clear the child's ability to think simultaneously in terms of the whole and its parts (e.g., "If you take all the flowers, you take the primulas too"). While he physically separates the flowers into primulas and other kinds, the child is able to reason both about the original whole and its part at the same time. His thought has *decentered* from exclusive preoccupation with the part or the whole.

Piaget also found that when the child of this age was asked the same questions about hypothetical objects, the subject often failed to give correct answers. Apparently, the child's classification is *concrete:* he understands the inclusion relations of a group of real objects, but fails to comprehend the same relations when imaginary classes are involved. The gap between hypothetical and concrete reasoning is another example of *vertical décalage.*

We may summarize by stating that the child from 7 to 11 has reached the most advanced stage as far as the classification of concrete objects is concerned: he can construct a hierarchical arrangement and understand the relations among the levels of the hierarchy. Piaget then proposes that this accomplishment can be described in terms of a logicomathematical model. Let us explore this idea.

Rationale for the Use of a Logicomathematical Model

We have seen that Piaget attempts to describe the basic processes underlying the classification of objects or events. He proposes that the stage 1 child (2 to 4 or 5 years) fails to construct hierarchical arrangements partly because after a short while he forgets the defining property (intension) which he has used to form a collection. The stage 2 child (5 to 7 years) can construct a hierarchy because of the ability to use a defining property to determine which objects go in a collection, but at the same time cannot understand inclusion relations because of the inability to simultaneously consider several immediately present collections and the larger one from which they were derived. The stage 3 child (7 to 11 years) can correctly answer questions concerning inclusion because of his ability to think of original classes and their derivatives at the same time.

Thus far, we have described these basic processes (the ability to think simultaneously of subclasses and larger classes) in terms of the ordinary language. Many psychologists believe that this is the proper procedure; but others, including Piaget, feel that descriptions of structure should be phrased, as much as possible, in a formal language like mathematics.

Let us consider first, however, some aspects of the use of the common language. Most psychological theories have been stated in this way. Freud, for example, wrote exclusively in German and not in logic nor mathematics, and no doubt there is not a single formula in the entire corpus of psychoanalytic doctrine. Another example from another point on the psychological spectrum is Tolman, an experimental psychologist, who produced his theories of learning in ordinary English and made use of only a few (and nonessential) symbols. Tolman and Freud are hardly isolated examples. Today, too, the major part of psychological theorizing is done in English, or Russian, and so forth. Several advantages are usually claimed for this procedure. The ordinary language may be richer and subtler than formal languages, and also it is generally easier to read than mathematics or logic.

However, another approach to this problem is possible. Piaget feels that for scientific purposes the ordinary language is fundamentally ambiguous and must be supplemented by formal approaches. Anyone even slightly familiar with the history of psychology knows that most, if not all, psychological theories stated in the common language have been vague and easily susceptible to misinterpretation. Even today there are many fruitless arguments over the meaning of words like "concept" or "ego" or "learning." As an example, let us consider the word "thought," which we have used without definition quite frequently. No doubt "thought" means quite different things to different readers. To some it may mean "ideas," and to some "consciousness"; to others it may mean "mental effort," "meditation," "concentration," "opinion," and so forth. Is it any wonder that a given psychological theory which uses words like this will elicit a variety of interpretations and, hence, considerable argument and misunderstanding? Perhaps a prime example of the difficulty is Piaget's own use of verbal theories in his early work. Considerable confusion still surrounds the terms "egocentrism," "moral realism," and so forth.

Piaget feels, then, that the ordinary language produces obscure and ambiguous psychological theorizing, and must therefore be supplemented, if not replaced, by other modes of description. The physical sciences have convincingly shown that mathematics is an extremely powerful tool for communicating certain precise ideas. Piaget—along with increasingly large numbers of other psychologists—feels that it would be fruitful for psychology to adopt a similar approach, and he himself has attempted to do so in the case of classification and other matters. Let us now explore his formal description of the structure of classification.

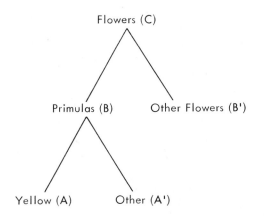

FIGURE 5   Classification hierarchy.

Grouping I

The formal description called a *Grouping*[3] begins with this situation: we have a classification hierarchy of the sort constructed by the 7- to 11-year-old children in Piaget's experiments (see Figure 5). This is what we start with (that is, it is a given) and the Grouping describes what the child can do with the hierarchy. At the top of the hierarchy that the child has constructed are the two classes, flowers which we shall symbolize as (C) and other things (C'). On the middle level of the hierarchy we find primulas (B) and other flowers (B'). On the lowest level there are yellow primulas (A) and primulas of other colors (A'). Each of the classes (A, A', B, B', C, C') is an *element* of the system. There is one *binary operator* that may be applied to the elements, namely, *combining*. We will symbolize combining by +, although the reader should be aware that combining classes is not precisely equivalent to adding numbers. The operator + is binary since it can be applied to only two elements at a time. Just as we can add only two numbers at any one time, so we can only combine two classes at a time.

Given the elements and the binary operator, the five *properties* describe the ways in which the operator may be applied to the elements.

The first property is *composition* (usually referred to in mathematics as *closure*) which states that when we combine any two elements of the system the result will be another element of the system. For example, if we combine the yellow primulas with the primulas of other colors, we get the gen-

[3]Our exposition of Grouping I is simplified and incomplete: for example, we have defined only one binary operator. We have kept the mathematical development at a very informal level. The reader interested in pursuing the matter should see Jean Piaget, *Traité de Logique* (Paris: Colin, 1949), and also J. B. Grize's formalization of Piaget's system as described in E. W. Beth and Jean Piaget, *Mathematical Epistemology and Psychology* (Dordrecht, Holland: D. Reidel Publishing Company, 1966).

eral class of primulas. This may be written as A + A' = B. Or if we combine the yellow primulas with all the primulas, we get all the primulas. We may write this as A + B = B. This property describes aspects of the child's ability to understand a hierarchy. For example, he can mentally construct a larger class by combining its subclasses.

The second property is *associativity,* which may best be illustrated in a concrete manner. Suppose we want to combine three classes such as yellow primulas, primulas, and flowers (A, B, and C, respectively). Remember that we cannot just add all three of them together simultaneously since the operator (combining) is binary; that is, it can be applied to only two elements at a time. Given this limitation, there are at least two ways of adding A, B, and C. We might first combine the yellow primulas and the primulas and get primulas. That is, we do A + B = B. Then we might combine this result (B) with flowers-in-general (C) and get flowers-in-general. Thus, we do B + C = C. To summarize, we first perform A + B = B and then B + C = C so that our final result is C. Another way of stating this is (A + B) + C = C.

There is yet a second way of combining the classes. We could start by combining the yellow primulas (A) with the *combination* of primulas and flowers in general (B + C) and finish with the same result: flowers-in-general, (C). Thus we can write A + (B + C) = C. Note that the final result of performing the operation by either method is C, so that the two methods may be considered equivalent. We may write this equivalence as (A + B) + C = A + (B + C). This equation expresses the fact that the child can combine classes in different orders and can realize that the results are equivalent.

The third property is *identity,* which states that there is a special element in the system (the "nothing" element), that produces no change when combined with any of the other elements. If we combine the nothing element with the yellow primulas the result will be the yellow primulas. If we symbolize nothing by 0, then we have A + 0 = A. More concretely, if we do not combine the yellow primulas with any of the other classes, then, of course, we still have the yellow primulas.

The fourth property is *negation* or *inverse,* which states that for any element (class) in the system, there is another element (the inverse) that produces the nothing element when combined with the first element. That is, if we add to the class of yellow primulas its inverse, then we are left with nothing. The inverse is equivalent to the operation of taking away the same class. If we start with yellow primulas and combine with this class its inverse, we are in effect taking away the yellow primulas with the result that we are left with nothing. We can write this as A + (− A) = 0 or A − A = 0. The inverse rule might apply to a train of thought like this: "Suppose I combine the yellow primulas with all of the other primulas. Then I have all of the primulas. But if I take away [inverse or negation] all

of the other primulas, then I am left again just with the yellow primulas.''
Note how this train of thought is *reversible*. First, the other primulas are
added, but later they are taken away, so that the thinker is once again at
the point where he started. Negation, then, is one kind of reversibility.

The inverse also may be used to express aspects of class inclusion.
Suppose we start with the class of primulas (B) and take away (or add the
inverse of) the primulas which are not yellow (A'). This operation leaves
us with the yellow primulas (A). We may write this as $A = B + (-A')$ or
$A = B - A'$. This type of reasoning underlies the child's ability to say
that there are *more* primulas than yellow ones, that the yellow primulas are
included in the class of primulas, or that the yellow primulas are only some
of the primulas.

The fifth property actually encompasses several aspects. One of them
is related to special identity elements. Suppose we combine the class of
yellow primulas with itself. The result is yellow primulas. We may write
this as $A + A = A$. In this equation, A functions as an identity element
like 0. Adding A to A is like adding 0 to A: the result, A, is unchanged.
Piaget calls this *tautology*. Another aspect is *resorption*. If we combine the
class of yellow primulas with the class of primulas, the result is primulas.
We may write this as $A + B = B$. Here, too, A functions as an identity
element. Adding A to B is like adding 0 to B; the result, B, is unchanged.
In a sense, this is another way of looking at inclusion relations. The yellow
primulas must be included in the class of primulas (or must be some of the
primulas) since adding the former to the latter does not change the latter.

These, then, are some of the aspects of Grouping I and are intended
as a formal description of the processes underlying the child's classification. The model involves elements (classes), the binary operator of combining, and five properties governing the application of the operator to the
elements.

Discussion of Grouping I

A few general remarks should be made concerning Grouping I.
First, Piaget's use of mathematics is not at all meant to imply that the child
understands the logicomathematical model in any explicit sense. It is obvious that most children have never heard of the special identity element, let
alone Grouping I. Clearly, the child is not a mathematician at this level.
In fact, he often cannot describe in *any* clear way, mathematical or otherwise, his procedure for solving a particular problem. His report is often
incoherent. Piaget uses the logicomathematical model, therefore, not to
characterize the child's consciousness, but to describe the processes underlying his classification.

Second, Grouping I is not metrically quantitative in the sense that it
does not involve numbers. The operations involve classes which may be of

any size. It does not matter whether there are 5 yellow primulas and 6 white ones, or 5,000 yellow primulas and 300 white ones. In both cases there are more primulas than there are white primulas, and so forth.

Third, we may expand on our earlier point that the Grouping is intended to describe the structure of the child's classification. Piaget is not interested in the minor details of the child's performance; that is, whether he is classifying flowers or fish or whether he first put the flowers in an arrangement and then the animals. Piaget instead attempts to capture the essence of the child's activities and to identify the processes underlying them. The Grouping is Piaget's way of describing these processes in a clear way. Therefore, the Grouping is not simply a protocol listing everything that the child does. It is instead an abstraction which describes basic processes like the ability to combine mentally two smaller classes into a larger one, or to take away one class from another.

The grouping also is a comprehensive and integrated structure. It is comprehensive since it describes the processes underlying basic classification activities. The Grouping describes the potentialities of the child, and not necessarily what he does in any one task at any one time. Let us suppose that a child constructs a hierarchy of classes. In doing so he may not make use of inclusion relations. In this case, the Grouping does not so much describe what the child actually does, but what he is capable of doing under the proper conditions.

Also, the Grouping is an integrated system in the sense that each of the properties does not stand alone but is related to all of the others. On the mathematical level, this is easy to see. The property of associativity describes the order in which elements may be combined, but the property of composition or closure is needed to interpret the result of the associative combination. In other words, associativity shows that two different orders of combining elements are equivalent, and composition reveals that both of these orders of combination result in another element which must be in the system. Thus, the property of associativity would be meaningless without the property of composition. We cannot have one property without the other. This feature of the Grouping is, of course, intended to reflect an important aspect of the child's activities: the child's successful classification (including the understanding of inclusion) presupposes an *interrelated whole,* a structure of mental operations. For example, suppose the child recognizes that there are more primulas than yellow primulas. This achievement implies a number of interrelated mental acts.

The child must be aware that the primulas (which are no longer present in a single collection) are the combination of yellow primulas and primulas of other colors ($A + A' = B$). The child must also be aware that when yellow primulas are taken away from the primulas, there remain primulas of other colors ($B - A = A'$). These, then, are some of the operations underlying the child's answer to a question concerning inclusion. When the child correctly answers the question, he may not first actually perform all these operations. However, they are implicit in his answer; he could not answer correctly if it were not possible for him to perform all the operations involved in the classification system. To summarize, any particular response that the child makes to a classification problem cannot be considered in isolation. His response presupposes a complex structure, and it is this which Piaget describes as the Grouping. The Grouping, in other words, describes the mental operations which make it possible for the child to "really" understand classification.

Fourth, the Grouping explains and predicts behavior. Insofar as the Grouping describes the processes underlying the child's classification, it may be said to explain performance. The Grouping states that the child can combine two classes to get a larger one. This operation, among others, underlies the child's ability to understand inclusion relations and in this sense explains it. Insofar as the Grouping is general it may be said to predict behavior. The Grouping is not limited to the objects Piaget used to study classification. Because the Grouping provides a description of structure, it goes beyond the details of any particular problem and allows us to predict what the child's performance is like on other similar tasks.

Fifth, Piaget has described several other Groupings all of which are intended to refer to the child's ability (from 7 to 11) to deal with concrete objects or thought about them. Therefore, stage 3 is termed *concrete operational*.

Sixth, toward the end of his life, Piaget began to feel that the Grouping model is not fully adequate as an account of the concrete operations. While the facts concerning children's performance on the classification tasks (and others as well) remain as well established as ever, the Grouping model suffers from several deficiencies. "[The Grouping] model . . . has generated little enthusiasm from logicians and mathematicians because of its unavoidable limitations . . . and consequent 'lack of elegance' " (Piaget, 1977b). (Indeed, one might even go further and claim that the logic of the model is not only inelegant, but not entirely coherent.) "[The Grouping model] . . . was too closely linked to the traditional model of extensional logic and truth tables" (Piaget, 1980, p. 5, quoted in Beilin, 1985). In view of these limitations, Piaget felt it is necessary to develop new formal models to characterize the essence of concrete operational thought. "A better way, I now believe, of capturing the natural growth of logical thinking in the child is to pursue a kind of logic of meanings" (Piaget, quoted in Beilin, 1985b). While Piaget did not have the time to develop such models in detail, he began the effort by introducing the notion of "correspondences," which we describe in our discussion of preoperational strengths. It is important to realize, as Beilin points out, "that Piaget was not irrevocably committed to a particular logic or abstract model; consequently, following Piaget's example, others are free to [select] the logical or mathematical models that best explain the data of cognitive development'' (Beilin, 1985, p. 112).

In brief, Piaget believed that while thinking is best described in terms of logical models, his own efforts in this area were not entirely successful. Hence it is necessary to expand the theory by developing new models. As Piaget claimed, he himself was the chief ''revisionist'' of Piagetian theory.

Summary and Conclusions

Piaget's early work (in the 1920s and 1930s) dealt with classification in a preliminary way. In the 1950s he returned to the problem, using the revised clinical method. He presented 2- to 11-year-old children with an array of objects to be classified. The findings were that in stage 1 (2 to 5 years) the child fails to use consistently a clear rule or defining property to sort the objects into different classes. He instead constructs graphic collections which are small partial alignments or interesting forms. In stage 2 (5 to 7 years), the child sorts the objects by a reasonable defining property and even constructs a hierarchical classification, but fails to comprehend inclusion relations. Stages 1 and 2 are termed *preoperational.* In stage 3, which is *concrete operational* (7 to 11 years), the child has a mature notion of class, particularly when real objects are involved. The child sorts them by defining properties, understands the relations between class and subclass, and so forth. To describe clearly the processes underlying the child's activities, Piaget proposes a logicomathematical model which he calls Grouping I. This Grouping involves some elements, a binary operator, and five properties relating the operator to the elements. Also, the Grouping is not metrically quantitative in the sense that it does not matter how big or small (in numerical terms) are the various classes involved. The child, of course is not conscious of the Grouping; rather the Grouping is intended to describe the basic structures of his activities. In his last years, Piaget recognized the shortcomings of the Grouping model and proposed the development of a new ''logic of meanings.''

Piaget stresses that the age norms describing classification are only approximate. A particular child may pass from stage 1 to stage 2 at 6 years and not necessarily at 4 or 5 years. One child may spend three years in stage 1 while another child may spend four years in the same stage. Piaget does maintain, however, that the *sequence* of development is invariant. The child must first be characterized by stage 1 before he can advance to stage 2 and then to stage 3. Piaget also points out that a child may not necessarily be in the same stage of development with respect to different areas of cognition. That is, a child may be in stage 1 with respect to classification, and in stage 2 of number development. Thus, a child may be slightly more advanced in some categories of thought than in others.

One important issue regarding classification, and indeed all the concepts studied by Piaget, is the generality of the findings for children in different cultures. Recently, much cross-cultural work has been carried out to determine whether children in different cultures employ the types of reasoning described by Piaget, and whether the sequence of stages is invariant across cultures, as Piaget proposes. Opper (1971; and in Dasen, 1977) has examined a number of Piagetian concepts, including classification, in rural and urban children in two Southeast Asian countries, Thailand and Malaysia. Like many other investigators (for a review, see Dasen, 1977), Opper finds that although the ages may vary, the *sequence* of development is the same in different cultures: first, Thai children are characterized by stage 1, then stage 2, and so on.

Moreover, Opper finds that Thai and Malaysian children present responses similar to those of Swiss children. For example, when a Malaysian girl in stage 2 of classification was asked whether there are more roses or flowers in a bunch of seven roses and two orchids, she responded, "There are more roses than flowers." The examiner said, "Show me the flowers." The child then pointed to the two orchids.

A Thai boy, in the same stage, was presented with seven roses and two lotus. He, too, maintained that there are more roses than flowers. *More roses.* —More than what?—*More than flowers.* —What are the flowers?—*Roses.* —Are there any others?—*There are.* —What?—*Lotus.* —So in this bunch, which is more, roses or flowers?—*More roses.* —Than what?—*Than lotus.*

Turning to the stage 3 child, we also find the same responses as the Swiss children. For example, a Malaysian girl said: *There are more flowers because if it's roses, it's only these* [pointing to roses], *but the flowers are plus these also* [pointing to orchids]. We see then that in many cases Thai and Malaysian children's arguments are virtually identical to those of Swiss children.

How can we evaluate Piaget's work on classification? On the one hand, Piaget has been very successful at what he has attempted to do. A number of independent investigators have confirmed that stage 1 classification takes unusual forms (e.g., Vigotsky, 1962), that young children experience genuine difficulty with class inclusion (Klahr and Wallace, 1972), and that the course of development with respect to classification is generally as Piaget has described (Kofsky, 1966). On the other hand, it should be pointed out that Piaget's approach to classification is of a very specific sort. He focuses mainly on the hierarchical structure of classes, for example, class inclusion. He is not particularly concerned with other aspects of concepts which now seem to be quite important. Thus Neisser (1967) has pointed out that everyday concepts are often vague and difficult to define, and Rosch (1973) has developed a new approach focusing on nonlogical aspects of children's concepts. The defining property or intension of a class is often quite vague, a particular object may fit into several classes simultaneously, the boundaries between classes may be fuzzy, and it may not be possible to form a simple hierarchy. In brief, Piaget's approach focuses on only one of many important aspects of classes.

RELATIONS

In Chapters 2 and 3 we have already reviewed several aspects of relations, a problem (like classification) with which Piaget has been concerned since his earliest work in psychology. We saw that in the sensorimotor period the infant displays precursors of relations. He can broadly discriminate within the dimensions of numerosity, intensity of muscular effort, and loudness of sounds (among other dimensions). In the case of numerosity, you will recall that Laurent said ''papa'' when Piaget said ''papa,'' that Laurent said ''bababa'' when Piaget said ''papa-papa,'' and that Laurent said ''papapapa'' in response to ''papapapapapapa.'' Laurent's imitation, although not exact, nevertheless implies an ability to discriminate or hear the difference among several sounds which differed in number of repetitions of one syllable. Similarly, in the case of muscular effort, Laurent appeared able to detect the difference among the variations in vigor with which he swung a chain, and also he was able to discriminate among sounds of different degrees of loudness. Thus, the infant can differentiate gradations within different kinds of stimuli: some things are louder than others, or more numerous, or bigger, and so forth. He can perceive differences in various aspects of his world. The ability to make such discriminations is a prerequisite for reasoning about differences.

   Piaget's early research on the child from about 5 to 10 years investigated reasoning about differences, but not the perception of differences. He presented children with this verbal problem (among others): ''Edith is fairer (or has fairer hair) than Suzanne; Edith is darker than Lili. Which is the darkest, Edith, Suzanne, or Lili?'' (*Judgment and Reasoning,* p. 87). The results showed that children from 5 to 10 years are unable to deal with problems of this sort, called *transitivity,* at a verbal level.

   As in the case of classification, Piaget returned to the problem of relations in his later work. Using the revised clinical method, he performed several interesting studies on *ordinal relations,* which we will now characterize briefly.

Some Properties of Ordinal Relations

   Piaget's definition of ordinal relations involves several features. Suppose we have several numbers, such as 17, 65, 25, 3, and 1,001. It is possible to arrange them in order of increasing size. We may use the symbol $<$ to stand for ''is a smaller number than'' and write $3 < 17 < 25 < 65 < 1,001$. The sequence is an ordering of the numbers with the smallest being first, the next smallest second, and so forth. Note that the absolute size of the numbers makes no difference. The second number does not have to be exactly one more than the first or exactly twice as big as the first. The last number, so long as it is larger than 65, may be of any size whatsoever. Also, we do not need to have zero as the beginning of the series. The only requirements for ordering the numbers are that they are different from one another, that at least one number is smaller than the rest, that another is larger than all the rest, and that any number in between the smallest and the largest is both larger than the one immediately preceding it in the series and smaller than the one immediately following it. Of course, orderings are not limited to numbers. We may also order sounds on the dimension of loudness. Suppose sound a is very soft, b is much louder than a, and c is slightly more loud than b. Then we have $a < b < c$, where $<$ means "is softer than." Again the precise degree of loudness does not affect the ordering.

Piaget's work deals with such matters as the child's ability to construct orderings or ordinal relations and to manipulate them in various ways. These studies, involving children from about 4 to 8 years of age, usually detect three distinct stages of development: stage 1 lasting from about 4 to 5, stage 2 from about 5 to 6, and stage 3 from about 7 and above. The first two stages are *preoperational,* and the last is *concrete operational.* While the age norms are approximate, the sequence is crucial.

Stage 1

One study was concerned with the ability to construct an ordering of a collection of ten sticks which differed only in size. We will call the shortest of the sticks (about 9 centimeters in length) A, the next larger B, and so on through J, the largest (about 16 centimeters in length). A differed from B by about .8 centimeters, and this also was true of B and C, and so on. Piaget presented the child with the sticks in a randomly organized array and asked him to select the smallest of the lot. After this was done, Piaget gave an instruction like this: "Now try to put first the smallest, then one a little bit bigger, then another a little bit bigger, and so on" (*Child's Conception of Number, CCN,* pp. 124–25). In another study the child was asked to make a staircase from the sticks.

When confronted with this problem, children in stage 1 showed several reactions, none of which was successful. Some children produced random arrangements of the sticks, like H, E, B, J, and so on. Other children managed to order a few of the sticks, but not all of them. An example of this reaction is $A, B, C, D, H, F, E,$ and so on.

Another strategy was to place the larger sticks in one collection and the smaller sticks in a second collection. Within each of these collections, however, the sticks were in a random order. A more advanced reaction

FIGURE 6   Ordering of sticks.

also appeared which may be considered a transition to the next stage. The child started with some stick, like *B*, apparently selected at random; then he took another stick, like *H*, and made the top of it extend slightly above the top of *B*; a third stick, for example, *A*, was made to extend slightly beyond the top of *B*; and so forth. The result was that the tops of the sticks form an ordering; *H* is slightly higher than *B*, and *A* slightly higher than *H*, and so forth, as in Figure 6. But the bottoms of the sticks also differed in a random way, and failed to lie on a straight line as they should. Thus, the child constructs an ordering, but only by ignoring the length of each stick. This procedure frees him from the necessity of comparing each stick with the one immediately preceding it and with the one to follow. One way of characterizing these activities is to say that the child focuses (centers) on one aspect of the problem (putting the tops in order) but ignores another, equally important aspect (arranging the bottoms in a straight line). To summarize, the child at this stage frequently cannot form a systematic ordering of any number of objects although he is sometimes able to order a few of them.

Stage 2

Presented with the same problem, children in the second stage generally succeed in constructing the ordinal arrangement of sticks, so that $A < B < C < D < E < F < G < H < I < J$. But the child does not build the orderings without difficulty. Sometimes he begins by ignoring the bottoms of the sticks, as in stage 1. Sometimes he makes many errors, like $A < D < B$, and so on, and takes a long time to recognize and correct them. The child continually rearranges his ordering, and shifts the sticks from one position to another. Essentially the child's procedure is one of trial and error, lacking an overall plan or guiding principle. For example, if he has chosen *A* as the smallest, he might then choose another small one, like

D, and line it up next to A. Then he might choose another small one, like C, and place it next to D and see that it is smaller than D. Since this is so, he might rearrange the sticks placing C after A but before D. After beginning with A, the child fails to look for a stick that is longer than A but smaller than all the ones remaining. If this rule is followed, then each step of the ordering can be constructed without any difficulty. However, the child at this stage does not employ such a logical procedure. He fails to make systematic comparisons between a given stick and the one immediately preceding it and all those following.

This tendency was further revealed by the addition of one more problem. After constructing the ordering A through J, the children were given a new collection of ten sticks, $a, b, c, d, e, f, g, h, i, j$. Each of these new sticks could fit in between a pair of sticks of the first series. That is, if the new set of sticks were ordered correctly along with the first set, the arrangement would be $A < a < B < b < C < c < D < d < E < e < F < f < G < g < H < h < I < i < J < j$. The child's task was to do precisely this; to fit the new sticks into the ordering already constructed (A through J), so as to make a new ordinal arrangement involving all twenty sticks.

Children of this stage had great difficulty with the problem. In fact, many failed to solve it. Part of one child's ordering was $C\ e\ d\ D$, and another produced $H\ g\ G\ I\ h\ j\ c$, and so forth. Other children succeeded in producing the correct ordering, but only after considerable trial and error.

These difficulties seem due to several factors. One factor appears to be that the child perceives the original series as a whole and finds it hard to break up the series into smaller units. Also, children of this stage do not approach the problem with a guiding principle. They fail to use a rule like, "Start with the smallest of a-j; insert it in between the pair of the smallest sticks in A-J; then take the smallest of b-j and insert it between the smallest pair of sticks in B-J; and so forth." Not only did the children fail to use a rule like this, but they also had difficulty in deciding that a given element of a-j was at the same time bigger than one stick in A-J and smaller than the next larger stick in A-J. To place d properly, the child must see that $d < E$ and that $D < d$. He must *coordinate* these two relations but fails to do so consistently. That is, some children would take e and, seeing that it was larger than B, would place it right after B. They failed to consider whether e was at the same time smaller than C, and therefore made an error.

After investigating the child's ability to construct an ordering and place new elements in it, Piaget went on to study the child's ability to construct equivalences between two separate orderings (which involve equal numbers of elements). To illustrate this, let us take a class with fifteen boys and fifteen girls and order each of these groups in terms of height. We find the shortest boy, the next-to-shortest boy, and so on, and we do the same for girls. We can see that the two orderings are equivalent in some ways and different in others. Some differences are that the height of the shortest boy may be 48 inches, whereas the height of the shortest girl is 44 inches. Also, the second shortest boy may be 4 inches taller than the shortest one, whereas the second shortest girl is only 1 inch taller than the shortest girl. Despite these real differences, there are important similarities between the two orderings. The boy who is 48 inches tall and the girl who is 44 inches tall, despite their difference in height, are equivalent in terms of their position in the ordering. They are both the shortest. The same holds true, of course, for the tallest boy and girl, the next to tallest, and so forth.

Piaget then raises the issue of whether the young child can recognize the equivalences between two distinct orderings. Does he understand that two objects, while differing in height, for example, can at the same time be equivalent in terms of their relative position in an ordering? To study the matter he first presented children with ten dolls, $A-J$, which were presented in a random display and which could be arranged in order of height; and with ten sticks, $A'-J'$, also randomly arranged, which could be ordered in size. The sticks were smaller than the dolls, and the differences between adjacent pairs of sticks were smaller than between pairs of dolls. The child was told that the dolls are going for a walk and that each of them must have the proper stick. The intention of the instructions, of course, was to get the child to produce an ordering of the dolls and of the sticks and to make each member of one ordering correspond to the appropriate member of the other ordering. Thus, doll A should have stick A', doll B should have stick B', and so on. Piaget calls this process the placing of orderings into one-to-one correspondence.

The results showed that children of this stage can produce a one-to-one correspondence of dolls and sticks, but only in a trial-and-error fashion. The most common procedure is to order the dolls (by trial and error) and then to order the sticks (by trial and error). Only after two separate orderings have been constructed are the elements of each put into one-to-one correspondence. That is, the child first identifies the largest doll, the next to largest doll, and completes the ordering of dolls; then he goes on to order the sticks. It is only after this is done that the child places the largest stick with the largest doll, the next to largest stick with the next to largest doll, and so forth. While this procedure works, it is somewhat cumbersome. An easier method is to begin by identifying the largest (or smallest) doll and the largest (or smallest) stick and immediately placing the two together. The second step is to choose the largest doll and stick of all those remaining and to place them together, and so forth. In any event, the child in this stage does succeed in setting the two orders into one-to-one correspondence. He seems to have established that the orderings are equivalent.

FIGURE 7   The equivalence of relative position (dolls and sticks).

The next problem concerns the stability of the equivalence established by one-to-one correspondence. Let us suppose that the sticks are placed very close together with their order preserved (as in Figure 7). The shortest stick is closest to the third tallest doll, the second stick is closest to the fourth tallest doll, and so forth. Does the child recognize that the second tallest stick is *still* equivalent to the second tallest doll, even though the former is now closest to the fourth tallest doll? That is, does the child *conserve* the equivalence of relative position when the overt one-to-one correspondence is destroyed?

Piaget presented this and similar problems to a number of children. He placed the sticks close together and asked which stick "goes with" which doll. Piaget discovered several methods of attacking the problem. The most primitive reaction is to assert that a doll is equivalent to the stick closest to it. Thus, the second largest stick and fourth largest doll are considered to belong together simply because one is below the other. The child's judgment is dominated by *spatial* relations. Other children try to solve the problem by counting, but they fail to do so properly. For example, one child said that the fourth largest stick was equivalent to the third largest doll. The reason for his mistake was that he noticed that there were three sticks preceding the fourth largest stick; he then counted out three dolls, stopped there, and identified the third doll with the fourth stick. This method is quite frequent among children of this stage; that is, they find a doll corresponding to the nth stick, counting the preceding $n - 1$ sticks, then count the dolls, stopping at the $n - 1$th element. The child confuses the position to be found (say, stick 4) with the number of preceding elements (3).

Stage 3

After about the age of 6–7 years, the child is successful in all of the tasks we have described. When asked to construct a single ordering of sticks differing in size, the child does so quite easily. The ordering is guided by an overall plan. The child usually begins with the smallest (or sometimes, with the largest), then the next smallest, and so forth, in sequence until the ordering is complete. This strategy may be characterized as starting with the smallest and continuing to take the smallest of everything that is left, until the sticks have been exhausted. When asked to place additional sticks (a–j) in their proper positions within the ordering (A–J) already constructed, the child does so with almost no errors. The process underlying this achievement is the comparison of one of the new sticks (say, d) with two in the original ordering simultaneously. That is, to ascertain d's proper position, the child determines that it is at the same time bigger than D but smaller than E. To phrase the matter differently, he coordinates two inverse relations—bigger and smaller than.

In a similar way the concrete operational child easily places two separate orderings into one-to-one correspondence. One child immediately put the biggest doll with the biggest ball (balls were sometimes used in place of sticks), the next to biggest doll with the next to biggest ball, and so forth. His strategy was to identify the biggest doll and ball of all those remaining and to place the two together at once. This procedure is more economical than that of the younger child who first orders the dolls, then the balls, and finally begins to put them together. When this one-to-one correspondence is destroyed, the child conserves the equivalence of relative position. He realizes that the smallest doll is still equivalent to the smallest ball and not to the ball to which it happens to be closest in space.

In summarizing the material on the concrete operational child, then, we can state that he is adept at understanding and manipulating ordinal relations. However, as in the case of classification, one limitation applies: he can deal with relations on a concrete level only; that is, when real objects or thoughts about them are involved. Nevertheless, his thought is far more advanced than that of the child in stages 1 and 2. The child can construct orderings, put two such orderings into one-to-one correspondence, and conserve the resulting equivalences. As in the case of classification, the processes underlying the child's ability to manipulate relations form integrated and comprehensive structures. Each of his mental operations cannot be understood without reference to the others of which he is capable. These processes must be interpreted in terms of complex *systems* of operations. To describe these systems, Piaget has developed several logicomathematical models, similar to Grouping I (although they, of course, deal with relations, not classes). Also, Piaget has investigated several other aspects of ordinal relations, such as *transitivity* (if $a > b$ and $b > c$, then $a > c$), which we will not cover here.

NUMBER

The ability to understand classes and relations, according to Piaget, is basic to mature concepts in many areas. The several groupings which describe the processes underlying the older child's performance in problems of classes and relations may also be used to characterize concepts of space, chance, geometry, and so forth. Since we cannot review all these concepts, we will concentrate on one that is particularly interesting and that has received considerable attention in the American and British research literature, namely, the concept of (whole) number.

First, we must understand what Piaget does and does not mean by the concept of number. He does *not* mean and is *not* interested in computational abilities as taught in the first few grades of school. Whether the child can add 2 and 2, or subtract 3 from 5, is not the issue. The reason for Piaget's lack of interest in these matters is that simple addition and subtraction of whole numbers, as well as other manipulations of them, can be carried out entirely by rote and without understanding. The child can simply memorize the addition and subtraction tables and fail to comprehend the basic concepts underlying them. Piaget does not deny that it is useful to memorize the facts of addition and subtraction; for purposes of computation, we all find it helpful to do so. He asserts, however, that for mature understanding of number, such rote memorization is not sufficient and must be accompanied by the mastery of certain basic ideas.

Among these ideas are one-to-one correspondence and conservation. Let us first consider one-to-one correspondence. Suppose we are presented with a collection or set of discrete objects as in Figure 8. The size of the objects, their color, and so forth are completely irrelevant. All that is required is that the set contain a finite number of discrete objects. We are then given a box of objects and are required to construct from it another set which has the same number property as the first set. It does not matter whether the objects in the second set (which we will call set B) are the same

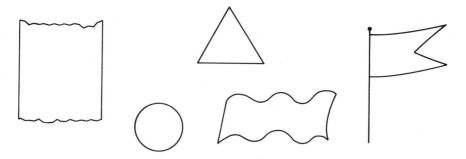

FIGURE 8   Collection of objects.

color, size, and so on as those in the first set (set A). Whether set A contains elephants and set B contains geraniums is irrelevant. The only requirement is that they have the same number. One way of constructing a set B so that it will have the same number property as A is by counting the objects in A (say, there are five) and then take out of the box the same number of objects. This procedure, which of course is quite adequate, probably occurs first to adults. But suppose we cannot count. Suppose we do not know the number of objects in set A. Even with these limitations there is a simple way of constructing a new set, B, which will have the same number property as A. This method merely involves putting next to each member of set A one, and only one, new object. These new objects, after the one-to-one correspondence has been established, form a set, B, with the same number as A. Of course we do not really have to physically place each new object next to one in A; we can note the one-to-one correspondence mentally. That is, we can "say to ourselves," "This new object corresponds to the first in the line of set A," and so on. The important idea is not the physical placing together of the sets, but the pairing of one member in set A with one in set B, however this is done.

Although very simple, the idea of one-to-one correspondence is basic and powerful, and may be used in a variety of situations. If we want to determine whether there are the same number of seats as people in an auditorium, all we have to do is ask everyone to sit down (with no one allowed to sit on anyone else's lap!). If all the people are in seats (in one-to-one correspondence with the seats) and if none of the seats is empty, then the numbers (whatever they may be) of people and seats are equal. If there are people standing, then this defines the relation of more people than seats. If there are empty seats, then this defines the relation of more seats than people. In brief, one-to-one correspondence establishes that any two sets—regardless of the nature of the objects comprising them—are equivalent in number. Counting or other procedures are not needed. Lack of one-to-one correspondence establishes that one set is larger than the other (and one smaller than the other).

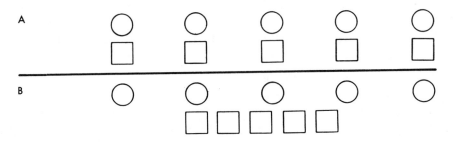

FIGURE 9   Conservation of number.

The second basic idea which Piaget investigates is *conservation*. Suppose that we have established that sets A and B are equal in number, as in Figure 9A. That is, we have put set A in a line, and below each member of set A we have put a new object. The line of the new objects is set B. Suppose that we then compress the members of set B, as in Figure 9B, so that the perceptual one-to-one correspondence is destroyed. Now each member of set B is not directly below a different member of set A. The problem is whether the two sets which now differ in physical arrangement still are equal in number. In other words, is the equivalence established in Figure 9A conserved when the rearrangement shown in Figure 9B is performed? To adults, this may seem like a foolish question. Of course, the equality of numbers has not changed! But the problem is whether children accept this simple and basic idea, too. If they do not, then their world of number must be very chaotic indeed. If quantity is seen to change whenever mere physical arrangement is altered, then the child fails to appreciate certain basic constancies or invariants in the environment.

Piaget has conducted a number of investigations on the child's understanding of these two basic ideas: one-to-one correspondence and conservation of the equivalence of two numbers. He finds that young children fail to understand these two notions and that a period of development is required before the child achieves the mental operations necessary for thorough comprehension of number. Let us now review the experiments.

Stage 1

To study the ability to construct sets of equivalent number, Piaget presented children with a variety of problems. The simplest of these involved placing before the child a row of six or seven pennies or buttons or sweets, and so on. The examiner then asked the child to pick out the "same number" or "as many" from a large collection of similar objects. Thus the child was given set A and was required to construct a second set, B, which was equivalent in number. The children were, of course, not told how to construct set B. Here is a protocol describing how a stage 1 child, 4

FIGURE 10   Failure to construct equal sets.

years and 7 months of age, dealt with the problem. Piaget had placed six sweets in a row and told the child that they belonged to his friend Roger:

> "Put as many sweets here as there are there. Those . . . are for Roger. You are to take as many as he has." (He made a compact row of about ten, which was shorter than the model.)—"Are they the same?"—*"Not yet"* (adding some).—"And now?"—*"Yes."*—"Why?"—*"Because they're like that"* (indicating the length). (*CCN,* p. 75)

The example makes clear the predominant tendency of this stage. The child does not use the method of one-to-one correspondence. Instead, he thinks that the two sets are equivalent in number if they have the same lengths. In Piaget's terms, the child *centers* on one dimension—the length—of set A (Roger's sweets or the model) and bases his construction of set B solely in terms of that one dimension. The result is pictured in Figure 10. The lengths of the two rows are equal, but their numbers are not. The new row is denser; that is, there are smaller spaces between the sweets, than Roger's row, but the child ignores this fact and concentrates only on the lengths. Since he fails to *coordinate* the two dimensions of length and density at the same time, he cannot construct sets equivalent in number except when very small numbers are involved, or except by accident.

In another investigation, Piaget tried to make the child understand the principle of one-to-one correspondence, and then performed the conservation experiment. In this study, set A was a row of ten vases and set B consisted of flowers. One child, 4 years and 4 months of age,

> put 13 flowers close together in a row opposite 10 vases rather more spaced out, although he had counted the vases from 1 to 10. Since the rows were the same length, he thought that the flowers and vases were *"the same."*—"Then you can put the flowers into the vases?"—*"Yes."*—He did so, and found he had 3 flowers [left] over. (*CCN,* p. 50)

The child, then, initially constructed set B so as to make it the same length as set A and thought that the two sets were therefore equal in number. The examiner then made the child construct a one-to-one correspondence between the flowers and vases; that is, the child put each flower in a vase. The result was ten flowers in ten vases (or two sets equivalent in number), and the three extra flowers were discarded. The question now is whether the child realizes that the two sets are really equivalent in number. Does the child *conserve* the equivalence despite a mere physical rearrangement of the objects? To find out, Piaget continued the experiment with the same child.

> The flowers were taken out and bunched together in front of the vases. [That is, they formed a shorter row than did the vases.] "Is there the same number of vases and flowers?"—*"No."*—"Where are there more?"—*"There are more vases."*—"If we put the flowers back into the vases, will there be one flower in each vase?"—*"Yes."*—"Why?"—*"Because there are enough."* (The vases were closed up and the flowers spaced out.)—"And now?"—*"There are more flowers."* (*CCN,* p. 50)

Note that after the child had himself established a one-to-one correspondence between the flowers and vases, he failed to conserve the numerical equivalence of the two sets. When the flowers were put into a shorter row than the vases, the child believed that the numbers were no longer equal and that now there were more vases. He maintained this even though he realized that the one-to-one correspondence could be reestablished; that is, that the flowers could be returned to the vases. Then when the row of vases was made shorter than that of the flowers, he changed his mind once again. He asserted that now there were more flowers. Clearly, this child centered on the lengths of the rows and used only this information to make judgments of equivalence or lack of equivalence of number. When the rows were the same length (as when the flowers were in the vases), he said that they were equal in number. When the rows differed in length, he believed that the longer line had the greater number.

Piaget also investigated the role of counting, questioning the way in which counting the two sets affects the child's judgment. One child, 5 years and 3 months of age, failed the conservation problem. He said that set A (six glasses) was greater than set B (six bottles) because one was longer than the other. Then the examiner said:

> "Can you count?"—*"Yes."*—"How many glasses are there?"—*"Six."*—"And how many bottles?"—*"Six."*—"So there's the same number of glasses and bottles?"—*"There are more where it's bigger* [that is, longer]." (*CCN,* p. 45)

This examination shows that while the child can count, the act is meaningless in dealing with conservation. Although he can recite a string of numbers, he does not comprehend what they signify. The fact that he counted six bottles and also six glasses does not imply to him that the sets are equal in number. For him, equality of number is determined solely by equality of lengths, and counting is an extraneous and irrelevant act, which does not assure either the equivalence of sets or its conservation.[4]

Stage 2

The child of this stage easily constructs two sets equivalent in number, but fails to conserve the equivalence when the sets are rearranged. Per, a child of 5 years, 7 months,

> had no difficulty in making a row of 6 sweets corresponding to the model. [Piaget uses "model" to refer to set A, the row to be copied, and "copy" to refer to set B.] The model was then closed up: *"I've got more."*—"Why?"— *"Because it's a longer line.* (The process was reversed.)—*Now there are more there, because it's a big line."* But a moment later, Per said the opposite: "Are there more here [referring to the longer row]?"— *"No."*—"Why not?"— *"Because it's long."*—"And there [the shorter row]?"— *"There are more there, because there's a little bundle"* [The child meant that the shorter row was denser].—"Then are there more in a little bundle than in a big line?"— *"Yes."* After this Per went back to using length as the criterion, made the two rows the same length again and said: *"Now they're both the same."* (CCN, p. 79)

The protocol shows that the child of this stage easily constructs a set equal in number to another. He also establishes the equivalence by the method of one-to-one correspondence. That is, in order to construct set B, he places a new sweet just below each in set A. But the one-to-one correspondence is not fully understood; it is just "perceptual." When set B is made shorter than set A, the child fails to conserve the equivalence which he so easily constructed. The protocol also shows that the child is ambivalent about the criteria used to establish equality or inequality of number. Sometimes he maintains that the longer row has more because it is longer; at other times he believes that the shorter row has more because it is denser. In Piaget's terms the child sometimes *centers* on the lengths (ignoring densities) and sometimes centers on the densities (ignoring lengths). This tendency is an improvement over what occurs in the previous stage, since the younger child (in stage 1) consistently centers on only one of the two dimensions, usually length, and does not consider the other, usually density, at all. By contrast, the child in stage 2 has widened the sphere of his centrations. He notices, albeit at different times, that both dimensions may be relevant and uses the information from either of these dimensions separately to make a judgment. This use of partial information is called

---

[4]Although it does not seem to help with conservation, counting is far from useless in children's arithmetic. Hebbeler has shown, for example, that young children make very good use of counting in doing addition. See K. Hebbeler, "Young Children's Addition," *Journal of Children's Mathematical Behavior,* Vol. 1 (1977), pp. 108–21.

regulations. We will see next how the child in the period of concrete operations *coordinates* the two dimensions.

Stage 3

The results of this stage are easy to describe. The child can now construct a set numerically equivalent to another set and can conserve their equivalence despite changes in physical arrangement. Here is a protocol illustrating this stage:

> "Take the same number of pennies as there are there [there were 6 in set A]." He made a row of 6 under the model, but put his much closer together so that there was no spatial correspondence between the rows. Both ends of the model extended beyond those of the copy. "Have you got the same number?"—*"Yes."*—"Are you and that boy [referring to the hypothetical owner of set A] just as rich as one another?"—*"Yes."*—(The pennies of the model were then closed up and his own were spaced out.)—"And now?"—*"The same."*—"Exactly?"—*"Yes."*—"Why are they the same?"—*"Because you've put them closer together."* (*CCN*, p. 82)

This protocol contains several interesting features. One feature is that in making set B equal to set A, the concrete operational child does not bother to place each element in B directly under each element in A. He does not need to rely on the perception of spatial proximity between the elements of each set. How then does he construct numerically equivalent sets? One method, of course, is simply to count the number of objects in set A, and then merely count out the same number for set B. Probably some children used this method, but Piaget concluded from his clinical examinations that other children did not use counting. They seemed to use the method of one-to-one correspondence, but in a more sophisticated way than the younger child. The concrete operational child's technique may be described as follows: to construct set B equal to set A, he puts out one penny for the first penny in set A, and so forth. It does not matter *where* he puts the members of set B. The only crucial requirement is that he match each member in set A with one and only one member in set B (a nonspatial one-to-one correspondence). The child must not forget to put out a penny for each member of set A (that is, he cannot skip any member of set A) and must not put out more than one penny for each member of set A (that is, he must not count any member of set A twice).

The process of establishing sets equal in number may be described in terms of classes and relations. As far as relations are concerned, the child uses the method of *vicariant ordering*. Suppose that set A (the model) is a line of pennies, and the child must construct a set B (the copy) from a large supply of candies. He begins by pointing at the penny on the extreme left and puts out a sweet. Then he points to the second penny from the left, puts out a sweet for it, and continues until the line of pennies has been exhausted. This process of pointing to one penny at a time, being careful to count each penny once and only once, is an ordering. It is equivalent to saying: "This penny comes first, this one second, this one third . . . ," and so forth. In a way, the ordering of pennies is like arranging a series of sticks or dolls in order of height. There is a first stick, a second stick, and so forth, just as there is a first penny and a second one. Therefore, something like the ability to construct ordinal relations underlies the child's construction of sets equivalent in number.

Despite the evident similarity, the two processes—constructing ordinal relations (as in ordering the sticks) and vicariant ordering (the pennies)—are not identical. In the case of the sticks, there is one and only one shortest stick which must come first in the series, one and only one second shortest stick which must come second in the series, and so forth. In the case of the pennies, it does not matter which penny is considered first in the series, which comes second, and so on. One could start counting at the extreme left, at the extreme right, in the middle or wherever one pleased, just so long as one is careful not to omit pointing to each of the pennies and not to point to any of them more than once. The ordering of pennies is called "vicariant" for this very reason: the order in which the pennies are counted does not matter.

Other aspects of relations are involved too. When putting out one and only one sweet for each penny, the child is *coordinating* two orderings. This is similar to the problem of dolls and sticks. Just as the child can give to the shortest doll the shortest stick, to the second shortest doll the second shortest stick, and so forth, so can he place the first sweet with the first penny, the second sweet with the second penny, and so forth. Of course, the one-to-one correspondence of pennies and sweets is vicariant, whereas the one-to-one correspondence of dolls and sticks is not. In the latter instance, there is one and only one stick (the shortest) which goes with the shortest doll, and so forth. In the case of pennies and sweets, it does not matter which sweet is placed into correspondence with any penny, so long as one and only one sweet is used for each penny.

The construction of equivalent sets also involves *classification*. To the child, the pennies in set A, for instance, are in some ways all the same and in some ways different from one another. They are different in that a certain penny is counted first, another one second, and so forth. They are the same in that it does not matter which is counted first, which second, and so forth. In other words, it is only the child's act of pointing to each in turn that differentiates the pennies; otherwise, they are all equivalent. Insofar as each of the pennies is an element equivalent to all the rest, they are all members of the same class. The same is true, of course, of the sweets in set B.

Thus far we have seen how the child's ability to construct sets equivalent in number may be analyzed into a number of component skills. Underlying the child's overt performance (e.g., placing on a table seven sweets corresponding to seven pennies) are a number of *concrete operations:* vicariant ordering, one-to-one correspondence of two vicariant orderings, and classification. Some of the operations involve classes and others relations. Thus, number is a union of classes and relations. The operations are *concrete* since the child can apply them only to immediately present objects or thoughts about them. They are *operations* since they are actions which the child performs mentally and which have the added property of being reversible. This means that for each particular mental action, for instance addition, the child can perform its opposite action, in this case subtraction, which leaves him where he started. As operations, they may also be described in terms of overall structures or systems, that is, in terms of the Groupings, an example of which we have given in the case of classification.[5]

In the stage of concrete operations, the child can also conserve number. After constructing two sets equivalent in number, the child recognizes that the sets remain equivalent despite mere physical rearrangement of the sets. If the seven sweets are compressed to make a short line while the line of seven pennies remains the same, the two sets are nevertheless still equal in number. The equivalence has been conserved.

What enables the concrete operational child to conserve while the preoperational (stages 1 and 2) child fails to do so? Recall the mechanism underlying the preoperational child's failure: centration. The younger child centers on only a limited amount of the information available. When the row of sweets is compressed, he notices only that the line of pennies is now longer than the line of sweets. He ignores the fact that the line of sweets is denser (has smaller spaces between adjacent elements), and bases his judgment only on the lengths. The preoperational child knows that *empirical reversibility* is possible: he realizes that if the sweets were returned to their original positions, there would be one sweet for each penny. This knowledge does not help, however; despite it, he feels that the number of a set changes when its appearance is altered. Perceptual factors have too strong a hold on the child at this stage. They are not yet sufficiently controlled by mental actions which can compensate for misleading information.

By contrast, the concrete operational child decenters his attention. He attends to both the relevant dimensions and uses this information in several ways.

---

[5]Strictly speaking, in the case of number Piaget uses a somewhat different logico-mathematical model, called the *Group*. The essential difference between the Groupings and the Group is that the fifth Grouping operation, tautology (e.g., $A + A = A$), is not used in the Group. Tautology does not apply to number since there $A + A = 2A$, not A. Therefore, the Group must be used for number.

1. He notices that the line of pennies has become longer than the line of sweets *and* that the line of sweets has become denser than the line of pennies. Moreover, he coordinates the two dimensions. He mentally manipulates the visual data available to him. This mental activity leads him to realize that while the length of the line of pennies increases (relative to the sweets) by a certain amount, the density of the line of sweets increases by an equivalent amount. In other words, the child conceives that the pennies' increase in length is balanced by, or compensated for, by the sweets' increase in density: there is a relation of *reciprocity* or *compensation* between length and density. In effect, one increase cancels out the other with the result that the sets remain equivalent in number. This reciprocity is one form of *reversibility*. Since the increase in length counteracts the increase in density, the result is a return, or a reversal, to the original situation, which is equal number.

2. The concrete operational child also comes to use the operation of *negation*. We have already seen that when the row of sweets is compressed, the concrete operational child realizes that the sweets' increase in density is reciprocated by the pennies' increase in length, and that, as a result of these reciprocal transformations, the number of the two sets remains equivalent. The concrete operational child is also able to imagine that these changes can be annulled or *negated*. He reasons that the action of contracting the sweets can be negated by the inverse action of spreading them out. The one action is annulled by the other. Such annullment or negation is another form of reversibility; that is, the child mentally reverses the action of contracting the row of sweets. As a result he attributes equal numbers to the two sets. Note that the stage 3 child both reverses the act of contracting and recognizes that the final result is the original arrangement of sweets and pennies. The stage 2 child, who is capable of *empirical reversibility*, recognizes that the sweets can be returned to their original position but does not focus on or appreciate the *act* of rearrangement. He attends to states, not transformations.

3. The concrete operational child sometimes uses an *identity* argument, reasoning that the numbers must be the same since the same objects are involved: nothing has been added or taken away.

The stage 3 child's thought is concrete in a special sense which Sinclair (1971), one of the most important Genevan investigators, expresses quite clearly: "Concrete operations . . . does not mean that the child can think logically only if he can at the same time manipulate objects. . . . *Concrete,* in the Piagetian sense, means that the child can think in a logically coherent manner about objects that do exist and have real properties, and about actions that are possible; he can perform the mental operations involved both when asked purely verbal questions and when manipulating objects. . . . The actual presence of objects is no intrinsic condition'' (pp. 5–6).

To summarize, the stage 3 child, having entered the period of concrete operations, can construct two sets equivalent in number, and can conserve this equivalence despite changes in appearance. Underlying these achievements are a number of thought processes. The ability to construct equivalent sets requires *vicariant ordering* and *classification*. The ability to conserve, which is acquired as a result of the decentration of the child's attention, is supported by three types of operations which are sometimes explicitly expressed in the child's justification of his response: *reciprocity, negation,* and *identity*. These are aspects of *concrete* operations, which may be described by the *groupings*. The child does not always perform all of the thought processes when presented with a problem of constructing equal sets, nor does he refer to all three arguments when asked for a justification of conservation. He might only refer to one or perhaps two of them. The child is, however, *capable* of performing all the concrete operations, although he may not always do so. In fact, after a period of time the concrete operational child takes conservation for granted. He immediately recognizes that number is conserved and does not need to prove conservation to himself by means of negation or reciprocity. When asked why number is conserved, he thinks that the question is silly and that the fact of conservation is self-evident. For him, conservation has become a matter of logical necessity. This is evidence that the child has acquired an underlying structure of mental operations in which each is dependent upon the other and none is performed in isolation. The stage 3 child's thought is concrete in the special sense that he can think coherently about and deal with real objects but not hypothetical entities.

In conclusion, Piaget's work on number has been extraordinarily productive. It has stimulated volumes of research on children's number, and many of Piaget's findings have been successfully replicated, even in non-Western societies (see Dasen, 1977). As we shall find in Chapter 6, the work has also had implications for educational curricula. Like many major contributions to psychology, the work has aroused a good deal of controversy, and several alternative views have been proposed (see, for example, Gelman and Gallistel, 1978; and Ginsburg, 1982).

CONSERVATION

Thus far, we have described only the conservation of number—that is, the child's ability to recognize that the numerical equivalence between two sets remains unchanged despite alterations of physical arrangement. Piaget has also investigated several other conservations which include continuous quantity, substance, weight, and volume. The *conservation of continuous quantity* may be defined by this situation. The child is presented with two identical beakers (A and B), each filled with equal amounts of liquid

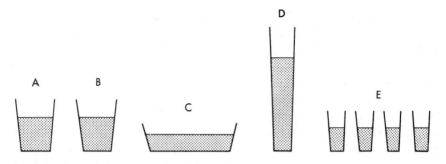

FIGURE 11   Conservation of continuous quantities.

(see Figure 11), and is asked whether the two glasses contain the same amount or not the same amount to drink. After he agrees to the equivalence of quantities, the liquid is poured by either the experimenter or the child from one of the two identical beakers (say, B) into a third, dissimilarly shaped beaker (C). The column of the liquid in the third class (and the glass itself) is both shorter and wider than that in the remaining original glass (A). The child is now asked whether the two beakers (now A and C) contain equal amounts. If he asserts that they do, he is asked to explain why. The liquid in C is then returned to the original beaker B, and the child is again asked if A and B contain identical amounts. The manipulation is repeated, this time with a glass (D) which is taller and thinner than the original beakers. Finally, the liquid of either A or B is poured into a set (E) of about three or four smaller glasses and the same questions are asked of the child. If the child continuously asserts in each case that the amount that has been poured from B into the different beakers is always the same as the amount remaining in the original beaker (A), then he has conserved continuous quantity. That is, the child recognizes that merely pouring the liquid from B to C or D or E, does not increase or decrease the quantity; the "amount" of liquid remains the same (or is conserved) whether it is in B or in C. Since the quantities A and B were equal, and since pouring the liquid of B into C does not change its quantity, then the quantities in A and C must also be equal. If the child does not consistently assert this equality, then he has failed to conserve.

    In the case of *conservation of substance,* the child is presented with two identical balls of plasticene (or clay, etc.). He is first asked whether there is the same amount of plasticene in both balls. If he does not think so, he is asked to take away or add some clay to make them identical. Then, the experimenter changes one of the balls to a sausage shape, while the child watches. The child must now decide whether or not the ball and the sausage have equal amounts of substance. As in the liquid situation, the ball is changed into a variety of different shapes. If the child consistently asserts that the ball and the new shapes do have equal amounts of substance, then he has conserved substance and has recognized that merely changing the shape does not alter the amount of matter involved.

To test the *conservation of weight,* the experimenter again presents the child with two identical balls of plasticene and places them on a balance. The child sees that the two balls weigh the same. Then they are removed from the balance and one ball is transformed into the shape of a sausage. The child is asked to anticipate the results of placing the ball and the sausage on the two sides of the balance. Will they still remain balanced or will one side be heavier than the other? The question is whether the child recognizes that weight is conserved despite changes in shape. Here again a series of changes are made to one of the balls and the question as to the identity of weight is repeated.

In the case of *conservation of volume,* two balls of plasticene are placed in two identical beakers, each filled with equal quantities of liquid. The child sees that the balls displace an equal volume of liquid in both beakers. Or, in the child's terms, the liquid goes up an equal distance in both cases. Then the balls are removed from the beakers, and one ball is changed into the shape of a sausage. The question now is whether the child recognizes that both ball and sausage continue to displace equal volumes, or whether the water goes up an equal amount in both cases.

All these conservations are similar. They involve a first phase in which the child must recognize that two amounts—liquid quantity, substance, weight, or volume—are equal. Most children above the age of 4 years are quite successful in this task. All the conservations also involve a visible transformation which may be done by either the child or the experimenter. While the child watches, or as a result of his own actions, the liquid is poured from one beaker to another, or the ball is changed into a sausage. It is quite apparent that no liquid or plasticene is added or taken away. It is also apparent that things now *look* different. The column of liquid is shorter and wider, and the ball is now a sausage. And, finally, all the conservations involve a second phase in which the child must once again judge whether the amounts in question are still the same. Of course, they are equivalent, and the issue is whether the child will recognize this or be misled by the observed changes in appearance.

Piaget's general findings are that there is a sequence of development with regard to each of the conservations. Children begin by failing to conserve and require a period of development before they are able to succeed at the task. For example, in the case of continuous quantities, children are not able to conserve until about the age of 6 or 7 years. In the first phase of the problem (two identical beakers, each filled with equal amounts of liquid), the youngest children, around 4 or 5 years of age, correctly conclude that the amounts of liquid are equal. Since the child has either poured out the liquid into the second beaker, or has told the experimenter when to stop pouring, this is not surprising. If asked to justify the identity, the child will say that the water comes up to the same level in each glass so that the amounts are equal. When the liquid in one beaker is poured into a third glass which is different in shape from the first two, the child now maintains that the amounts are no longer equal. One glass has more to drink than the other. Asked to explain his answer, he says that the glass with the taller column of liquid has the greater amount. This judgment of amounts is tied exclusively to the heights of the columns of liquid: when the heights are the same (as in phase 1), the child thinks that the amounts are the same; when they are different (as in phase 2), then the amounts must be different too.

In stage 2, the child of 5 or 6 years vacillates in his responses to the conservation problem. While he usually fails to conserve, his approach to the problem varies from time to time. In the second phase of the experiment (when one beaker is shorter and wider than the other), the child sometimes says that the taller beaker has more to drink, and sometimes maintains that the wider one has the greater amount. Unlike the stage 1 child, he does not concentrate exclusively on the heights of the columns of liquid, but sometimes bases his judgments on the widths as well.

In stage 3, the child is capable of conservation. When asked why the amounts do not change after the pouring, he gives at least one of several reasons. One is that if the liquid in C were returned to its original container, B, then the two initial beakers, A and B, would contain identical columns of liquid. This is the *negation* argument. A second reason is the *identity* argument: it's the same water. You haven't added any or taken any away. A third argument, involving *compensation* or *reciprocity,* is that the third glass, C, is shorter than the original beaker, A, but what C lost in height was compensated by C's gain in width; therefore, the amount in C must be equal to the amount in A.

Toward the end of his life, Piaget returned to the problem of conservation and stressed the role of *commutability*. In one experiment, Piaget (1979) presented children with a conservation of substance problem of the following type. A ball of clay is presented and then a piece is removed. The child is asked if the ball has the same amount, and says no, since something has been taken away. The piece that had been removed from one side of the ball was placed on the other side and the child was again asked if the ball has the same amount now (with the piece added to the other side) as did the original ball. Piaget finds that under these conditions, children assert conservation at a very young age. They say essentially that "It's the same thing, you took it away and then put it back and it's always the same" (p. 21). In other words, the children have understood "that there is displacement, and that when one displaces, what is added at one place has been taken away from another place" (p. 21). This Piaget calls "commutability" and claims that it is one important factor in conservation. Commutability bears a similarity to the notion of compensation.

In the case of conservation of substance, weight, and volume, a similar progression to that of quantity appears. In the first stage, the child fails to conserve apparently because of a concentration on only one of the stimulus dimensions involved. That is, in the case of weight he may say that the sausage is heavier than the ball because the former is longer. In the second stage, he again fails to conserve, although now he vacillates between the two dimensions involved. For instance, he may sometimes believe that the ball is heavier because it is wider and at other times assert that the sausage is heavier because it is longer. In the third stage, the child conserves, for reasons similar to those cited for continuous quantities.

While all the conservations follow a similar course of development, there is a striking irregularity as well—the phenomenon of *horizontal décalage*. This refers to the fact, which has been well substantiated, that the child masters the conservation of discontinuous quantity and substance at about age 6 or 7; does not achieve stage 3 of the conservation of weight until age 9 or 10; does not understand the conservation of volume until approximately 11 or 12. In each case the arguments used are the same, sometimes even involving the same words. But having mastered conservation in one substantive area, like substance, the child is not able to generalize immediately to another area like that of weight. First, he acquires conservation of discontinuous quantity and substance, and then weight, and then volume. The décalage, or lack of immediate transfer, illustrates how concrete is the thought of the child during the ages of about 7 to 11 years. His reasoning is tied to particular situations and objects; his mental operations in one area may not be applied to another, no matter how useful this might be.

GENERAL CHARACTERISTICS OF THOUGHT

We have reviewed the development of various aspects of thought: classes, relations, number, and conservation. It would seem useful at this time to take a broader look at some general characteristics of cognitive development.

Underlying Patterns of Thought

There are striking regularities in the child's cognitive development. In each of the two major periods of development discussed in this chapter (preoperational and concrete operational), the child uses distinctive patterns of thought to approach different substantive problems. There appear to be some general patterns which characterize the thought of the preoperational child and some other patterns manifested in the concrete operational child's cognition.

Consider, first, the child from about 4 to 7 years in the preoperational period. (Remember that this age designation is only approximate, since a child as old as 9 or 10 years typically shows a preoperational approach to the conservation of volume.) One general characteristic of cognitive activity during this period is *centration*. The child tends to focus on a limited amount of the information available. In the conservation of number, he judges two sets equal when they are the same length and ignores another relevant variable, the density. In the conservation of continuous quantity, the child judges two amounts equal when the heights of the columns of liquid are the same and ignores the width. In the construction of ordinal relations (the problem of ordering ten sticks in terms of height), he succeeds only by considering the tops of the sticks and ignoring the bottoms, or vice versa. In all these problems, the preoperational child deploys his attention in overly limited ways. He focuses on one dimension of a situation, fails to make use of another, equally relevant dimension, and therefore cannot appreciate the relations between the two. (The notion of centration is somewhat similar to Piaget's earlier concept of juxtaposition which is the tendency to think in terms of the parts of a situation and not integrate them into a whole.)

By contrast, the concrete operational child is characterized by *decentration*. He tends to focus on several dimensions of a problem simultaneously and to relate these dimensions. In the conservation of number, he coordinates length *and* density: two sets have the same number when the first is longer then the second but the second is denser than the first. In the conservation of continuous quantity, he recognizes that amounts are equal when one column of liquid is at the same time taller but narrower than a second. In the construction of ordinal relations, he determines whether a given object is simultaneously bigger than some objects and smaller than others. In all these problems, the concrete operational child attends to several aspects of the situation at once. Centration and decentration are general patterns of thought, underlying structures.

The two major periods of development can be characterized in other ways as well. The thought of the preoperational child is *static* in the sense that it centers on states. In the conservation of substance he focuses on the shape of plasticene (sometimes a ball and sometimes a sausage) and ignores the transformation, that is, the change from one state to the other. In the conservation of continuous quantity he focuses on the heights of the columns of liquid and not on the act of pouring. He lacks adequate representations of an object's shift from one position to another. In general, he concentrates on the static states of a situation and not on its dynamic transformations.

The concrete operational child, on the other hand, is attuned to changes. In the conservations he concentrates on the transformation: the act of pouring the liquid, or spreading apart a set of objects, or deforming a ball into a sausage. He forms more or less accurate images of the changes which have taken place, and, therefore, can reason, for example, that as a set expands in length it simultaneously decreases in density.

The preoperational child's thought lacks *reversibility*. He may be able to predict an empirical reversibility as, for instance, in the case of the liquids where he would agree that if the water were poured back into B, there would be the same quantity as before. But this empirical reversibility does not change the fact that now he believes there is more (or less) water in the new glass C. It is as if pouring from B to C, and from C to B were totally unrelated actions. The older child, on the other hand, realizes that pouring from C to B reverses or negates the action of pouring from B to C and is aware that it is the same action performed in another direction. By carrying out the action mentally, that is, by reversing the pouring in his mind, he is able to ascertain that the quantity of water in C (the lower wider glass) is the same as in B. He can perform a mental operation which leads him to a certain conclusion, and then do the reverse of this operation which enables him to return to his original starting point.

The concrete operational child can also perform another type of reversibility when operating on relations. This is reciprocity. For instance, in the example of liquid quantity, when the child says that one glass is longer and thinner, whereas the other is shorter and wider, he is canceling out the differences between the two glasses by an action of reciprocity. One difference balances out the other, with the result that they have a reciprocal relationship.

To summarize, the preoperational child's thought is irreversible and attentive to limited amounts of information, particularly the static states of reality. The concrete operational child focuses on several aspects of a situation simultaneously, is sensitive to transformations, and can reverse the direction of thought. Piaget conceives of these three aspects of thought— centration-decentration, static-dynamic, irreversibility-reversibility—as interdependent. If the child centers on the static aspects of a situation, he is unlikely to appreciate transformations. If he does not represent transformations, the child is unlikely to reverse his thought. By decentering, he comes to be aware of the transformations, which thus lead to reversibility in his thought. In conclusion, we can see that one aspect of thought is not isolated from the rest. Even though the nature of the system may vary with the development of the child, thought processes form an integrated system.

Invariant Sequence

Another striking regularity in cognitive development involves *invariant order:* the sequence of activities (for example in classification, partial alignments, collections, class inclusion) assumes an invariant order despite wide variations in culture. Cross-cultural research provides relevant evidence on this issue. Within Western cultures children progress through the various stages in the order described by Piaget. In the case of conservation of continuous quantities, for example, research shows that Swiss, British, American, and Canadian children first fail to conserve, then vacillate in their response, and later conserve with stability. While children in these cultures do not necessarily achieve the various stages at the same average ages, the sequence of development—the order of the stages— seems identical in all cases. Even in other and very different cultures, like the Thai or Malaysian, the same sequence of stages and type of responses appear. Children in Thailand, for example, exhibit classification activities which are virtually identical to those used by Western children, and proceed through the sequence of stages in the order described by Piaget (Opper, in Dasen, 1977). There is great cross-cultural generality in Piaget's findings. At the same time, we must make one qualification: apparently, members of some cultures do not advance as far in the sequence of stages as do Westerners. Thus, for whatever reasons, in some cultures, individuals may not complete the stage of formal operations. Not everyone achieves the highest level possible in terms of Piaget's stages. Yet, until their progress terminates, these individuals proceed through the sequence of stages in the standard order. While the ultimate level of development may differ among cultures, the sequence seems to be invariant, as Piaget proposes. The phenomena described by Piaget are thus nearly universal, occurring across extreme variations in culture and environment. Piaget has surely captured something very basic in human cognition.[6]

Irregularities

Piaget has gone to great lengths to dispel some misinterpretations concerning his theory. In particular, he shows that there are certain *irregularities* in development. He points out, first, that the ages at which the stages occur vary considerably both within and among cultures. Not all Genevan children attain stage 3 of number development at 6 or 7 years, and children in Martinique lag behind Genevans by approximately four years. In Thailand, urban children attain stage 3 at the same time as children in Geneva, but rural Thai children lag behind by approximately three years. In Malaysia, rural children attain the number concept one year ahead of urban children, who in turn lag behind Swiss children by two years. Thus the rate of development seems to vary from group to group. Second, the course of an individual's development is continuous.

---

[6]Recently, Gelman and Baillargeon (1983, p. 171) have argued that the phenomenon of invariant sequence is not as clear-cut as Piaget suggests. They describe research showing that in some areas some children do not exhibit the stages in the order predicted by Piaget. This seems to present serious difficulties for the theory.

The child is not characterized by stage 1 one day and by stage 2 the next day. Rather, the transition is gradual, occurring over a long period of time, and the child exhibits many forms of behavior intermediary between the two stages. Indeed, an individual child's behavior takes many forms in addition to those Piaget describes as being typical of the various stages. Piaget's stages are idealized abstractions; they describe selected and salient points on an irregular continuum of development. Third, the child is not always in the same stage of development with regard to different areas of thought. The child may be characterized by stage 2 in the case of classes, and stage 1 in the case of relations. It is unlikely, however, that he will be in stage 1 for classes and stage 3 for relations. Only infrequently does one find extreme discrepancies between stage levels in different areas. Fourth, as we have already seen, there exists the phenomenon of *horizontal décalage*, in which the child displays different levels of achievement in regard to problems involving similar mental operations; for example, he may be able to conserve substance but not number.

Preoperational Strengths

Piaget (*On the Development of Memory and Identity*, 1968) tries to correct a widespread misconception concerning preoperational thought. Typically, we characterize the young child as intellectually *incompetent* since he cannot conserve, cannot use reversibility, and cannot decenter. Piaget feels that this view is exaggerated; as a result of recent research, Piaget proposes that the preoperational child possesses a number of important intellectual strengths which must not be overlooked. In particular, the young child is capable of *identity, functions,* and *correspondences.*

While unable to conserve, the young child nevertheless appreciates certain basic identities. For example, in the standard conservation problem, the young child recognizes that the *same liquid* is transferred from one beaker to another even though one looks quite different from the other. He sees that the basic substance does not change, even though its appearance is altered and even though he falsely believes that the *amount* of liquid has changed. He appreciates identity but fails to conserve quantity.

Piaget proposes that the notion of identity may derive from the child's perception of his own body's growth. With Gilbert Voyat, Piaget asked children to draw themselves when they were babies, when they were a little bigger, and so on; then the experimenters questioned the children concerning the maintenance of their identity despite obvious physical changes. The experimenters also posed similar questions concerning the identity of other objects, including plants. The results showed that children easily appreciated their own identity despite changes in size, and were less likely to accept the continuing identity of a plant over its various changes in appearance. Perhaps, then, the notion of identity derives from the child's perception of his own body's growth and later is generalized to the world of objects.

The preoperational child can also perceive functional relations in the environment. One example of such *functions* (given by Sinclair, 1971) involves the opening of a curtain: "the child understands that when one pulls the cord of a curtain, the curtain opens; the farther one pulls, the farther the curtain opens" (p. 4). In other words, there is a functional relation, a co-variation between pulling and opening, and the child perceives that the two factors are positively related. (There may even be precursors of functions in infancy: this example is reminiscent of the infant Laurent who seemed to realize that the more vigorously he shook a chain, the louder would be the sound produced by the attached rattles.) It is very important, of course, for the child to recognize such functional relations in the environment: they pervade it. The taller the person, the stronger he is likely to be; the harder one hits another child, the more likely is the child to protest and even cry; the bigger the glass, the more milk it holds. Despite limitations in other areas of thought (for example, centration), the preoperational child has some appreciation for basic functional relations, and this is of great value to him in coping with the environment.

At the same time, Piaget points out that these functions are incomplete: they constitute only a *semilogic*. For one thing, the child's appreciation of functions is imprecise. To return to the example of the curtain, the child does not realize exactly how the pulling of the cord is related to the opening of the curtain and cannot quantify the results with any degree of precision. Another Piagetian experiment makes this clear. Children were presented with three toy fish, 5, 10, and 15 centimeters long, respectively, and were told to feed each fish its proper diet of meatballs. The middle-sized fish should get twice as many meatballs as the smallest, and the largest fish three times as many. Preoperational children understood the functional relation between size of fish and number of meatballs only in an imprecise way. They realized that the larger the fish, the more it needs to eat. But they were not able to work out the function in a precise manner (for example, by giving 2, 4, and 6 or 3, 6, and 9 meatballs to the respective fish).

Toward the end of his life, Piaget (1979) stressed the role of "correspondences." He used this notion to refer to the child's tendency to compare objects or events, to determine the ways in which they "correspond," or are similar and different. This tendency appears at all levels of development, from infancy onward, although it takes different forms at different levels.

For example, an infant first hits a toy parrot to make it swing and then applies the hitting scheme to other hanging objects as well. In a sense he has compared the new object with the familiar parrot and noted the similarity between them (the correspondence of one object to another).

Note: A black marble and a white marble are glued to a plate, with the white one above the black one (as in Figure 12A). Then the plate is rotated so that black one is above the white one (as in Figure 12B).

First Plate   Rotated Plate
A   B

FIGURE 12   Correspondence of Marbles.

The preoperational child displays different forms of correspondence. For example, in one experiment, Piaget (1979) showed children two objects on a rotating disk. Imagine that the objects are a white marble and a black marble, glued to a dish, as in Figure 12A. When the marbles are on the left (Figure 12A), the white is above the black. When the dish is rotated so that the marbles are on the right (Figure 12B), then the black is above the white. The preoperational child observes the situations—the marbles on the left and on the right—and gradually notes the correspondences between them. The child sees that when the marbles are on the left side, the white is higher, but when they are on the right, the white becomes the lower. At first, the child's approach is simply "empirical": to record the facts without interpreting them. But "the child discovers suddenly that there is a general order" (p. 24). He determines, in other words, that there is a reversal of position. It's not just that the white is higher in one situation and lower in the other, but that the white has *switched positions*. This insight then gradually leads the child to another: the positions were switched because a transformation took place. The rotation of the dish caused the switch in position.

We see then that the child begins by comparing two states, noting some basic similarities and differences (the switch in position). These correspondences are important because they pave the way for the child's appreciation of transformations. And as we have seen, an appreciation of transformations is at the heart of concrete operational thinking.

In brief, preoperational thought is not characterized solely by incompetence. Young children appreciate certain basic aspects of identity, perhaps as a result of experience with their own bodies. They also understand, albeit in an imprecise manner, various simple functional relations in the environment. They detect correspondences, and this leads them to an appreciation of transformations. In dealing with young children one must be aware of these strengths as well as of the commonly cited limitations, as Gelman and Gallistel (1978) and other contemporary writers concur in maintaining.

The Concept of Stage

Piaget's theory describes a sequence of *stages*. For example, in the case of the conservation of number we have reviewed the transition from centration to decentration. Now it is important to consider the nature of such stages. What does Piaget mean by *stage* and how useful a concept is it?

According to Piaget (*Biology and Knowledge,* 1971a, p. 17) the notion of stage is used when the following three conditions are fulfilled. First, there must be an *invariant sequence* of activities. Thus, in the case of conservation, there is, first, a failure to recognize equivalence; then there is vacillation; and, finally, there is success. The order of appearance of the activities is the same for all children. Second, each stage in the sequence is characterized by an *underlying structure,* a core system determining the child's overt behavior. Thus, underlying the child's failure to conserve is the strategy of centration—the tendency to focus on limited amounts of information. Third, each of the structures *prepares the way* for a succeeding one. Thus, in the case of conservation, the initial centration prepares the way for a vacillation among the available dimensions, and this in turn leads to the subsequent decentration. In brief, Piaget proposes that stages are characterized by invariant sequence, underlying structures, and successive integrations.

Piaget also emphasized that despite the existence of stages, development is *continuous.* The child does not enter a new stage overnight; instead, the changes are gradual, and indeed barely perceptible from close-up. Piaget explained this in terms of the *scale of measurement.* If we look closely at a child's development, observing every day and thus using a fine scale of measurement, it is hard for us to see dramatic changes; from one day to the next we will not notice differences in stages. But if we stand back, observing the child infrequently and thus using a crude scale of measurement, we will be impressed with changes; from one year to the next we will see progress from one stage to the next.

We have already reviewed research concerning the notions of invariant sequence and underlying structure. Cross-cultural study demonstrates that the sequence described by Piaget is extremely widespread, if not universal. Also, there seem to be distinct underlying patterns or structures in each of the major periods under consideration—preoperational and concrete operational. Consider next Piaget's third condition for the existence of a stage—the requirement that each stage prepare the way for the next. While it is hard to adduce evidence supporting this notion, it seems to have a certain amount of face validity; for example, a focus on two dimensions seems naturally to follow from a focus on one. In brief, the evidence concerning invariant sequence, underlying structures, and successive integrations seems to support Piaget's proposition concerning the existence of major stages of development.

At the same time, the stage notion suffers from a number of difficulties. One, already alluded to, is the existence of irregularities in development. We have seen that the child is not always in the same stage with regard to different areas of thought. Thus, he may be in stage 1 with respect to classes and stage 2 in the case of relations. Also, the phenomenon of *horizontal décalage* is very striking: the child may display different levels of achievement in regard to very similar areas of thought. Thus, he may conserve substance but not number. The existence of these irregularities seems dissonant with the notion of distinct underlying patterns or structures of thought characterizing the major stages of development. If the patterns are so strong and pervasive, why are the *décalages* so striking?

Another difficulty with the stage notion is that the structures presumably underlying a stage may also be implicated in stages occurring earlier in the sequence. Thus we have recent evidence by Trabasso (1975), for example, to the effect that under certain conditions, preoperational children can perform concrete operational tasks. If the same structures underlie behavior at different stages, do we not then have to alter our notion of stages? The issue of stages is extremely complex and is now the subject of considerable rethinking (for an excellent discussion see Flavell, 1985).

Indeed, toward the end of his life, Piaget seems to have rethought the stage notion himself. The last ten years of Piaget's research revolved largely around issues of cognitive change and development and did not employ stage notions to any significant degree. In this sense, Piaget became less of a "structuralist" (one who deals with the analysis of mental structures underlying the stages) and more of a "functionalist" (one who deals with the factors determining development). As we shall see in Chapter 6, Piaget's theory of equilibration placed the emphasis on gradual changes or in effect on many fleeting substages. What was important for the later Piaget was not a concept of broad, stable stages, but a theory of the continuous change and development of the child's intellectual structures.

MENTAL IMAGERY

After his brief examination during the 1920s of the *content* of thought, Piaget's main concern has been with the *operative* aspect of cognition. This refers to *actions* used to deal with or even change the world. These actions may be either overt or internal. Examples of overt actions abound in the sensorimotor period. The infant kicks to shake a rattle, or uses a stick to draw an object close. The present chapter has covered two major subdivisions of internalized actions: the isolated and unrelated actions of preoperational thought and the structured and coordinated ones of concrete operational thought.

Piaget has also shown an interest, albeit a lesser one, in the figurative aspect of cognition. This refers to three ways in which the child produces an account of reality. One is perception, a system which functions by means of the senses and operates on an immediately present object or event. It is through perception that the child achieves a record of the things in the surrounding world. This record is often inexact, as in the case of the visual illusions. A second subdivision is imitation, by which the child reproduces the actions of persons or things. It is true that imitation involves actions on the part of the child, but these actions nevertheless fall under the figurative aspect since they produce a copy of reality but do not modify it. A third portion of the figurative aspect is mental imagery. As we saw in Chapter 3, mental imagery refers to personal and idiosyncratic internal events which stand for or represent absent objects or events. When we "picture" to ourselves our first bicycle, or the stroll we took last week, then we are using mental imagery. As we see from this last example, the topic of memory is closely bound up with the figurative aspect of thought. Memory (recall) typically involves retaining knowledge gained through the figurative mode.

In recent years, Piaget has conducted important investigations into two important aspects of figurative cognition, specifically imagery and memory. His theory stands in stark contrast to the traditional *empiricist* view of these matters. The latter assumes that perception stamps on the individual a literal copy of reality. Given sufficiently frequent repetition of the initial event, a mental image mirroring the reality is formed and is stored in memory. If there is no further experience with the original event, the memory image gradually fades, losing its fidelity to the reality; it is forgotten. Piaget criticizes this traditional view on several grounds. Most important, he believe that reality does not simply impose itself on a passive organism. Rather the individual assists in the construction of his own reality. His intellectual activities—the operative mode of thought—serve to shape the results of encounters with the environment. The resulting figurative knowledge is not simply a copy of reality. This theme—the influence of operative structures on figurative knowledge—dominates Piaget's discussion of mental imagery and memory. We will now consider these two topics in succession.

History

Mental imagery was one of the first topics studied by experimental psychologists. At the end of the nineteenth century, the school of Wundt used the introspective method to analyze the nature of mental imagery. The Wundtians believed that images were composed of a bundle of sensations tied together by means of association. At the beginning of the twentieth century, the study of imagery fell into disrepute for two reasons. First, the Wurzburg psychologists found that much of thought did not seem to involve imagery at all, and second, the behaviorist revolution which occurred in the United States maintained that the introspective method was a poor one. The behaviorists felt that the data of introspection—one's impressions of one's own consciousness—were not public enough. How could another psychologist determine if an introspection were reliable and accurate? As a result of the behaviorist attack on the method of introspection, the study of imagery was considered "unscientific" and was largely abandoned. Recently, however, psychologists have shown a renewed interest in the ancient problem of imagery, and the topic is once again becoming central to experimental psychology (Neisser, 1976).

In contrast to modern investigators, Piaget has been studying imagery since at least the 1930s. In Chapter 3 we discussed Piaget's work on imagery in the young child up to the age of 4 years. If you will recall, this theory proposed that mental images do not occur until about the middle of the second year. Before this time the child did not possess mental representations of the environment and, as a result, reacted mainly to events occurring in the present. After imagery makes its appearance the child can represent to himself both events that occurred in the past and objects that are no longer perceptually present. Also, according to Piaget's theory, imagery results from imitation. At first, the child overtly imitates the actions of things or people; later, his imitation becomes internalized and abbreviated. It is through this internal activity that images arise. Clearly, Piaget's views contrast strongly with Wundt's. Images are not merely bundles of sensations, imposed by the environment and connected by association; rather, the construction of images involves the activity of internalized imitation.

Later, with Inhelder, Piaget returned to the study of imagery (1971). His later work deals with children above the age of 4, and poses a number of interesting questions. For example, are there different types of images at different stages of intellectual development? If so, what is the relation between the images and the mental operations of a given stage?

Method

While these questions are interesting, the study of mental images is very difficult, especially in the case of children. Images are personal, idiosyncratic events which cannot be viewed directly. One cannot "see" another person's imagery; the investigator must, therefore, infer their existence and nature from other phenomena, such as a verbal report. Piaget has used a variety of methods to study imagery. One of these methods is to ask a person to describe his own images. But language is not fully adequate for this task, or even for describing something as concrete as the immediate perception of an object. We are never able to convey by words the precise nature of what we see. In our attempt to describe percepts, we inevitably emphasize certain features and neglect others. We have difficulty in describing shades of colors, or gradations of textures. We cannot give an impression of the entire percept at once, but must describe its details in sequence, and thereby often lose the essence of the whole. If language so poorly conveys perceptual events which continue to remain before our eyes for further inspection, how much more difficult is it to describe mental images which often are fleeting and unstable?

Another method of studying mental images is by drawing. Here the person is asked to draw an object previously presented. Since the object is no longer present, he must produce an image of it to yield the drawing. The drawing, therefore, gives some insight into the nature of the image, which is the internal "picture" of the object. The method of drawing, however, presents several shortcomings. Drawing is not a simple and direct reflection of images; it also involves other processes. Some persons have poor memory. If they have forgotten their image of an object, they cannot very well draw it. Other persons simply cannot draw well. It is not their image that is at fault, but their artistic skill.

A third method attempts to bypass the shortcomings of original drawings. The subject is given a collection of drawings made by the experimenter, and must select from them the one most closely corresponding to his image of what he had previously observed. This method, of course, is not affected by variations in subjects' artistic abilities and reduces the difficulties created by a poor evocative memory. But even the method of selection from a collection of drawings is not altogether satisfactory. One problem is that the drawings presented are not likely to be exact copies of the person's mental image. The drawings may omit details of the original image or add new features. In either event, the subject's choice does not give a fully accurate indication of his image.

To study imagery, Piaget has used all these methods—verbal report, drawing, and selection of drawings—either alone or in combination. As is customary with the explorations carried out by the Geneva school, the methods were supplemented by verbal questioning carried out in the clinical manner.

Major Findings

One experiment was concerned with *kinetic images,* or the imagery of an object's movement. Children from about 4 to 8 years of age were presented with two identical blocks, one on top of the other (see Figure 13A).

A

B

FIGURE 13   Movement of blocks.

Each subject was asked to draw the situation, and generally did this quite well. Then the top block was moved so that it slightly overlapped the bottom one, as in Figure 13B. After the child had had a chance to look at this for a while, the top block was returned to its original position (Figure 13A). The child was then asked to draw the block in its displaced position (Figure 13B), which was, of course, no longer visible. After this, a collection of drawings was presented. This contained a correct rendering of Figure 13B as well as an assortment of incorrect drawings which represented errors typically made by children of this age. (This technique is similar to the use of countersuggestions in the interview.) The child was asked to select the drawing which he felt corresponded most closely to what he had seen. In the final step another control was added. The top block was once again displaced, and the child was asked to draw the situation while it was present. If the child could accurately draw the blocks when present, then any of his previous errors of drawing (when the blocks were absent) must be due to faulty imagery or memory and not to faulty drawing ability.

To summarize, the child first drew the displaced blocks after they were no longer visible; then he selected from a group of drawings one resembling the displaced blocks; and finally, when the displaced blocks were once again before him, he drew them.

The findings show that before the age of 7 years, children can draw the displaced blocks quite correctly when they are present, but not when they are absent; nor can the children choose a drawing which corresponds to the situation. In general, children of about 4 and 5 years produced and selected drawings of the types A through E (see Figure 14), whereas children of 6 years made errors like those of types F and G. It was only at 7 years that over 75 percent of the subjects both drew and chose the correct drawings.

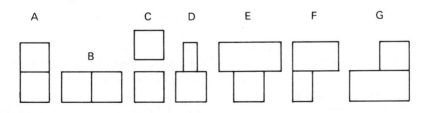

FIGURE 14   Drawing of blocks.

A cross-cultural study of this problem in Thailand (Opper, 1971) shows that Thai children make the same types of errors as do Swiss children, although it is not until 10 years of age that 75 percent of the Thai subjects make correct drawings of the two blocks.

The responses of the younger child would seem to indicate that he forms only a very general picture of the situation, that is, that one block has been moved. When asked to draw the exact details, he is unable to do so. The child therefore reproduces this general impression of movement by detaching the top block from the bottom (cf. C), by a symmetrical movement of shrinking or enlargement of one of the two blocks (cf. D and E), or, finally, by the retention of one common boundary or identical line for the two blocks, in addition to making changes on the other side of the blocks (cf. F and G). His image does not appear to correspond to the actual situation. The child seems to center on one dimension, that is, on one particular aspect of the situation—for example, the overlapping of the top block in drawings E and F, or the overlapping of the bottom block in drawings D and G. However, the child does not coordinate the movement of one block with the final state of the two blocks. Apparently the child does not analyze the situation in sufficient detail but merely forms a global impression of what has happened. He is aware that the block has moved, but the intimate details of the movement and the ensuing displacement seem to have escaped his attention. As a result, his mental image is inadequate.

A second type of imagery is *static* imagery. In this instance the image reproduces a collection of objects, a scene, or a picture—in brief, any situation in which the elements remain unchanged in either shape or position. Piaget finds that the child is able to produce adequate static imagery earlier than kinetic.

We have reviewed only a small sampling of Piaget's experiments on imagery. Their results, together with those of a great many more studies, have led Piaget to draw the following general conclusions concerning imagery and its relation to intelligence as a whole. First, imagery develops in a gradual manner. The evolution of imagery is not as dramatic as that of the cognitive operations which display a clear-cut sequence of stages. There appears to be only one major turning point in the development of images. This seems to occur at around the age of 7 or 8 years and corresponds to the onset of the period of concrete operations. Before the break, that is, from the age of 1½ to about 7 years, the child seems capable of producing with any degree of accuracy only static images, and even these are far from perfect. The child cannot represent correctly the movements of an object or even simple physical transformations; the images produced for such situations are grossly deformed.

Piaget believes that the reason for this deficiency is one aspect of operative cognition, namely, a tendency to concentrate on the initial and final states of a given situation and to neglect the intervening events which are responsible for the changes. We have already seen this tendency, which is called *centration,* operating in the case of conservation. If you will, recall the situation where the child was presented with a line of vases, each of which contained a flower. The flowers were removed from the vases and spread apart. When this occurs, the young child usually believes that there are more flowers than vases, since the line of flowers is now longer than the line of vases. He has *centered* on the lengths and ignored a number of other factors. He has failed to decenter and to consider the density of the lines, as well as their length, and he has ignored the intermediary transformation (the removal and spacing of the flowers). Thus, the child focuses mainly on the initial and final states (the flowers in the vases and the flowers spaced out) and fails to integrate these impressions with all else that has occurred. Thus, before the age of 7 or 8 imagery is extremely static. As a result, the child produces a distorted picture of reality characterized by an emphasis on superficial features which are each isolated from others and not coordinated into a coherent whole.

From about the age of 7 years onward, however, the child becomes capable of producing images which can reproduce kinetic situations. This improvement is due to the fact that he can now imagine not only the initial and final states, but also the intermediary transformations. His imagery has become less static. Of course, it is never possible to reproduce *all* the intervening events, since in some cases (like the pouring of liquid), they occur rapidly. But the child recognizes that a sequence is involved and that there has been a series of intervening steps between the initial and final states.

A final question concerns the relation between dynamic images and the concrete operations. Kinetic images occur at approximately the same time that the child becomes capable of the concrete operations; what then is the relation between the operative and figurative aspects of thought at this stage? On the one hand, we have already seen that operative cognition influences the nature of the child's imagery. Thus, the concrete operational child's decentration contributes to the dynamic nature of his imagery. In Piaget's theory, figurative cognition (here, imagery) is dominated by operative cognition (here, the concrete operations). On the other hand, images can play an auxiliary role in thinking. For example, consider the number conservation task involving flowers and vases. The concrete operational child can form accurate transformational images of the displacement of the flowers. After the transformation has been done, he correctly pictures the way in which the flowers have been removed from the vases. The ability to form images of this sort does not *guarantee* that the child can conserve number; as we have already seen, the processes underlying conservation are not solely perceptual or imaginal. Nevertheless, the child who has a correct image of the transformation is certainly ahead of the child who does not. In other words, images are a useful and necessary auxiliary to thought during the concrete operational stage. By providing relatively accurate representations of the world, images assist the process of reasoning although they do not cause it.

Summary and Conclusions

Images represent absent objects or events. They are "symbols," in the sense of bearing some resemblance to the object represented, and are personal and idiosyncratic. Images do not give as complete and detailed a reproduction of the object as is provided by direct perception. Images first make their appearance around the middle of the second year of life, and they arise from a process of imitation which gradually becomes internalized. Until the age of approximately 7 years, the child is only able to produce approximately correct mental images of static situations. He concentrates on states rather than on transformations. The limited imagery of the child is partly the result of immature operative structures. As these structures develop, so does his imagery. After the age of about 7 years, the child becomes capable of correct kinetic imagery. This new ability permits a further understanding of reality: the child now has available a more accurate and detailed rendering of the events on which to focus his reasoning.

MEMORY

Memory, too, is influenced by operative cognition. Before exploring this, it is necessary to begin by clarifying some terminology.

Definitions

In ordinary language, we use the words "memory" or "remember" in several different senses. Here is an anecdote to illustrate the point. An adult has not ridden a bicycle since childhood, some years ago. Now his own child gets a bicycle and asks whether the adult "remembers" how to ride. "Of course, I remember how to ride a bicycle," says the adult. Asked (skeptically) to prove it, the adult get on, and pedals around a bit. Despite the lack of practice over a long period of time, he is able to ride very smoothly, much to the surprise of the child who owns the bicycle and who now wonders whether he will get to ride it. As the adult is pedalling down the street, he "remembers" riding the bicycle which he owned as a child. He has a fairly clear mental picture of its overall shape and form, as well as the places in which he rode.

This example illustrates two very different kinds of "memory." In the first kind, the adult *remembers how to do something*. Although there has been no practice for many years, he has not lost general bicycle-riding skills. He "remembers" how to ride not just a specific bicycle, but any bicycle. Through experience, he has acquired a physical skill of a general nature, and remembers it. In this instance, we use the term *memory* to indicate that the past still exerts an influence on the present. The adult's ability to ride a bicycle, acquired through a set of earlier learning experiences, was somehow preserved within him. Note that after childhood this ability existed as a potential, since until this incident he did not actually engage in the behavior. Note, too, that the element of earlier learning is crucial to the definition. It would not make sense to say, "I remember how to sneeze," since sneezing was never learned. Yet it *would* make sense to say, "I remember how to keep from sneezing" since that *was* learned. In brief, this is one valid use of *memory:* a person can retain, over a period of time, a behavioral potential which is the result of previous learning.

The other sense of *memory* is quite different. When the adult "remembers" riding his childhood bicycle, he is referring to a specific event and thing in the past. He has a hold on a particular slice of his own history. He "remembers" a bicycle with wide tires, and a heavy frame—a Schwinn, in fact. He remembers riding it up Commonwealth Avenue to a park with a certain kind of path. This kind of *memory* is more specific and concrete than the first. In this kind of remembering, the adult retains specific events or things from the past; in the other kind of remembering, he preserves the general skills acquired in the past. Often the two types of memory occur together. A person remembers how to type (thus preserving the general ability) and also remembers the specific typewriter used in his early lessons (thus retaining information concerning a specific thing from the past). But the two types of memory do not have to coexist. A person may remember how to type and yet may have totally forgotten the specific typewriter or his early lessons. Similarly, a person may remember the typewriter and lessons, but not remember how to type. Thus, we have used some examples of physical skills to illustrate a distinction between two types of memory.

In the intellectual domain, Piaget's theory (Piaget and Inhelder, *Memory and Intelligence, MEM,* 1973) proposes a similar distinction between "memory in the wider sense" and "memory in the specific sense." The former refers to "the conservation of the entire past, or at least of everything in the subject's past that serves to inform his present action or understanding" (*MEM,* p. 1). More precisely, memory in the wider sense refers to the "conservation of schemes," to the retention of acquired patterns of behavior or thought, like the concrete operations. By contrast, memory in the specific sense "refers explicitly to the past," to specific events or things or persons in an individual's history. Another way of looking at the distinction is to say that memory in the wider sense involves the *operative* aspect of thought: it is the way in which general operations or ways of doing things are preserved over time. Memory in the specific sense is generally *figurative:* it preserves information concerning specific things—a face, an object, an activity. (These "things" include actions, but only specific actions that are thought to have actually occurred, not the potential for actions of a general type.)

Piaget goes on to propose some further distinctions concerning memory in the specific sense. This type of memory—and we shall now simply use the word *memory* to refer to it—may take one of several forms. Perhaps the most primitive is *recognition.* This occurs when a person encounters things (an event, person, thing, etc.) previously experienced and "has the impression of having perceived them before (rightly or wrongly, for there are false recognitions)" (*MEM,* p. 5). Thus, we see someone known before, and "say to ourselves" that the person is familiar, even though his name may elude us and we cannot recall where we knew him. Similarly, the baby in the sensorimotor period recognizes faces and places when they are encountered. Or the baby shows through his abbreviated schemes that he recognizes a toy he has played with. *Recognition,* then, is one form of (specific) memory, involving an impression of familiarity upon an encounter with a previously experienced object.

Recall is a much more sophisticated and difficult form of memory. It involves producing a mental account of a previously experienced thing in the total absence of that thing. One example would be remembering your childhood bicycle or your first grade teacher. *Recall* sometimes involves a mental picture, sometimes words, sometimes an odor. The crucial aspect of *recall* is that the individual produces some kind of mental representation of the previously experienced event.[7] It is evident that recall is closely linked with the semiotic function, already discussed, since the latter involves the formation of mental representations for absent things or events.

The General Hypothesis

Piaget's main interest is in the functioning of memory in the specific sense—recognition and recall. How does specific memory operate?

According to some empiricist views, memory works in the following manner. An individual perceives an object and stores within him its replica or trace. The more frequently or recently the object is perceived, the stronger the trace, and hence the stronger and more accurate the memory. In this classic view, memory is simply a copy of something real, and the accuracy of the copy depends on such factors as frequency, recency, and the like. Note that in the classic view, the individual is mainly passive: things impose themselves on him; they make an impression on him; they

---

[7]There can be instances of false recall. Piaget himself falsely remembered being the object of an abortive kidnap attempt when he was a child.

form a trace in him as a piece of chalk leaves a record on a slate (hence the expression *tabula rasa,* or blank slate).[8]

Piaget's view is different. He proposes that the child does not simply record reality in a passive manner, storing a copy in the warehouse of memory. Instead, as Piaget sees it, the child *assimilates* and *interprets* reality, so that memory is in part a function of the child's intellectual operations. Memory stems not only from experience but from intelligence. This, then, is the general hypothesis with which Piaget begins his empirical investigations. Given this theoretical framework, Piaget goes on to investigate the specific ways in which mental operations affect memory, especially recall.

Experiments on Memory of a Series

To study the influence of knowing on remembering, Piaget conducted several experiments, one of which involved memory for a series, a topic already reviewed in this chapter. Children of various ages were shown ten wooden sticks, already arranged in a complete series, from smallest to largest. Each child was "told to take a good look at it and remember what he has seen." Then about a week later, each child was asked to recall the series by drawing it or by tracing it out with his fingers on the table. After this, the experimenter determined the child's stage of development with respect to seriation by giving him the usual tests. The experimenter also obtained a check on the child's drawing ability by having him copy a series of sticks available to direct perception. This copy could then be compared with the child's drawing from memory to determine if distortions in the latter stem from mere drawing deficiencies. In brief, the experiment involved (1) determining children's intellectual level with respect to seriation, (2) presenting them with a completed series to remember, and (3) measuring recall by finger tracing and drawing. Furthermore, (4) a measure of drawing ability was taken so that this factor could be controlled.

What should happen in such an experiment? According to the classic view, the series impresses itself on the passive subject, and the accuracy of

[8]Piaget's exposition of the classic view probably refers to theorists like Ebbinghaus, who in the nineteenth century invented nonsense syllables and spent many years of his life memorizing them himself. He was his only subject and deserves some sort of prize for an immense capacity for boredom. In recent years, however, theorists of memory have given up both the inclination themselves to memorize nonsense syllables (although may require their subjects to do it) and theoretical accounts which treat the subject as passive. Many modern theories are in substantial agreement with Piaget on the issue of activity. For a comparison of Piaget's theory with others, as well as an excellent critique of Piaget's work, see L. Liben, "Memory from a Cognitive-Developmental Perspective: A Theoretical and Empirical Review," in *Knowledge and Development,* W. F. Overton and J. M. Gallagher, eds. (New York: Plenum Press, 1977), Vol. I, pp. 149–203.

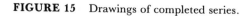

FIGURE 15   Drawings of completed series.

recall depends on the extent of the subject's experience with it and on similar factors. The child's drawings should to some degree mirror the reality which impinges on him. Piaget's view is much different: the child actively assimilates the reality into his intellectual system and this process of interpretation determines the nature and quality of recall. In the present instance, a stage 1 child may distort his memory of the series in accordance with his immature intellectual operations, and this will be reflected in his drawing and tracing. Note that the result of this is not a drawing which is simply a pale copy of the reality. Rather, it is a drawing which is systematically distorted in line with the child's intellectual operations.

Consider a few examples of this. One child made a drawing like that in Figure 15A, involving several identical long lines and several identical short ones. This drawing was similar to the child's actual arrangement of the sticks during the test of seriation: he made one bunch of large sticks and another bunch of small sticks, but did not accurately seriate within each bunch. Another child produced a drawing like that in Figure 15B. This, too, was similar to his actual arrangement of the sticks. He made the tops of the sticks increase in order of size, but totally ignored the bottoms. (When asked to copy a well-formed series immediately in front of them, these same children produced far more accurate drawings. This allows us to conclude that drawing skill in itself is not at issue.) By contrast, children in stage 3 who could accurately seriate were accurate in recall, as indicated by veridical drawings and tracings.

These findings can be taken to support Piaget's theory. The individual's memory is influenced and organized to some degree by his intellectual operations. *The child recalls not what he has seen but what he knows.* In the present instance, stage 1 children's recall is distorted by their immature seriation schemes. (We shall see cases later where the effect is of a different sort.) At the same time, Piaget points out that the results are not entirely clear-cut. Some stage 1 children make perfectly accurate drawings. Their mental operations do not seem to intervene so forcefully in the act of recall. Instead they seem to focus on the appearance of the series—on its "figurative aspects"—and manage to recall it very well, much as they would recall (and draw) a circle or a tree or a staircase. It is hard to explain why some stage 1 children show the distorting effects of intellectual operations while others do not.

In brief, while there is some variability, the results show that intelligence—the intellectual operations—structures the child's recall. Knowledge interacts with perception to produce what is remembered.

The Development of Memory

According to Piaget, there is a general developmental progression from the early appearance of accurate recognition to the later use of accurate recall. Memory begins in a crude fashion during the sensorimotor period. At this time, the infant shows evidence of recognition. Through overt or abbreviated behavior, he demonstrates that a toy or a person is familiar. The infant does not seem capable of more demanding forms of memory, especially recall (this of course involves evoking a mental representation of absent objects or events). It is only with the onset of the semiotic function, at about 18 months, that the child becomes capable of mental representation and hence recall. Earlier, in another context, we cited the example of Jacqueline, at 1;11(11), who upon returning from a trip, was able to report on events which had occurred earlier: "Robert cry, duck swim in lake, gone away" (*Play, Dreams, and Imitation*, p. 222). This is an example of recall in a child who is just beginning to give evidence of the use of the semiotic function. In brief, infants show signs of recognition memory, whereas recall, as one aspect of the semiotic function, begins to appear only at about 18 months.

As we have seen, once recall appears, its functioning is influenced by the intellectual operations. Now we shall see that this influence can have developmental aspects. Piaget's experiments on memory for a series shed light on this issue. We already know that the child's recall after one week is distorted in line with his current stage of seriation. But what happens to recall over a longer period of time, say, six to eight months? According to the classic view, the memory trace simply fades, and this fading becomes more complete as time goes on. In Piaget's view, matters are more complex than that. In many cases, there may well be some deterioration of memory over a long period of time. And yet there are other possibilities as well. Memory, which depends on intelligence, therefore exhibits developmental changes which correspond to the development of intelligence. Indeed, Piaget's theory leads to the prediction that under certain circumstances, recall may actually *improve* over time.

In the case of seriation, the matter works as follows: the stage 1 child sees a well-ordered series and assimilates it into his intellectual operations. Since these are immature, one week later the child inaccurately recalls the sticks as a collection of small ones and a collection of large ones. His intelligence has organized recall poorly. Then over a period of time, the child's mental operations develop and he enters stage 3. Now, asked to recall the sticks, he remembers a well-formed series. His memory has improved over time because his intellectual structures have developed more fully.

This is indeed precisely the result which Piaget discovered. Of twenty-four stage 1 children, twenty-two showed improved recall (as measured by drawings) when they advanced to a later stage seven or eight months after the initial testing.

Several comments should be made at this point. First, independent investigators have had a hard time replicating this result (for example, Samuels, 1976). A good deal of careful research, with adequate controls, needs to be done to pin down the effect. It is particularly important to obtain direct measures of the child's assumed intellectual development. Second, it is important to recognize that Piaget's theory does not always predict improvement in long-term recall. Improvement can be expected to occur only if the initial recall was distorted by immature intellectual operations and if these operations subsequently improve. This is a very special case, however, and often does not occur. For example, suppose a child learns someone's name and tries to recall it a year later. Memory for the name is likely to deteriorate regardless of the child's stage of development. The child's advancement from stage 1 to 3 of concrete operations will have no particular bearing on the recall of names, since the recall is merely figurative with no logical operations involved. Here is another example, which may seem paradoxical. Suppose a stage 1 child is shown a badly formed series. After one week he accurately remembers the badly formed series because he has assimilated it into his immature mental operations. Then, over the next year, the child's mental operations advance and he has reached stage 3. Now when asked to recall the sticks, he produces a well-formed series which is the product of his current intellectual structure. Unfortunately, this is inaccurate recall, since the initial series was badly formed. This example is a case of an improvement in intellectual status leading to a deterioration in recall. (Several studies cited by Liben, 1977, actually obtain this kind of result.) The main point of Piaget's theory is not that memory necessarily improves over time—it seldom does— but that memory is influenced by developing intellectual operations, and not just by real events.

Summary

Piaget distinguishes between two types of memory. *Memory in the wider sense* refers to the individual's ability to retain over time the potential to exhibit learned schemes or operations. *Memory in the specific sense* refers to the individual's ability to retain over time information concerning particular events, things, or persons. Specific memory may take one of several forms, the most important of which are *recognition* (an impression of familiarity on an encounter with a previously experienced object) and *recall* (evocation of the past through mental representations). Piaget's general hypothesis is that specific memory is influenced by intelligence—the intellectual operations. Intelligence serves to organize and shape memory. Piaget rejects the classic view in which events are seen to impress themselves on a passive observer, leaving a trace or a simple copy of the reality.

Piaget's experiments on memory for a series demonstrate that after one week, recall is influenced by the individual's stage of intellectual development. Presented with a well-formed series, some children recall not what they have seen, but what they know about the series. It is important to note, however, that there is some variability in these results. According to Piaget, there is a general developmental progression from recognition memory to recall. Infants show signs of recognition; recall does not seem to appear until the onset of the semiotic function at about 18 months.

After it appears, recall is influenced by the development of intellectual structures. The general hypothesis states that as intellectual structures develop, they exert corresponding developmental effects on recall. Indeed, under certain circumstances, recall may actually improve over time. Piaget has shown that in the case of seriation, recall becomes more accurate as children advance from one intellectual stage to the next. It is important to note, however, that this result is not easily replicated and that Piaget's theory does not always predict improvement in recall over time. Instead, the main point of Piaget's theory is that memory is influenced and organized (but not necessarily *improved*) by developing intellectual operations, and not simply by real events. Memory is the result of an interaction been knower and known.

CONSCIOUSNESS

We have seen how the child develops operative and figurative aspects of thought. By the age of 7 or 8 years, he achieves some success at classifying and ordering objects, at producing mental images, and at remembering. These cognitive processes, both figurative and operative, work mainly on an unconscious level. Now we will assume a different level of analysis to consider a new topic which Piaget has recently studied, namely, the child's awareness and verbalization of his own thought processes.

In studying the issue of consciousness, Piaget's general strategy is first to have the child solve a problem and second to determine his awareness of the methods of solution (*The Grasp of Consciousness, GC,* 1976b). In one investigation, Piaget used standard seriation tasks, involving such materials as a set of cards varying in height and width, or a set of barrels varying in both height and diameter. Each child's task was to arrange the objects in order of increasing (or decreasing) size. He was told, for example, to "make a nice line of barrels." As soon as the child began to do this, the investigator asked him to describe what he was doing or was about to do. Sometimes the child was asked "how he would explain to a friend what should be done" (*GC,* p. 301). After the child completed the first series (successful or not), he was asked to repeat it and to describe and explain his actions as he went along. The purpose of this repetition was to ensure that the child knew what was expected of him.

Suppose that a child succeeds at the seriation tasks just described: he produces an accurate ordering in terms of length of the rods or size of the barrels. Given this, we may inquire into the child's *consciousness* or *cognizance* of seriation. It is important to begin by clarifying what is meant by Piaget's usage of *consciousness* or *cognizance*. Piaget uses these terms to refer to the child's ability to produce a coherent verbal account of the mental processes underlying his behavior. By this definition, the child is conscious or cognizant of his thought processes if he says, for example, "I always look for the biggest one, then I put it aside and look for the biggest one out of all the ones that are left." In Piaget's usage, *consciousness* refers to an awareness and verbalization of one's own thought processes. Not only is the conscious child able to do something; he is also explicitly aware of how he does it.[9] Note that Piaget does not use consciousness to refer to the elementary and fleeting perception of the immediate situation. Thus the term is not used to refer to the child's awareness that there are toy barrels on the table or that his hand is moving toward them, and so on. While such elementary awareness appears very early in life and is no doubt highly prevalent, it is not the subject of Piaget's investigation. In brief, Piaget is interested in the child's explicit knowledge of his thought processes, and not merely in the crude awareness of ongoing activities.

Several questions then arise with respect to consciousness. It is especially interesting to inquire into the temporal relations between action and cognizance. There are of course several possibilities. One alternative is that action and cognizance emerge simultaneously. As one develops so does the other, and it is impossible to determine the direction, or even existence, of causality. A second possibility is that consciousness comes first, and thus directs the subsequent action. Perhaps the child first conceptualizes his action and this helps him to perform it. A third possibility is just the reverse. Perhaps successful behavior precedes cognizance of it. The child may be able first to perform certain actions, and only later, upon reflection, does he become aware of his behavior.

The behavior of one of Piagets' subjects, STO, at 6-1, working at seriation, sheds some light on these issues. On his first attempt, STO failed to complete a successful series. He could not arrange cards in order of size and put the smallest ones in the center of the line. He said, "I've made a staircase that goes up or down." The examiner responded that the staircase should go down all the time, "but first tell me how are you going to make it?" STO responded: "I'm going to put the big one, another big one, another big one, the middle-size one, the smaller middle-size one, the smaller middle-size one, and the smaller middle-size one" (*GC,* p. 312). STO proceeded to produce a good series, with only one mistake, which he easily corrected. On subsequent trials, the same sort of thing happened: STO produced good series but poor verbal descriptions.

According to Piaget, this example shows that STO's seriation was far in advance of his consciousness of it. STO could order the cards in a fairly systematic way and yet could refer only in an imprecise manner to "another big one, another big one," or to "the smaller middle-size one, and the smaller middle-size one." Other children exhibit similar behavior. For example, they use an extremely systematic procedure for seriation (like selecting the smallest and then the smallest of all those left) and yet can say only that they first took a small one, then another small one, and

---

[9]Recently, Flavell and others have been investigating a similar topic, which they term "meta cognition," and which involves the child's knowledge about his own knowledge. (For a review, see J. H. Flavell, *Cognitive Development* (Englewood Cliffs, N.J.: Prentice-Hall, Inc., 1985.) An example is whether the child is aware of using systematic strategies to aid in memory.

so on. Piaget concludes from data like these that, in general, the child's successful activities—including operative activities like seriation—precede cognizance of them. The child can act and think effectively before he can verbalize or be conscious of his actions or thoughts.

How does consciousness of problem solving develop? Piaget proposes that at first the child is only dimly aware of goals. For example, he wants to make a "staircase." The child then gradually develops various strategies for achieving his goal, for example, random placement or systematic selection of the largest. At first, he is quite unaware of these strategies, just as the 3-month-old baby is not conscious of the procedures which he uses for getting his thumb into his mouth. He acts, successfully or unsuccessfully, but does not explicitly analyze his actions. With development, however, the child observes his own activities and reflects on them. He interprets his actions; he tries to "reconstruct" them on the plane of thought. At first, this process of interpretation may lead to distortion and misunderstanding. Piaget has observed many cases in which the initial consciousness was in error—where the child did not accurately see what in fact he had done. But gradually, the reconstruction becomes more and more accurate. The child's reflection on his own activities allows the development of explicit knowledge concerning both his problem-solving processes and the objects under consideration. In this way, the child learns about himself and about the objects surrounding him. He develops abstract concepts that can be verbalized.

Piaget's position has much to recommend it. It seems useful to make a distinction between at least two levels of knowledge. There does seem to be a kind of "action knowledge" or "how-to knowledge" in which we solve problems using means of which we are unaware. Thus STO could seriate, but without consciousness of his method. At the same time, there is also another level of abstract knowledge, in which we can explicitly formulate our methods of solution and even the principles underlying them. Thus a child cannot only seriate but explicitly understands the principles which he uses. The process of transforming action knowledge into abstract knowledge may be crucial for human learning. There is a good deal of wisdom built into our behavior, and a major task for learning may consist in making explicit what in a sense we already know unconsciously.

While these are useful points, Piaget's investigations in this area seem to suffer from a major weakness, namely, an overreliance on verbalizations as a source of evidence. In these studies, verbalization is taken as the main, or even only, source of evidence for consciousness or cognizance. Thus STO is said to lack consciousness of his actions, since his language is inadequate. But STO's repetitive use of vague terms like "the smaller middle-size one" may not accurately reflect the true level of his consciousness. Seriation is hard to express in words, and perhaps STO could conceptualize it but was unable to offer adequate descriptions of the process. Piaget's interpretation seems weak in this regard. At the same time, despite the difficulties, Piaget's research raises extremely provocative issues requiring a good deal of further study.

GENERAL CONCLUSIONS

While criticisms may and should be made, and while revisions are necessary, Piaget's theory is an enormously significant accomplishment. Indeed, on reviewing Piaget's later work on the child from 2 to 11, one is struck above all by the incredible creativity and diversity of his contribution. Between 1940 and 1980, Piaget revolutionized the study of the child. He introduced a score of fascinating problems and experimental tasks— conservation is only one example—which for a long time dominated research in child psychology. More important, he offered an extraordinarily deep and subtle theory of cognitive development, which continues to inform our understanding of the mind's growth.

5

Adolescence

Thus far we have reviewed the sensorimotor period (birth to 2 years), the preoperational period (2 to 7 years), and the concrete operational period (7 to 11 years). In Piaget's theory the final period of intellectual development is that of *formal operations,* which begins at about age 12 and is consolidated during adolescence.

There are several major themes which run through Piaget's account of adolescent thought. One is that the adolescent's system of mental operations has reached a high degree of equilibrium. This means, among other things, that the adolescent's thought is flexible and effective. He can deal efficiently with the complex problems of reasoning. Another major theme is that the adolescent can imagine the many possibilities inherent in a situation. Unlike the concrete operational child, whose thought is tied to the concrete, the adolescent can deal with hypothetical propositions. He can compensate mentally for transformations in reality; this is one of the determinants of equilibrium.

These general conclusions are based on a number of studies performed by Inhelder and Piaget,[1] on adolescent reasoning (*The Growth of Logical Thinking from Childhood to Adolescence, GLT,* 1958). These studies,

[1]For purposes of brevity, we subsequently refer to the work on adolescence as Piaget's; nevertheless, Inhelder's contributions should be recognized.

which use the revised clinical method, describe the adolescent's performance on various problems involving scientific concepts. In a typical investigation, a number of adolescents were given several problems based on classical physics, chemistry, or other disciplines. In each case the adolescent was presented with some apparatus or materials (a pendulum, a balance, etc.) and was required to explain how they work. Each subject was allowed to manipulate the apparatus, and to do experiments—in short, to behave as a scientist. The investigator kept a detailed record of the adolescent's activities and occasionally asked a few questions if verbal clarification seemed necessary. Piaget's major question, of course, is not whether the adolescent can come up with the "right" answer. Rather, the issue is whether and how the adolescent's thought differs from that of the younger child. Piaget's interest is in how the adolescent copes with scientific problems, how he experiments, and how he reasons about the observed data. As we shall see, Piaget's theory of adolescent thought is stated in terms of two logical models—the sixteen binary operations[2] and the INRC group. These two models together describe the period of formal operations. Since the models are quite complex, we will consider only limited portions of Piaget's theory.

THE SIXTEEN BINARY OPERATIONS

The Pendulum Problem

In one investigation all subjects were presented with the following situation. A pendulum was constructed in the form of an object hanging from a string, and the subject was shown how to vary the length of the string, how to change the weight of the suspended object, how to release the pendulum from various heights, and how to push it with different degrees of force. The subject was required to solve what is essentially a problem in physics, to discover which of the four factors, that is, length, weight, height, or force, alone or in combination with others, affects the pendulum's frequency of oscillation (the number of swings within a given interval of time). The correct solution, of course, is that the major causative factor is the length of the string: the shorter the string, the more frequent the oscillation. To solve the problem, the subject was allowed to experiment with the pendulum in any way he pleased. He could, for instance, make the pendulum heavy or light and see what happened. The

---

[2]The model of the sixteen operations is actually a special case of a larger and more comprehensive system called the *combinatorial system*. This special case applies to situations involving two values (e.g., p and $\bar{p}$) of each of two factors (e.g., p and q). With a greater number of factors, more complex models are necessary and can be generated from the combinatorial system.

examiner played a limited and nondirective role, recording the subject's experiments and verbal statements, and intervening in the course of events to question the subject on a few points that were not clear. In addition, the examiner also asked the subject to prove his assertions when he did not voluntarily do so. To summarize, the subject assumed the role of a scientist seeking an answer by empirical means to a classical problem in physics, and the examiner recorded his behavior.

To show the true measure of the adolescent's accomplishment, we will first present a brief account of how children in the preoperational and concrete operational periods deal with the problem. Preoperational children below 7 years of age approach the task in a very haphazard way. First, the "experiments" which they devise reveal no overall plan or pattern. These younger children seem to make random tests which in fact yield little information of value. For example, one child began by pushing a long pendulum with a light weight, then he swung a short pendulum with a heavy weight, and then he removed the weight altogether. Such a procedure can tell one nothing about the role of weight or length for reasons that should be clear (and if they are not, they will be later). Second, the child does not even report the results accurately. He hypothesizes, for instance, that his pushes influence the frequency of oscillation, and reports that this is what occurs when in fact it does not. Apparently the child's expectations influence his observations, and this attitude is hardly a mark of scientific objectivity. Third, the child's conclusions are faulty and unrelated to the evidence. This may occur because the child reports the results inaccurately; for example, he may mistakenly perceive that frequency of oscillation increases as the pendulum is pushed more vigorously. On other occasions the conclusions are inaccurate because the child reasons about the results in a faulty way. For example, if he (correctly) perceives that a short, heavy pendulum swings with greater frequency than a long, light one, he may incorrectly conclude that weight, and not length, is the causative factor.

The concrete operational child shows considerable improvement in his intellectual ability. He investigates a number of potential determinants of oscillation and observes the results in an accurate way, perhaps even discovering the correct answer. But there are many features of his procedure which are unsystematic and illogical and which require further development. Consider this protocol:

> BEA (10;2) varies the length of the string [according to the units two, four, three, etc., taken in random order] but reaches the correct conclusion that there is an inverse correspondence: *"It goes slower when it's longer."* For the weight, he compares 100 grams with a length of two or five, 50 grams with a length of one and again concludes that there is an inverse correspondence between weight and frequency. (*GLT*, pp. 70–71)

The child performed well in two respects. First, his answer was at least partially correct, although he mistakenly inferred that weight played a role too. Second, he observed all the results correctly: for example, the short, light pendulum *did* swing with greater frequency than the long, heavy one. His objectivity as a scientific observer is no longer in doubt; expectation does not influence observation.

But there were two important deficiencies in the child's approach. First, he did not design the experiments properly. To investigate the role of weight, he compared a short, light pendulum with a long, heavy one. This is not the proper procedure. What he should have done was compare a short, light pendulum with a short, heavy one and a long, light pendulum with a long, heavy one. That is, he should have *held length constant* to test the effects of weight, and vice versa. Second, the conclusions drawn from the empirical results (which were, as we noted, correctly observed) were imperfect. The judgment that there was an inverse relation between weight and frequency of oscillation (the heavier the weight, the less frequent the oscillation) does not follow from the observed data. This kind of faulty reasoning can be seen even more clearly in another subject, who (correctly) observed that a short, heavy pendulum swings with greater frequency than a long, light one. From this result, he concluded that both length and weight were determining factors; that is, increased length caused less frequent oscillation, and increased weight caused more frequent oscillation. This, of course, is not necessarily the correct inference. In the absence of further information, one cannot decide among three possibilities: (1) the foregoing interpretation, (2) that increasing the length slows the oscillation, while weight is irrelevant, and (3) that adding weight increases the frequency, while length is irrelevant. Unfortunately, the child did not design his experiment so as to provide the information necessary for deciding among the alternatives, and without sufficient justification unwisely settled on one of them.

Consider, on the other hand, the behavior of the adolescent in the period of formal operations. After passing through a transitional stage, which we will not discuss here, the adolescent performs well at three aspects of the problem: (1) he plans the tests adequately, or designs the experiment properly, (2) he observes the results accurately, (3) and he draws the proper logical conclusions from the observations. Here is an example:

> EME (15;1), after having selected 100 grams with a long string and a medium-length string, then 20 grams with a long and short string, and finally 200 grams with a long and short, concludes: *"It's the length of the string that makes it go faster or slower; the weight doesn't play any role."* She discounts likewise the height of the drop and the force of her push. (*GLT*, p. 75)

TABLE 1   ARRANGEMENT OF
OSCILLATION EXPERIMENT

	Length	Weight	Oscillation
1.	long	light	?
2.	short	light	?
3.	long	heavy	?
4.	short	heavy	?

Let us consider in turn each of the three aspects of the adolescent's behavior.

1. *Designing the experiment.* From the outset, and before carrying out any tests, the adolescent believes that there are several possible determinants of the frequency of oscillation. The causative factor could be length, weight, or any other of the factors present. Furthermore, she realizes that it is also conceivable that some combination of factors might be responsible: perhaps weight and length combined increase oscillation while neither by itself is a sufficient cause. In other words, the adolescent begins by imagining a series of purely hypothetical results; before acting, she conceives of all the possibilities. The evidence for this assertion is that later she proceeds to test all *possible* causes of oscillation. The systematically exhaustive way in which she performs the test suggests that she must have imagined all of the possibilities at the outset. Also, these imagined possibilities are abstractions of a sort. While she considers length, for instance, as an isolated and independent determinant of oscillation, it is the case that in reality length never stands alone; it is always accompanied by other factors such as weight. A swinging pendulum is never just long or short; it also has a certain weight, is released from a particular height, and so forth.

The adolescent's next step is an attempt to discover which of the many possibilities is operative. She uses a method which involves holding some factors constant while varying others. EME's approach was to first test a long string with 100 grams, then a shorter string with 100 grams, then a long string with 200 grams, and finally a short string with 200 grams. A schematic overview of her procedure is given in Table 1.

Note that four possibilities are tested, and that they involve holding one factor constant and varying another. In the case of the first two steps, the weight is light and the string is either long or short. In the case of steps 3 and 4, weight is heavy and the string may be long or short. Thus in both steps 1 and 2, and in 3 and 4, weight is held at one level (or is constant) while length is varied. If length is a causative factor, then its effects should be manifest in a comparison of 1 versus 2 and in a comparison of 3 versus 4.

We can easily arrange Table 1 to show the strategy of holding length constant while varying weight. Table 2 shows more clearly what is, of

TABLE 2 ALTERNATIVE
ARRANGEMENT OF OSCILLATION
EXPERIMENT

	Length	Weight	Oscillation
1.	long	light	?
3.	long	heavy	?
2.	short	light	?
4.	short	heavy	?

course, already contained in Table 1, namely, that the four tests can be used to get information on the role of weight. If one compares 1 and 3, for example, the length is long in both cases, while weight changes.

Actually, for purposes of illustration, we have simplified the matter somewhat. In dealing with length and weight, the adolescent also holds constant the other factors—height of the drop and force of the push—since varying them would confuse the results. All these variables are held constant so that the effects of the two factors, length and weight, may be assessed. Also, after testing the effects of length and weight, EME went on to do the same for the height of the drop and force of the push.

The adolescent's procedure seems very reasonable, of course, and one might even consider a detailed description of it to be trivial; surely, everyone would go about the problem in this way. But as we have seen before, for example, in the case of conservation, what is obvious and trivial to the adult is not necessarily apparent to the child. Similarly, in the case of designing experiments, the child in the concrete operational period does not always follow the "obvious" procedure. Remember the child whose *only* comparison involved a short, light pendulum versus a long, heavy one (steps 2 and 3 of Table 3), and who felt that this test resulted in sufficient information for firm conclusions.

2. *Observing the results.* It comes as no surprise that the adolescent, like the concrete operational child but not like the preoperational period child, observes the empirical results without bias.

3. *Drawing logical conclusions.* When the adolescent performs the four-step experiments shown in Tables 1 and 2, she obtains the results shown in

TABLE 3 OBSERVED RESULTS,
OSCILLATION EXPERIMENT

	Length	Weight	Oscillation
1.	long	light	infrequent
2.	short	light	frequent
3.	long	heavy	infrequent
4.	short	heavy	frequent

TABLE 4   RESULTS NOT OBSERVED,
OSCILLATION EXPERIMENT

	Length	Weight	Oscillation
1.	long	light	frequent
2.	short	light	infrequent
3.	long	heavy	frequent
4.	short	heavy	infrequent

Table 3. It should be clear from Table 3 that whenever the pendulum is short, it swings with greater frequency; and whenever it is long, it swings with lesser frequency. None of the other factors has any effect on oscillation.

Table 4 shows the results which were not observed. The reason for presenting this table will be clear later.

To introduce Piaget's use of logic, we will simplify the tables by means of a few abbreviations. If we let p stand for short and $\bar{p}$ for long, q stand for light and $\bar{q}$ for heavy, r for frequent and $\bar{r}$ for infrequent, and T (true) for observed result and F (false) for nonobserved result, then we have Table 5. In that table, p and q are the factors and r is the result. T and F merely indicate whether the result was observed or not. For example, line 1 says that it was observed (T) that a long ($\bar{p}$), light (q) pendulum swung with low frequency ($\bar{r}$). Line 7 says that it was not observed (F) that a long ($\bar{p}$), heavy ($\bar{q}$) pendulum swung with high frequency (r).

What does the adolescent conclude from this pattern of observed and nonobserved results? In regard to weight, Table 5 shows that it is observed that when heavy or light, the pendulum swings with low or high frequency. Consequently, the weight makes no difference whatsoever on the frequency of oscillation. Piaget writes this conclusion as q * r (read: weight is irrelevant to oscillation) and calls it *tautology* or *complete affirmation*.

TABLE 5   SYMBOLIZATION OF OSCILLATION
EXPERIMENT

	Length	Weight	Oscillation	Result
1.	$\bar{p}$	q	$\bar{r}$	T
2.	p	q	r	T
3.	$\bar{p}$	$\bar{q}$	$\bar{r}$	T
4.	p	$\bar{q}$	r	T
5.	$\bar{p}$	q	r	F
6.	p	q	$\bar{r}$	F
7.	$\bar{p}$	$\bar{q}$	r	F
8.	p	$\bar{q}$	$\bar{r}$	F

(Clearly, it could be shown in the same way that force and height are also irrelevant.)

In regard to length, Table 5 shows that it is observed that a short pendulum always swings frequently and a long one infrequently (and it is *never* observed that a short pendulum swings with low frequency and a long one with high frequency). Therefore, the length of the pendulum fully determines the frequency of oscillation, and height is irrelevant. Another way of saying that is that short length is a necessary and sufficient cause of frequent oscillation.

In propositional logic, the pattern of results for length and oscillation may be described by a relation usually called "reciprocal implication" and is written $p \supseteqq r$. Thus, the adolescent has found that $p \supseteqq r$ (length determines oscillation), whereas q * r (weight is irrelevant).

To summarize, the adolescent begins in the realm of the hypothetical and imagines all the possible determinants of the results. To test hypotheses, the adolescent devises experiments which are well ordered and designed to isolate the critical factors by systematically holding all factors but one constant. She observes the results correctly, and from them proceeds to draw conclusions. Since the experiments have been designed properly, the adolescent's conclusions are certain and necessary.

The Bending of Rods

To investigate another aspect of adolescent thought, Piaget presented subjects with a problem involving the bending of rods. We shall first review the logical conclusions drawn from the results of the experiment, and later see how this form of reasoning differs from that observed in the case of the pendulum problem.

Piaget presented the subjects with a series of rods which were attached to the edge of a basin of water. The rods were in a horizontal position (parallel to the water). The rods differed in (1) composition (steel, brass, etc.), (2) length, (3) thickness, and (4) cross-section form (round, square, rectangular). In addition, (5) different weights could be attached to the end of the rod above the water. The subject's task was first to determine which of the rods bend enough to touch the water, and then to explain the results. As in the case of the pendulum problem, the subject was allowed to vary the factors in any way. He might place on the apparatus a long, thin, round, steel rod with a heavy weight; a short, thin, square, brass rod with a light weight; or any other kind that he preferred. Again, the examiner's role was nondirective; mainly he noted the subject's tests and remarks and initiated a few questions to clarify uncertain points.

Here is a protocol of one adolescent's behavior:

TABLE 6 DESIGN OF RODS
EXPERIMENT

	Length	*Weight*	*Bending*
1.	long	heavy	?
2.	long	light	?
3.	short	heavy	?
4.	short	light	?

DEI (16;10): "Tell me first [after experimental trials] what factors are at work here."—"*Weight, material, the length of the rod, perhaps the form.*"—"Can you prove your hypotheses?"—[She compares the 200 gram and 300 gram weights on the same steel rod.] "*You see, the role of weight is demonstrated. For the material, I don't know.*"—"Take these steel rods and these copper ones."— "*I think I have to take two rods with the same form. Then to demonstrate the role of the metal I compare these two* [steel and brass, square, 50 cm. long and 16 mm.^{2} cross section with 300 grams on each] *or these two here* [steel and brass, round, 50 and 22 cm. by 16 mm.^{2}]: *for length I shorten that one* [50 cm. brought down to 22.] *To demonstrate the role of the form, I can compare these two*" [round brass and square brass, 50 cm. and 16 mm.^{2} for each.]—"Can the same thing be proved with these two?" [brass, round and square, 50 cm. long and 16 and 7 mm.^{2} cross section.]—"*No because that one* [7 mm.^{2}] *is much narrower.*"— "And the width?"—"*I can compare these two*" [round, brass, 50 cm. long with 16 and 7 mm.^{2} cross section]. (*GLT*, p. 60)

It should be clear from the protocol that the adolescent's procedure is highly systematized. DEI considered that any one of several factors may be involved in determining the flexibility of the rods. For example, an increase in weight or an increase in length may make the rod bend. To test these hypotheses, the adolescent employed the method of varying one factor at a time while holding the others constant. To test the role of weight, for instance, DEI put first a 200 gram weight and then a 300 gram weight on the *same* rod. Because it was identical in the two cases, the rod obviously held constant the factors of material, length, and the like, while only weight varied.

We will now examine the adolescent's procedure in detail. For purposes of economy, let us suppose that only two factors, that is, length and weight, were present in the problem. In that case, a full account of the adolescent's procedure is given by Table 6. This shows that when steps 1 versus 2 and 3 versus 4 are compared, length is held constant and weight varied. And when 1 versus 3 and 2 versus 4 are compared, weight is held constant and length varied. This procedure should be familiar to the reader, since it is the same as that employed in the pendulum problem.

DEI correctly observed the results given in Table 7, which also lists the data *not* observed.

TABLE 7   RODS EXPERIMENT

	Length	Weight	Bending
		Results Observed	
1.	long	heavy	great
2.	long	light	great
3.	short	heavy	great
4.	short	light	little
		Results Not Observed	
5.	long	heavy	little
6.	long	light	little
7.	short	heavy	little
8.	short	light	great

For example, line 2 says that the subject *did* observe a long, light rod bend a great deal, and line 5 says that the subject did not observe a long, heavy rod bend just a little. At first, the results may seem somewhat confusing. Rows 1 and 2 show that long rods bend a lot, but line 3 shows that short rods also bend a great deal. Similarly, lines 1 and 3 show that heavy rods bend a great deal, but line 2 shows that light rods do so also. Perhaps the results may be clarified if we consider the outcomes for each factor separately. Table 8 shows the results for length (ignoring weight). It should be clear from the table that a long rod always bends a lot, whereas a short rod may bend a great deal or just a little.

Table 9 shows the same pattern of results in the case of weight. Again, the obvious interpretation is that heavy rods are always observed to bend a great deal (and never just a little), whereas light rods may either bend a little or a lot.

Before we continue, let us symbolize the results once again: Table 10 first presents the case of both length and weight, and then shows the cases of length and weight separately. p stands for long length, $\bar{p}$ for short

TABLE 8   LENGTH AND BENDING

	Length	Bending
		Results Obtained
1.	long	great
2.	short	great
3.	short	little
		Results Not Observed
4.	long	little

TABLE 9   WEIGHT AND
BENDING

Weight	Bending
Results Observed	
1. heavy	great
2. light	great
3. light	little
Results Not Observed	
4. heavy	little

length; q for heavy weight, q̄ for light weight; r for great bending and r̄ for
little bending; and T for an observed result, and F for result not observed.
For example, line 4 under "weight alone" says that the subject did *not*
observe (F) a heavy (q) rod bending only a little (r̄).

The adolescent draws the following conclusions from the pattern of
observed and nonobserved results. First, length is a cause of the rod's
bending. Whenever there is a long rod, it always bends. But do not short

TABLE 10   SYMBOLIZATION OF RODS
EXPERIMENT

	Length	Weight	Bending	Result
		Both length and weight		
1.	p	q	r	T
2.	p	q̄	r	T
3.	p̄	q	r	T
4.	p̄	q̄	r̄	T
5.	p	q	r̄	F
6.	p	q̄	r̄	F
7.	p̄	q	r̄	F
8.	p̄	q̄	r	F
		Length alone		
1.	p		r	T
2.	p̄		r	T
3.	p̄		r̄	F
4.	p		r̄	F
		Weight alone		
1.		q	r	T
2.		q̄	r	T
3.		q̄	r̄	T
4.		q	r̄	F

TABLE 11   THREE LOGICAL RELATIONS

	Length	*Bending*	*Results showing implication*	*Hypothetical results showing:* Reciprocal *implication*	*Tautology*
1.	p	r	T	T	T
2.	p̄	r	T	F	T
3.	p̄	r̄	T	T	T
4.	p	r̄	F	F	T

rods also bend (at least sometimes) and does this not contradict the hypothesis? The adolescent reasons that the hypothesis of causality is not disconfirmed. A special kind of cause—sufficient cause—is involved. In the present case, a long rod is always *sufficient* to cause bending. But the fact that the rod sometimes bends also when the length is short means that length is not the only causative factor. In other words, length is not *necessary* for bending; other factors may cause bending too. Second, the adolescent concludes that weight also is a sufficient cause of bending. Whenever the rod is heavy, it bends. But as was the case with short length, sometimes light weights bend and sometimes they do not. Again, the result depends on what other factors are present. To summarize, the adolescent makes the judgment that both length and weight are *sufficient* to cause bending, although neither one alone is *necessary*. In propositional logic, these results may be represented by a relation "implication," and are written p ⊃ r, q ⊃ r (read: length implies bending, weight implies bending).

Perhaps we may achieve a better understanding of implication if we contrast it with reciprocal implication (previously observed in the pendulum problem). Table 11 shows both the pattern of implication and the (hypothetical) pattern of reciprocal implication in the case of length in the rods problem.

The implication column states, as we have already seen, that long rods always bend a great deal, and that short rods bend either a little or a great deal. The (hypothetical) reciprocal implication column says that long rods always bend a great deal, and that short rods *always* bend only a little. Therefore, in this hypothetical case only length causes bending. It should be clear from the table that reciprocal implication and implication differ only in the pattern of T's and F's (observed results and non-observed results). Finally, to review further, consider the last column, showing tautology or complete affirmation. This hypothetical case states that all possible combinations of length and bending can be observed. A long rod bends both a little and a lot, and so does a short rod. Clearly, then, length is irrelevant to bending. Thus, we have reviewed p ⊋ r (reciprocal implication), p ⊃ r (implication), and p * r (tautology).

TABLE 12   THE SIXTEEN BINARY OPERATIONS

		The four possible outcomes of an experiment			
		_1._	_2._	_3._	_4._
Length		p	p	p̄	p̄
Bending		r	r̄	r	r̄
Name of operation		_All ways in which four possible outcomes can be observed or not observed*_			
1. Negation		F	F	F	F
2. Conjunction		T	F	F	F
3. Inverse of implication		F	T	F	F
4. Inverse of converse implication		F	F	T	F
5. Conjunctive negation		F	F	F	T
6. Independence of p to r		T	T	F	F
7. Independence of r to p		T	F	T	F
8. Reciprocal implication		T	F	F	T
9. Reciprocal exclusion		F	T	T	F
10. Inverse of independence of r to p		F	T	F	T
11. Inverse of independence of p to r		F	F	T	T
12. Disjunction		T	T	T	F
13. Converse implication		T	T	F	T
14. Implication		T	F	T	T
15. Incompatability		F	T	T	T
16. Tautology		T	T	T	T

*Only number 14, implication, is actually observed in the case of rods. The rest are hypothetical.

The Other Binary Operations

In describing the adolescent's behavior on the various scientific reasoning problems, we have thus far covered three logical relations: p $\gtrless_{\subset}$ r, p $\supset$ r, and p * r. In Piaget's system, there are thirteen more, and the whole set is called the _system of sixteen binary operations_. Rather than discuss each of the sixteen operations in detail, we will instead merely list them all, in terms of patterns of observed and nonobserved results and briefly discuss only a few operations. Suppose, again, we have the variables of long length (p) and short length (p̄); great bending (r) and a little bending (r̄). There are four combinations of p, p̄, r, and r̄. These are shown on the top of Table 12. They correspond to possible outcomes of the experiment. It could conceivably occur that a long rod (p) bends a lot (r) or a little (r̄) and that a short rod (p̄) bends a lot (r) or a little (r̄): these are the four possible outcomes of an empirical test. Each of the possible outcomes may be observed (T) or not observed (F). It is possible for all of them to be observed or for only some to be observed, while others are not observed. In other words, there are a large number of ways in which the experiment might turn out in terms of observed and nonobserved results. Table 12 lists all the ways in which the four outcomes may be observed or not observed. (It is, of course, understood that instead of p and r, we could have a and b or any other symbols, and that instead of length and bending, we could have weight and oscillation or any other factors; Table 12 is completely general.) For example, row 2 says that if we did the experiment we could observe that long length produces great bending (p and r) and could fail to observe that long length produces little bending (p and r̄) and that short length produces a great deal of bending (p̄ and r) or little bending (p̄ and r̄).

We have already seen parts of the table before. For example, in connection with the pendulum problem we have seen that the pattern of observed and nonobserved outcomes shown in row 16 is tautology, or p * r. Row 14 is implication, p ⊃ r, the obtained relation in the rod experiment, and row 8 is reciprocal implication, p ⊋ r, also found in the pendulum experiment. The other rows involve analogous logical operations.

For example, suppose we did an experiment and obtained the hypothetical results shown in row 2. Then, column 1 says that it is observed (T) that long (p) rods bend a lot (r), while it is not observed (F) that long (p) rods bend a little (r̄), and that short (p̄) rods bend a little (r̄) or a lot (r). In other words, all we know from the experiment is that long rods bend a great deal. This pattern of results is called "conjunction" and is written as p ∧ r. It means merely that long rods *and* great bending go together: the two occur in conjunction. While this operation seems a bit unnatural in the present context of rods and bending, there are many other situations in which conjunction makes as much sense as we hope implication does here.

Such, then, are the sixteen binary operations. We have seen how the adolescent uses three of them and have briefly reviewed what the rest are like. Now let us consider another feature of the adolescent's thought, the INRC group.

THE INRC GROUP

Thus far we have seen how the adolescent draws conclusions from the pattern of observed and nonobserved results of an experiment. These conclusions may be stated in terms of logical operations, like p * q or p ⊃ q. In other words, to this point we have been concerned with how the adolescent derives from the results of an experiment the proper logical relations among the factors involved. Each of the sixteen binary operations is a logical relation of this type. These logical relations are usually called "functions," and that is the terminology we will use here.

Following the analysis of functions, Piaget goes on to describe how the adolescent manipulates the conclusions which he has derived from an experiment. For this purpose, Piaget introduces another logical model, the INRC group. We will see how the INRC group is an attempt to specify the rules which the adolescent uses in manipulating or transforming functions. There are four such rules: identity (I), negation (N), reciprocity (R), and correlativity (C). We will consider two of them.

Reciprocity

To illustrate R, let us return to the problem of the bending rods. If you will recall, after designing the experiment properly (using the method of holding constant all factors but one), and observing the results accurately, the adolescent came to the conclusion that length was a sufficient cause of bending ($p \supset r$) and that weight was also a sufficient cause of bending ($q \supset r$). Another way of phrasing each of these statements is to say that (1) a long rod which is light will bend and (2) a heavy rod which is short will bend. In terms of our symbols, (1) may be written as $(p \wedge \bar{q}) \supset r$, and (2) may be described as $(\bar{p} \wedge q) \supset r$. To restate these functions once again, $(p \wedge \bar{q}) \supset r$ says that a rod which is long (p) and ($\wedge$) light ($\bar{q}$) implies ($\supset$) bending (r); $(\bar{p} \wedge q) \supset r$ states that a rod which is short ($\bar{p}$) and ($\wedge$) heavy (q) implies ($\supset$) bending (r). In the course of his experiments, then, the adolescent has come to the conclusions which may be described in terms of both of the propositional functions just given. (He has also come to similar conclusions about the other factors in the experiment—material, cross-section, etc.—but we shall ignore these for the moment.)

Having derived the conclusions, the adolescent discovers that in the case of each rod, one factor *compensates* for the other. (Recall our discussions of compensation in the case of conservation.) In the first rod the weight is light, but the length compensates for this and causes the rod to bend. In the second rod the length is short, but the increased weight makes up for this and produces bending. Another way of looking at the matter is as follows. Suppose we observe that a rod of a given weight and length bends a certain amount. Imagine further that we want to keep the amount of bending exactly as it is and make the length shorter. The way to do this is to increase the weight—that is, compensate for a decrease in length by an equivalent increase in weight. Or, conversely, if we want to decrease the weight while maintaining the same degree of bending, we would have to increase the length.

Thus far, the adolescent has come to conclusions about the factors causing bending in each rod, and has also noticed, again in the case of each rod separately, that one factor compensates for the other to produce a given degree of bending. In one rod, length makes up for weight—$(p \land \bar{q}) \supset r$—and in the second, weight makes up for length—$(\bar{p} \land q) \supset r$.

Next, the adolescent sees a certain relation between the compensations affecting each rod: reciprocity is involved. That is, by linking his separate conclusions about each rod, the adolescent realizes that the compensation within one rod is the reciprocal of the compensation within the other. While in one rod length makes up for the weight, the reciprocal (weight making up for length) holds in the other rod.

Piaget again states the adolescent's reasoning in logical terms. If you will recall, the functions intended to describe the adolescent's initial conclusions were $(p \land \bar{q}) \supset r$ and $(\bar{p} \land q) \supset r$. Now, to describe the adolescent's understanding of the relation *between* these conclusions, we may write $(p \land \bar{q}) = R (\bar{p} \land q)$, or a long, light rod is the reciprocal (R) of a short and heavy one. Thus, we see how two separate functions, $(p \land \bar{q})$ and $(\bar{p} \land q)$, are related to one another by means of one operation of the INRC group, namely, R, or reciprocity. This is intended to describe how the adolescent perceives relations between his conclusions.

Negation

To illustrate the rule N, consider the following study. Piaget presented the subjects with another problem from physics. Subjects were shown an apparatus in which a spring device launched balls, one at a time, across a horizontal track. The balls were of various weights and volumes. The task was to predict where the balls would stop on the track. In addition, subjects were asked to explain the results. Piaget was particularly interested in whether subjects would come to discover the principle of inertia. This states, in essence, that if no factors impede the motion of the ball, then it will forever maintain a uniform rectilinear motion; it will keep going at the same speed. Of course, under normal conditions, several factors are always present to impede movement. Friction slows the ball as a function of its weight, air resistance impedes the ball as a function of its volume, and the irregularities of the track, among other factors, hinder motion, too. The result of all these interfering factors is that one can never observe the operation of inertia in a pure state. In other words, since the real world always and unavoidably contains impediments like friction or air resistance, it is impossible to view enduring, uniform rectilinear motion. The conservation of motion by inertia is a theoretical possibility, not an empirical fact. For Piaget, the interesting problem is how the subject discovers an ideal principle which is not observable.

The adolescent goes about solving the problem in a systematic way. As we have already seen, he designs a series of experiments properly and uses the method of holding constant all factors but one. Since we have covered this matter before, we will not review it again. The adolescent's observations allow the construction of several valid statements concerning the behavior of balls on the horizontal plane. DEV (14;6), for example, concludes that a ball "stopped because the air resists . . . the bigger they are, the stronger the air resistance" (*GLT*, p. 129). He and other adolescents are successful in identifying additional factors, too—for example, that friction stops the ball. We can conclude, then, that using the experimental procedures already discussed, adolescents are able to derive legitimate causal statements about the forces impeding a ball's motion.

Once again, Piaget describes the adolescent's conclusions in terms of propositional logic. Letting p = the ball's stopping, q = the presence of friction, and r = the presence of air resistance, Piaget writes $p \supset q$ (read: stopping implies friction) and $p \supset r$ (stopping implies air resistance). The functions may be combined into $p \supset (q \vee r)$, where "$\vee$" stands for "or." Furthermore, the function can be expanded to $p \supset (q \vee r \vee s \vee t \vee \ldots)$, where s, t, and . . . indicate an indefinite number of other factors. Thus far, then, the adolescent's thought merely illustrates several of the sixteen binary propositions, again a matter we have already reviewed.

Next appears the step which is of particular interest. After coming to a conclusion which may be described by the function $p \supset (q \vee r \vee s \vee t \vee \ldots)$, "the subject asks himself what should be the result of the negation of all these factors, this negation implying a corresponding negation of statement p, that is slowing down. This is equivalent to the assertion of the continuation of motion:

$$\bar{q} \cdot \bar{r} \cdot \bar{s} \cdot \bar{t} \ldots \supset \bar{p}." \ (GLT, \text{ p. } 130).[3]$$

That is to say, the adolescent begins with conclusions concerning the stopping of motion. The conclusions may be described in terms of the function $p \supset (q \vee r \vee s \vee t \ldots)$ or stopping implies friction, and so on. Then the adolescent transforms the original function by the operation of negation, N, which is one of the INRC group. The result of this transformation is a new function, namely, $\bar{q} \wedge \bar{r} \wedge \bar{s} \wedge \bar{t} \ldots \supset \bar{p}$. The new function states the principle of inertia: it reads, the absence of friction ($\bar{q}$), and ($\wedge$) the absence of air resistance ($\bar{r}$), and ($\wedge$) the absence of all other impeding factors ($\bar{s} \bar{t} \ldots$) implies ($\supset$) the absence of stopping ($\bar{p}$). Since the precise logical rules for applying negation are rather complex, they will not be covered here. The important point is that the adolescent has used certain rules to transform the initial conclusion into yet another. This transformation allows him to discover the principle of inertia which he cannot observe in the world of fact. Without manipulating the initial conclusion, and thus going beyond the evidence provided by reality (the factors causing stopping), the adolescent could not achieve the statement of

[3]Piaget uses "." as we have used "$\wedge$." Both mean "and."

the ideal (the principle of inertia). It is the adolescent's mental operations, his reasoning, rather than his observations, which allow him to discover the ideal possibility. The operation N is simply Piaget's attempt to describe *how* the adolescent manipulates the initial conclusions to go beyond them.

Further Aspects of the INRC Group

Thus far we have discussed two operations of the INRC group: negation and reciprocity. As we have seen in the discussion of conservation in Chapter 4, negation and reciprocity are both forms of *reversibility,* that is, ways of reversing the operations of thought. Of course, the reversibility of the period of formal operations differs from that of the period of concrete operations. In the latter case, operations on concrete objects may be reversed; in the former case, operations on hypothetical propositions (functions) may be reversed.

Piaget goes on to discuss two further aspects of the INRC group, I and C, which we will only mention here. I is an identity operator: when applied to a function, I leaves it unchanged. C is more complex. Applied to a function, C changes conjunction ($\wedge$) to disjunction ($\vee$), and vice versa, but leaves everything else unchanged.

THE LOGICAL MODELS

We could go on to describe further aspects of the logical structures or models. Piaget's discussion is quite extensive and complex. It is also very technical. Piaget has a tendency to elaborate on the logical features of his models. He stresses, for instance, that the sixteen binary operations have *lattice* properties and that the INRC operations form a *group* of four transformations. We will not review these logicomathematical features of the models, since a proper exposition requires far more mathematical development than lies within the scope of this book. (For example, to define a lattice we must introduce the notions of *partially ordered set, relation,* and so on). Instead, we will offer a few general comments on Piaget's models.

First, like the groupings that were discussed in connection with concrete operational thought, the sixteen binary operations and the INRC group are *not* intended to imply that the adolescent understands logic in any explicit way. Most adolescents do not know propositional logic or group operations. Piaget does not use logic to describe the adolescent's explicit knowledge, but to depict the structure of his thought. Piaget is interested in how logical thinking *mediates* the adolescent's problem solving.

Second, the logical models are qualitative, not quantitative. The adolescent comes to conclusions like "length is involved in oscillation" or "thinness causes bending in rods." His conclusions are statements which do not involve numbers; therefore, the model of the statements must also be nonnumerical. Neither the sixteen binary operations nor the INRC group involve numbers. For example, a statement of implication might be "the addition of weight causes bending." Implication would not be expressed by a statement like, "the addition of 5 pounds causes 4 inches of bending."

Third, the logical models are intended to describe the underlying structure of adolescent activities. It is not the case that the models exactly duplicate the adolescent's performance in full detail. The models are not simply protocols which list everything that the adolescent does; instead, they are abstractions which are intended to capture the essence of his thought. For example, in one study, adolescents were required to discover the factors causing the stopping of a roulette wheel type of device. Subjects performed certain tests and made a number of verbal statements. While the details of the study are not of interest to us at the moment, we will review part of one protocol to illustrate the function of Piaget's logic.

The following operations can be distinguished in his protocol:

1. Disjunction $(p \lor q)$. . . . It's either the distance or the content (or both).
2. Its inverse, conjunctive negation $(\bar{p} \cdot \bar{q})$: changing the position of the boxes verifies the hypothesis that neither weight nor color is the determining factor.
3. Conjunction $(p \cdot q)$: both content and distance are effective.
4. Its inverse, incompatibility . . . the effect of the magnet is incompatible with moving the boxes from the center for the needle may stop without the boxes being moved and vice versa, or neither occurs. (*GLT,* p. 103)

Piaget's account continues for twelve more steps. Note that for almost everything that the adolescent says or does, there is a corresponding logical representation. Piaget is able to translate almost the entire protocol into logical form. Such logical representations have the advantage of describing the basis of the adolescent's activities in a *general way.* The logical statements go beyond the details of the particular problem and describe fundamental intellectual skills which the adolescent uses in many situations.

Fourth, like the groupings, both the system of sixteen binary operations and the INRC group are integrated systems. According to Piaget, none of the sixteen binary operations or the INRC group exists in isolation from the others. An operation like implication, for example, does not stand alone; it is part of a larger system which makes implication and other operations possible.

Fifth, like the Groupings, the formal operations describe the adolescent's *competence.* Both the sixteen binary operations and the INRC group describe the capacities of the adolescent, and not necessarily what he does on any one occasion at any one time. It may be, for example, that factors of fatigue or boredom prevent an adolescent from displaying the full extent of his capacities. The models do not describe the actual performance, which may be deficient, but define the adolescent's capability.

Sixth, the models may be said to explain and predict behavior. There is explanation in the sense that the models describe basic processes underlying the adolescent's approach to problems. We can say that the adolescent solved a particular problem *because* his thought can utilize the logical operations of implication or negation, and so forth. Such a structural description is one kind of explanation. Also, there is prediction in the sense that the models are general. That is, having knowledge of the basic structure of his intellectual activity, we can predict what his performance will be like in general terms in other, similar tasks. Since the models describe the essence of his thought, we can predict how the adolescent will operate on problems that are similar in form to the ones with which Piaget presented.

These, then, are the goals of Piaget's theory: to develop formal systems which are clear, adequately descriptive, and general. It is now possible to consider how successfully Piaget's models fulfill his stated intentions. A judgment of this type is unfortunately not a simple matter. For one thing, the models may be successful in some respects but not in others. Also, considerable knowledge of logic is necessary for a fair evaluation of the system. And finally, no model ever definitive. It is always possible to revise a given model, to state it in another language, to modify its features, and so forth. Consequently, we will limit our comments to a few points.

First, it is not entirely clear that a binary logical model is fully appropriate. (A binary model is one in which only statements involving two truth values may be made; for example, the rod is long or short, or heavy or light.) Recall that Piaget feels that one of the advantages of binary propositional logic is that it can deal with nonnumerical statements. While this feature of the model is no doubt often advantageous, there are times when it is not. Sometimes, the adolescents' methods and conclusions are not binary in the way Piaget describes. For example, in the rods problem, PEY (12;9) concluded, "The larger and thicker it is, the more it resists" (*GLT*, p. 56). Note that PEY did not deal just with large and small rods, as propositional logic demands, but with the entire continuum of size. The same is true of thickness and resistance, with the result that the conclusion applies to rods of *all* possible gradations of largeness and thickness. Thus, PEY's statement is not restricted merely to two values (long and short) of each factor. Or consider EME's behavior in the pendulum problem. To assess the role of weight, she tested first a 100 gram weight, then a 20 gram, and finally a 200 gram. Thus, the weight did not assume just the two values of heavy and light as is necessary for binary propositional logic, but rather involved a scale with three distinct values. It would seem necessary, then, to alter the model to bring it closer in line with data of this sort.[4]

Second, some authors believe that children fail to use many of the sixteen binary operations described by Piaget. Neimark (1975, p. 558) describes several studies showing that some children seem to solve the Piagetian problems without *any* hypothetico-deductive reasoning, and others use only conjunction and implication. Further research is needed in this area, for perhaps these studies did not adequately assess competence.

Third, the weight of the evidence seems to support Piaget's general characterization of adolescent thought, but does not necessarily confirm the details of his logical models. As Neimark (1975) puts it, "All of the research reviewed supports the validity of formal operational thought as an empirical phenomenon distinct from concrete operations. . . . The research does not, however, shed much light upon the precise nature of the changes or the variables which affect them" (p. 572). In brief, while Piaget's work points to some important characteristics of adolescent thought, it is not clear that the logical models accurately describe them.

GENERAL CHARACTERISTICS
OF ADOLESCENT THOUGHT

We have reviewed in some detail the adolescent's methods of problem solving, and have illustrated aspects of the sixteen binary operations and the INRC group. Until this point, the description of Piaget's theory has of necessity taken an extremely technical form, and we are aware that some readers may not have followed every p and q. Fortunately, Piaget also discusses adolescent thought in a more general way, and it is to this discussion that we now turn.

Adolescent thought may be considered in terms of several broad characteristics. First, the adolescent makes reality secondary to possibility. To understand this point, let us consider first the behavior of the younger, concrete operational child. Given the oscillation problem, the child makes various experiments and observes the results quite carefully. He may correctly judge that short pendulums swing more rapidly than long ones; or in the rods problem, he may decide quite accurately that rod A bends more than rod B, which in turn bends more than rod C, and so forth. Thus, to solve the problem the child can efficiently perform the concrete operations, as in ordering the degree of bending of rods. But there

---

[4]The reader interested in pursuing a critique of the logical aspects of the models is urged to consult an incisive paper by C. Parsons, a logician. See C. Parsons, "Inhelder and Piaget's 'The Growth of Logical Thinking'," *British Journal of Psychology*, Vol. 51 (1960), pp. 75–84. See also R. H. Ennis, "Children's Ability to Handle Piaget's Propositional Logic: A Conceptual Critique," *Review of Educational Research*, Vol. 45 (1975), pp. 1–41.

are several major deficiencies in this procedure. The child begins his experiments with little foresight and does not have a detailed plan for carrying them out. The concrete operational child does not consider all the possibilities before he begins. Instead, he is limited to thought concerning empirical results—concerning things that are available to immediate perception. He fails to make consistent use of the method of holding constant all factors but one. The part played by possibility is very small indeed; it is restricted to the simple extension of actions already in progress. After the child has ordered a set of rods in terms of the extent of their bending, for instance, he could, if given several new rods, place them in appropriate positions in the series. The concrete operational child does not consider possibilities on a theoretical plane. Instead, he works efficiently with the concrete and real and has the potentiality to do to new things what he has already done to old ones.

For the adolescent, on the other hand, possibility dominates reality. Confronted with a scientific problem, he begins not by observing the empirical results, but by thinking of the possibilities inherent in the situation. He imagines that many things *might* occur, that many interpretations of the data *might* be feasible, and that what has actually occurred is but one of a number of possible alternatives. The adolescent deals with *propositions,* not objects. Only after performing a hypothetical analysis of this sort does the adolescent proceed to obtain empirical data which serve to confirm or refute the hypothesis. Furthermore, he bases experiments on deductions from the hypothetical and therefore is not bound solely by the observed. In the pendulum problem, he might suppose that length is a causative factor, and then deduce what must occur if such a hypothesis were true. The experiment is then designed to test the deduction. Thus, the adolescent's thought, but not that of the concrete operational child, is hypothetico-deductive.

The second distinctive feature of formal operations is their "combinatorial" property. For purposes of contrast, recall again the behavior of the concrete operational child. When confronted with several factors which might influence an experimental result, the child of this stage usually tests each of them alone, but fails to consider all their combinations. On the other hand, when given the task of discovering which mixture of five colorless chemicals produces a yellow liquid, the adolescent combines them in an exhaustive way. He mixes one with two, and one with three, and one with four, and so forth, until all combinations have been achieved. This is another way, then, in which possibility dominates the adolescent's encounters with reality. If, like the concrete operational child, the adolescent had not beforehand conceived of all the possibilities, he would have designed a more limited set of experimental situations.

It can be said, then, that adolescent thought has achieved an advanced state of equilibrium. This means, among other things, that the adolescent's cognitive structures have now developed to the point where they can effectively adapt to a great variety of problems. These structures are sufficiently stable to assimilate readily a variety of novel situations. Thus, the adolescent need not drastically accommodate his structures to new problems. This does not mean, of course, that the adolescent's growth ceases at age 16. He has much to learn in many areas, and Piaget does not deny this. Piaget does maintain, however, that by the end of adolescence, the individual's ways of thinking, that is, his cognitive structures, are almost fully formed. While these structures may be applied to new problems with the result that significant knowledge is achieved, the structures themselves undergo little modification after adolescence. They have reached a high degree of equilibrium.

The adolescent's thought involves a number of additional features. First, the adolescent's thought is flexible. He has available a large number of cognitive operations with which to attack problems. Given some preliminary statements, the adolescent can manipulate them by means of the INRC group to derive definitive conclusions. This ability is completely lacking in the concrete operational child. The adolescent is versatile in thought and can deal with a problem in many ways and from a variety of perspectives. Second, the adolescent is unlikely to be confused by unexpected results because he has beforehand conceived of nearly all the possibilities. In the pendulum problem, for instance, it would not at all surprise the adolescent if it occurred that the only determinant of oscillation were the combination of weight and length with neither factor by itself being effective; this result was one of the possibilities considered. For the younger child, however, the same result might be seen as inconsistent and incomprehensible, since it contradicts the simple relationships which the child can understand. Third, the adolescent's thought is now simultaneously reversible in two distinct ways.[5] That is, he has available both the operations N and R, each of which involves a kind of reversibility. In less technical terms, this means that his thought can proceed in one direction and then use several different methods for retracing its steps to return to the starting point.

The effect of the adolescent's intellectual achievements is not necessarily limited to the area of scientific problem solving. Piaget finds repercussions of formal thought on several areas of adolescent life, although his remarks probably hold more particularly for certain subgroups within European cultures than for American culture. In the intellectual sphere, the adolescent has a tendency to become involved in abstract and theoretical matters, constructing elaborate political theories or inventing complex

---

[5]The concrete operational child has available the two forms of reversibility too, but they are not integrated into one system. Negation applies only to classes and reciprocity only to relations. See *Growth of Logical Thinking*, Chap. 17.

philosophical doctrines. The adolescent may develop plans for the complete reorganization of society or indulge in metaphysical speculation. After discovering capabilities for abstract thought, he then proceeds to exercise them without restraint. Indeed, in the process of exploring these new abilities the adolescent sometimes loses touch with reality and feels that he can accomplish everything by thought alone. In the emotional sphere the adolescent now becomes capable of directing emotions at abstract ideals and not just toward people. Whereas earlier the adolescent could love his mother or hate a peer, now he can love freedom or hate exploitation. The adolescent has developed a new mode of life: the possible and the ideal captivate both mind and feeling.

We may now make some comments concerning the actual use of the formal operations. First, as we have already mentioned, Piaget does not mean to say that the typical adolescent of the formal stage *always* employs all or some of the formal operations in scientific problem solving, but rather that he is *capable* of doing so. Various factors may prevent their use. Under conditions of fatigue or boredom, for instance, the adolescent may not fully display the organization of thought available to him. Piaget's model of formal operations describes the adolescent's optimum level of functioning, and not necessarily his typical performance.

Second, we can inquire into the generality of the formal operations. Are all adolescents capable of them? Are the formal operations universal? The evidence seems to show that they are not.[6] In Western cultures, some adolescents do not seem capable of the formal operations; in some non-Western cultures, the formal operations seem to be completely absent, even in adults.

Why this apparent lack of universality? For one thing, Piaget's original subjects may have been a rather special group. Piaget points out that his subjects were taken from the "better schools in Geneva" and that "we cannot generalize to all subjects the conclusion of our research which was, perhaps, based on a somewhat privileged population" (*Intellectual Evolution from Adolescence to Adulthood, IE,* p. 6). Presumably Piaget's subjects were both affluent and well trained in school science. Their stimulating environments and educational training may have contributed to the early development of the formal operations. Perhaps other adolescents, lacking both stimulating environments and sound education, develop intellectually at a much slower rate, with the result that the formal operations do not appear until adulthood. Furthermore, "perhaps in extremely disadvantageous conditions, such a type of thought will never really take shape" (*IE,* p. 7). This indeed may be what happens in some existing societies. In

[6]For a review of the literature, see E. Neimark, "Intellectual Development During Adolescence," in F. D. Horowitz, ed., *Review of Child Development Research,* Vol. IV (Chicago: University of Chicago Press, 1975).

brief, some adolescents may not give evidence of formal operations because an unstimulating environment slows down their rate of development or fails to promote their development entirely.

There is, however, another possible interpretation, which Piaget fa-
vors. Perhaps adolescents and adults use formal operations only in situations which are compatible with their interests and professional concerns.
As Piaget states, "All normal subjects attain the stage of formal operations
[no later than] 15 to 20 years. However, they reach this stage in different
areas according to their aptitudes and their professional specializations"
(*IE,* p. 10). Piaget points out that the experimental tasks used to investigate the formal operations were of a very special sort: they involve traditional science experiments for which Piaget's privileged children were well
prepared by their education. By contrast, other children who are less well
educated or who grow up in another culture are placed in a disadvantageous position by these special tasks. Piaget says of such less well-educated
adolescents: "They would be capable of thinking formally in their particular field, whereas faced with our experimental situations, their lack of
knowledge or the fact that they have forgotten certain ideas that are particularly familiar to children still in school or college, would hinder them
from reasoning in a formal way, and they would give the appearance of
being at the concrete level" (*IE,* p. 10).

Piaget's point is extremely important: one cannot infer the lack of
competence from a subject's failure at some conventional task which is
inappropriate to his interests or culture. One must always search for "ecologically valid" tasks which are personally relevant to the individual child
or to members of a "primitive" culture. These points are too often ignored by researchers whose methodological concerns fail to extend beyond
finding an easy way to test large numbers of subjects.

When care is taken to employ "ecologically valid" tasks, the results
are often quite surprising. Consider the following example of research on
the Kalahari Bushmen, who are expert hunters. Instead of administering
tests using the pendulum problem, two Western scientists set up a "semi-
nar" with several adult Kalahari to discuss hunting. Under these conditions, the Kalahari showed a high level of formal operational thought:

> As scientific discussions the seminars were among the most stimulating
> the Western observers had ever attended. Questions were raised and tenta-
> tive answers (hypotheses) were advanced. Hypotheses were always labeled
> as to the degree of certainty with which the speaker adhered to them, which
> was related to the type of data on which the hypothesis was based.
>
> The process of tracking, specifically, involves patterns of inference, hy-
> pothesis testing, and discovery that tax the best inferential and analytic ca-
> pacities of the human mind. Determining, from tracks, the movements of
> animals, their timing, whether they are wounded and if so how, and predict-
> ing how far they will go and in which direction and how fast, all involve

repeated activation of hypotheses, trying them out against new data, integrating them with previously known facts about animal movements, rejecting the ones that do not stand up, and finally getting a reasonable fit, which adds up to meat in the pot. (Tulkin and Konner, 1973, pp. 35, 36)

In brief, some adolescents and adults fail to show evidence of the ability to use formal operations on some tasks. This may be due to a lack of environmental stimulation which results in a slowing down or stoppage of development. Or it may be due to the use of limited testing procedures which are biased in favor of adolescents from particular backgrounds. Perhaps all adolescents can use formal operations in situations of interest to them. Piaget leans toward this last interpretation.

Finally, we may ask how the stage of formal operations is attained. Why does the child pass beyond the period of concrete operations to reach a later state of equilibrium? Piaget is not very explicit on this point, and only gives an outline of a solution. He maintains, first, that it is conceivable that neurological development occurring around the time of puberty provides the basis for the appearance of formal operations. But neurological change is not sufficient: there are cultures whose members lack formal operations but not, presumably, the requisite neurological development. Second, Piaget maintains that the social environment also plays a role. Education in school or other instruction may hasten or retard the development of formal structures. It is also true that the level of intellectual accomplishment of a given culture may affect the cognitive development of its members. But the social environment explanation is not sufficient. One cannot teach a 5-year-old formal operations: the individual must be ready for them by having developed the proper preliminary cognitive structures. In other words, the child must prepare for the development of formal operations by first developing the skills of the concrete period. A third consideration is that the individual's experience with things plays a role. If the adolescent has never had a chance to experiment with anything, he will not develop formal structures. Experience, however, is not a sufficient hypothesis to explain the attainment of formal operations. The 4-year-old and the 14-year-old, given the same experience, will not benefit from it in the same way. Fourth, and finally, the child's own activity is crucial in this development. This is the "equilibration" factor. When the child in the concrete operational period attempts to apply his intellectual methods to complex situations (for example, the scientific problems already covered), he sometimes meets with contradiction and failure. When this happens, the child attempts to resolve the contradictions, and to do so must reorganize the concrete operations. Change begins with the felt inadequacy of the current state of affairs and proceeds by a process of internal reorganization so that previous structures integrate to form new ones.

To summarize, cognitive advance occurs as a function of appropriate neurological development, a proper social environment, experience with things, and internal cognitive reorganization. We shall elaborate on Piaget's theory of development in the next chapter.

SUMMARY AND CONCLUSIONS

In the stage of formal thought, the adolescent develops the ability to imagine the possibilities inherent in a situation. Before acting on a problem which confronts him, the adolescent analyzes it and attempts to develop hypotheses concerning what *might* occur. These hypotheses are numerous and complex because the adolescent takes into account all possible combinations of eventualities in an exhaustive way. As the adolescent proceeds to test his ideas, he designs experiments which are quite efficient in terms of supporting some hypotheses and disproving others. He accurately observes the results of the experiments, and from them draws the proper conclusions. Moreover, given some conclusion, he can reason about it and thereby derive new interpretations. The adolescent's thought is now so flexible and powerful that it has reached a high degree of equilibrium. Not all adolescents succeed at the usual tests of formal operations. There are at least two possible interpretations of this fact. Perhaps some adolescents lack sufficient education and stimulation. Or perhaps, as Piaget proposes, some adolescents use the formal operations only in areas which are of personal relevance but which nevertheless are not usually measured by the conventional Piagetian tests. If the second interpretation is reasonable, then psychologists need to invent testing procedures which are attuned to the individual adolescent's concerns. Piaget describes the process of adolescent thought in terms of two logical structures or models, the sixteen binary operations and the INRC group. He believes that such models are clear and capture the essence of the adolescent's mental activities.

Piaget has made a valuable contribution to our understanding of adolescent thought. First, Piaget's findings suggest that there are basic differences between the adolescent and younger child as far as scientific reasoning is concerned. It seems clear that as age increases there is an improvement in systematic experimentation, in the design of crucial tests, in attempts to isolate variables, in the appreciation of the complexity of problems, and in the ability to draw reasonable conclusions from empirical data. Second, Piaget has made a beginning in the task of developing formal models to describe and explain the adolescent's behavior. While we have doubts as to the adequacy of the proposed logical system, it is nevertheless true that Piaget is one of the very few theorists of child development who have even attempted to construct models of this sort. Third, Piaget has made an interesting proposal concerning the role of personal interests in the development of adolescent thought. This proposal has important implications for methods of testing in both domestic and cross-cultural research.

6

Learning, Development, and Education

LEARNING AND DEVELOPMENT

We have now described the major periods of intellectual development—sensorimotor, preoperational, concrete operational, and formal operational—and the stages within them. We have postponed until now consideration of the *transition mechanisms.* Why is it that the preoperational child's thought advances to a higher level? Why does the adolescent develop formal operations? In short, what factors produce the transition from one stage to the next? Piaget feels that mental growth involves two processes: *learning in the narrow sense* and *learning in the broad sense,* or *development.* The first of these, *learning in the narrow sense,* is provoked by external events and limited to certain situations; the second, *development,* is a much wider phenomenon, with broad implications. We will begin by discussing learning and development and then turn to the four factors underlying the process of development.

The Nature of Learning and Development

For Piaget, the term "learning" may be used in two senses. *Learning in the narrow sense* involves the acquisition of new information or new responses restricted to a specific situation. (Note the parallel with *memory in the specific sense.*) For example, in school geography, the child learns the names and locations of the states and their capitols. This kind of learning is obviously specific to particular cultural contexts and is of little generality. By virtue of an accident of birth, the American child learns about the fifty states; if transported to Canada, the child would then have to learn the names of the provinces and their capitols. Learning of this type, then, is important—but it is specific and cannot be generalized.

By contrast, *learning in the broad sense,* or *development,* involves the acquisition of general thought structures which apply to many situations. (Note the parallel with *memory in the wider sense.*) For example, the child acquires some general ways of thinking about the states and their capitols. Learning in the wider sense is involved when the child develops such notions as that a state cannot be in two locations at the same time or that the United States must be larger than any individual state (class inclusion). Learning of this type involves structures which are general and which can be transferred from one situation to another. They are not taught through specific instruction.

To take another example, if the young child observes that a ball of clay repeatedly weighs the same despite changes in shape, he may learn that the weight of this particular clay ball remains constant (conservation of weight). The child may even predict that the weight will continue to be the same for any new change in the same ball. In other words, as a result of repeated empirical observations or external reinforcements, the child will have learned a law for a particular situation. This does not necessarily mean, however, that he has understood why the weight remains constant. Also, the child may be unable to generalize the law to other situations with other objects. It is only when the child develops the structures of concrete operational thought that he understands the reasons for the conservation of weight and can generalize to new situations. To summarize, specific learning may enable the child to deal with a particular problem involving weight, but learning in the wider sense, or development, is necessary for him to acquire thought structures capable of generalization. We see, then, that there are important differences between learning in the specific sense and development.

Piaget proposes that, of the two processes, development (learning in the wider sense) is the more fundamental. First, as we have already seen, development results in the acquisition of general cognitive structures as opposed to specific information or responses. Second, development makes possible meaningful learning in the specific sense. The child can appreciate the meaning of an external reinforcement or of new experiences in general only when his structures have reached a certain stage of development through the process of equilibration. The child can profit from external information—for example, reinforcement or an adult's explanation—only when his cognitive structure is sufficiently prepared to assimilate it.

Thus, information concerning the states and their capitols will only be a rote recitation unless the child understands what a capitol is and how a state relates to the country of which it is a part. Similarly, the spoken number words "one, two three . . ." are only meaningless sounds unless the child possesses some general structures of thought enabling him to understand that "one" is less than "two," and so on. Genuine learning occurs when the child has available the necessary mental equipment to make use of new experiences. When the requisite cognitive structure is present, he can learn from the world and come to understand reality; when the structure is absent, new experience has only superficial effects. If there is too great a disparity between the type of experience presented to the child and his current level of cognitive structure, one of two things is likely to happen. Either the child transforms the experience into a form which he can readily assimilate and consequently does not learn what is intended; or else he merely learns a specific response which has no strength or stability, cannot be generalized, and probably will soon disappear. It is for this reason that the child's learning, in school or out, cannot be accelerated indefinitely. There are some things he is not ready to learn because the necessary cognitive structure is not yet present. If forced to deal with such material, the child does not achieve genuine learning.

Finally, Piaget maintains that learning in the specific sense cannot account for development. As we shall see, the general cognitive structures develop through a complex process involving four factors—maturation, experience (physical and logicomathematical), social transmission, and equilibration—and consists of far more than the mechanical acquisition of new information or responses. For Piaget, learning in the specific sense cannot explain development. Instead, development explains learning.

Piaget and his colleagues in Geneva (Inhelder, Sinclair, and Bovet, 1974) have conducted a number of studies into children's learning in the broad sense and the possibility of accelerating the acquisition of various logical structures. The findings shed some light on the processes of development. The general plan of these studies was first to administer a diagnostic pretest to determine each child's developmental level. After this, the children went through a series of training sessions which presented a range of problems, each of which was designed to elicit a different cognitive operation. The aim was "to arouse a conflict in the child's mind" so that he might attempt a coordination among the various operations and thereby achieve a higher level of development. The investigators carefully observed and questioned children in conflict situations to see whether and how learning occurred. Some time later, the children were given two diagnostic post-tests, the second about four to six weeks after the first to identify the effects of training and determine whether the changes observed were long-lasting and stable.

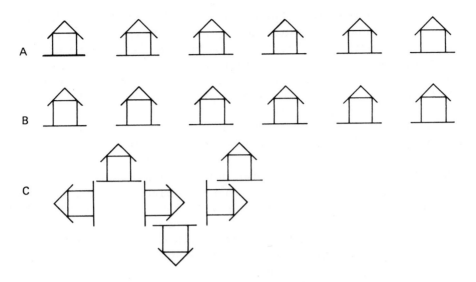

FIGURE 16   Sticks and houses.

Consider one of the Genevan studies. Children were presented with two straight lines of sticks with small houses glued onto each (see Figure 16). The lines (A and B) were identical in length and had the same number. Each child easily recognized that length and number were the same. Then as the child watched, line B was rearranged into configuration C, which obviously looks much different. The experimenter then asked a series of questions concerning both length and number: "Are there the same number of houses here as there? Is this road just as long as the other?" The aim was to place the child in conflict with respect to different aspects of the problem; the child might realize, for example, that number does not change when the configuration is transformed, but at the same time he may fail to conserve the length. If such a conflict is produced, how does the child deal with competing schemes? Does the conflict produce learning?

Through studies like these, Inhelder, Sinclair, and Bovet were able to discover fine distinctions in the learning process. In particular it appears that the learning process involves four steps. In the first, the child keeps the two modes of reasoning separate and does not realize that a conflict is involved. He says that there is the same number of houses in A and C but that A is much longer. Repeated questioning does not help the child to see the contradiction. In the second phase, the child begins to appreciate the conflict. He sees that the two roads, A and C, which he thinks are of different lengths, nevertheless have the same number of sticks in each; now the child understands that this presents something of a problem. Once the child perceives a discrepancy, he tries to reconcile it in some way. The third step involves "compromise solutions." Here, the child uses an inappropriate method to resolve the conflict. For example, he may break a stick in half so that the longer row in fact has more sticks as well! The fourth step involves a legitimate coordination of the two schemes. In the situation cited, the child sees that he must perform certain compensations; he sees, for example, that although the end points of row A go beyond those of row C, row C has more zigzags than does A and that these compensate for the overlap of A.

Inhelder, Sinclair, and Bovet make several general points about their findings. One is that the child's ability to profit from training depends on his initial developmental level. These investigators found that children in stage 1 generally progressed very little or not at all in response to training; while those at a transitional level showed considerable progress. The reason for the discrepancy is that the stage 1 children could not perceive the conflict which the training was intended to induce, while the transitional children were able to see it. According to this view, the child will not experience conflict unless his schemes are sufficiently developed. If they are not, then no amount of questioning the child or demonstrating different arrangements of objects will produce conflict and hence intellectual development. Conflict (and the resulting learning) can be provoked only when the child is ready for it. This perspective has important implications for education and we shall return to it later.

A second point is that a major form of conflict occurs when different cognitive subsystems—for example, length and number—operate simultaneously and when one of these schemes has reached a more advanced state than the other.

Third, the studies highlight the central role of the child's activity and initiative. In particular, the phenomenon of compromise solutions shows that strategies are not simply imposed on the child; rather he plays a major role in inventing them.

Fourth, the investigators summarize their findings as follows:

> [At first there is] . . . an application of existing schemes to an increasing variety of situations. Sooner or later, this generalization encounters resistance, mainly from the simultaneous application of another scheme; this results in two different answers to one problem and stimulates the subject seeking a certain coherence to adjust both schemes or to limit each to a particular application, thereby establishing their differences and likenesses. The situations most likely to elicit progress are those where the subject is encouraged to compare modes of reasoning which vary considerably, both in nature and complexity, but which all, individually, are already familiar to him. (Inhelder, Sinclair, and Bovet, 1974, p. 265)

We see, then, that development involves a conflict among existing schemes, the child's assimilation of new problems into those schemes, and a self-regulated adjustment or progression of the current modes of thought. Piaget refers to this as *equilibration,* which constitutes one of the four factors of development that we shall now discuss.

Factors Underlying Development

Maturation. As you will recall, Piaget's theory proposes that specific heredity equips the child with various physical structures which affect intellectual development. Some of these physical structures result in automatic behavioral reactions. For example, when the lips are stimulated, the baby sucks; this occurs because the appropriate reflex is activated through a "prewired" physical mechanism. The automatic behavioral reaction is a kind of "innate knowledge"; because of heredity, which reflects the evolution of the race, the baby implicitly "knows what to do" in the feeding situation. Reflexes, however, play a minor role in intellectual development. In human beings, physical structures given by specific heredity typically exert *indirect* effects on intellect. Thus, the baby is born with eyes that permit him to see only certain frequencies of light, to perceive depth, and to detect objects in front of the body but not behind. The eyes do not provide the baby with a previously written encyclopedia of knowledge—with a stock of innate ideas. Instead, they give the baby ways of knowing; they both set limits on and provide opportunities for intellectual functioning. In brief, the physical structures provided by specific heredity are organs of knowing which determine the rough outlines of intellectual growth but do not specify its content.

Consider now how maturation enters the picture. The physical structures, including the central nervous system, take time to reach their highest level of development. The brain of the newborn, for example, is smaller and lighter than that of the adolescent. It is obvious that immature physical systems often contribute to deficits in cognitive functioning. The simplest example involves motor coordination. The newborn's muscles and other structures are not sufficiently developed to permit walking. Since he cannot get around in the world, the newborn obviously can know very little about it. Other examples abound. One of the factors underlying the newborn's inability to speak is undoubtedly an underdeveloped articulatory apparatus. One of the variables producing his weakness at abstract reasoning is in all probability an insufficiently mature brain. It is clear, then, that immature physical systems can retard development.

It is also obvious that the healthy growth of physical systems contributes, at least indirectly, to intellectual advance, although the details of the process are largely unknown. When leg muscles develop, the baby becomes mobile and can learn about previously inaccessible things and events. Also in infancy, "the coordination between grasping and vision seems to be clearly the result of the myelinization of certain new nerve paths in the pyramidal tract" (Piaget, "Problems in Equilibration,"

1977b, p. 7). In the most general sense, as the brain and the central nervous system mature, they make it possible for the child to use thought and language. In Piaget's view, the question is not *whether* maturation has an effect, but how *important* the role of maturation is and *how* it operates. Some years ago Gesell proposed that maturation is the chief factor explaining development. According to this hypothesis, the process of physical maturation is the most important and direct influence on all aspects of psychological functioning. Piaget feels that this position is too extreme for several reasons.

One is our lack of understanding of the maturation of the central nervous system. How can one base a theory on maturation when so little is known about it? Second, it is clear that maturation does not explain everything. For example, children in Martinique reach the concrete operational stage about four years later than do children in Switzerland. It would seem unlikely that Swiss children's brains are four years more mature than those of the children in Martinique. A much more likely explanation is that cultural factors contribute heavily to the differences in development. In Piaget's view, then, physiological maturation undoubtedly affects cognitive development—often in ways we do not understand—but it is not the only factor.[1]

Experience. A second influence on development is contact with the environment. To acquire the notion of object permanence, the infant must obviously experience things disappearing and reappearing. To classify objects, the child must first perceive them. To speak a language, the infant must hear people talking. Piaget feels that contact with the environment leads to two types of knowledge: *physical* and *logicomathematical*. On the one hand, *physical experience* leads to the knowledge of *observables*. Observables refers to the properties and characteristics of objects, such as shape, color, size, and so on, that are perceived by a person. Physical knowledge of observables is obtained by a process of *empirical abstraction* (called *simple abstraction* in Piaget's early works). The child encounters an apple and, through perceptual activity, "pulls out" or abstracts some of its properties. Now the child "knows" that it is round and that it is red. Or he lifts a block, and in the process discovers that it is heavy. If, however, he lifts two blocks and notes that one is heavier than the other, this would no longer be purely physical knowledge. By comparing the two blocks, he has created a relationship of "more" or "less" heavy that is not given directly in the blocks themselves. This second type of knowledge is

[1]Lenneberg has proposed a sophisticated theory of maturation to explain the development of language. This theory, which is far superior to Gesell's, is in many respects congruent with Piaget's and deserves to be taken seriously indeed. See E. H. Lenneberg, *Biological Foundations of Language* (New York: John Wiley & Sons, Inc., 1967).

logicomathematical. In physical experience, then, a child uses empirical abstraction to extract directly from the objects themselves a knowledge of their physical properties.

Piaget makes several points about physical knowledge.[2] One is that it is a major influence on development: there is a "vast category of knowledge acquired by means of the experience of external objects" (*Biology and Knowledge, BK,* p. 335). A good part of intellectual development is learning what things are really like.

Second, the process of obtaining physical knowledge involves more than just empirical abstraction. Piaget maintains that "It is impossible for there to be direct and immediate contact between subject and objects. . . . Any kind of knowledge about an object is always an assimilation into schemes" (*BK,* p. 335). The data of experience are always interpreted in terms of a larger intellectual framework of schemes, concepts, and relationships. The child does not simply perceive the properties of a particular apple in isolation. Rather, he perceives and understands them in relation to all the other apples he has known. A particular apple is perceived as "red" as a result of its assimilation to the conceptual scheme of apples, of which redness is one characteristic. Implicit comparisons with other (more or less red) apples experienced in the past give meaning to the redness of this particular apple. But the action of comparing similarities and differences between a present object and a scheme that has been constructed on the basis of past experiences calls for more than empirical abstraction alone.

> The abstraction of any information from an object . . . requires the use of tools of assimilation of a mathematical nature: relationships, one or several classes (or action "schemes" at the sensorimotor level, which are already a type of practical concept), correspondences, functions, identities, equivalences, differences, etc. . . . Clearly, these tools . . . are not extracted from the objects. They are therefore due to the person's own activities. (*Adaptation Vitale et Psychologie de L'Intelligence, AV,* p. 82, trans. by the authors)

In brief, physical knowledge, or the knowledge of observables, is essential to development, but can only be built up within a larger framework because it requires certain mental tools which have been created by means of previous logicomathematical experience.

Logicomathematical experience involves knowledge acquired from reflection on one's own actions, not from the objects themselves. The con-

---

[2]Piaget himself has given relatively little attention to physical experience, despite his estimate of its importance. In developmental psychology, this topic is usually treated under the rubric of perceptual development, and the most important theory in the area is E. J. Gibson's. See E. J. Gibson, *Principles of Perceptual Learning and Development* (Englewood Cliffs, N.J.: Prentice-Hall, Inc., 1969).

FIGURE 17   Two sets.

cept of logicomathematical experience is a difficult one, and we shall now try to explain it by means of an example.

Suppose that a child encounters two sets of objects, as in Figure 17. Set A is arranged in a straight line and set B in a circle. The child examines the sets, accurately perceiving that each element is a square, that one set is arranged in a line, and the other in a circle. This is the child's *physical experience* of the sets, and it yields accurate knowledge concerning certain properties of shape, form, and layout. But, while essential, physical knowledge alone does not tell the child something very crucial about the sets: regardless of surface appearance, they have the same number. To gain this knowledge, the child requires a different kind of experience, *logicomathematical experience,* in which knowledge is not a direct result of perceiving objects, but of reflecting upon actions performed on objects. To illustrate the logicomathematical factor, Piaget cites a friend's childhood experience. At the age of about 4 or 5 years,

> he was seated on the ground in his garden and he was counting pebbles. Now to count these pebbles he put them in a row and he counted them one, two, three up to 10. Then he finished counting them and started to count them in the other direction. He began by the end and once again found he had 10. He found this marvelous. . . . So he put them in a circle and counted them that way and found 10 once again. (Piaget, 1964, p. 12)

Through repetitions of counting and recounting, of arranging and rearranging, the child grasped an important property of number: it stays the same despite different orders of counting and despite differing physical arrangements.

How did this learning take place How did the child come to know something about the equivalence of number? Piaget maintains that empirical abstraction was not sufficient to produce this knowledge. In a sense, the child learned nothing about pebbles: he already knew that they are small, dark, smooth objects. The physical properties of the pebbles were known, and they did not ''say'' anything to the child about number.

In Piaget's view, the child learned about number not through direct physical experience with the pebbles themselves, but by considering his own actions. A process of *reflective abstraction* (as opposed to *empirical abstraction*) is involved. The child first notices one of his own actions. In this case, he sees that he has counted the row in one direction, getting 10, and that he has counted the row in the opposite direction, also getting 10. This perception of his own actions interests the child; it surprises him. Next, "the action noted has to be 'reflected' (in the physical sense of the term) by being projected onto another plane—for example, the plane of thought as opposed to that of practical action" (*BK,* p. 320). The child reflects (transposes) his action of counting to the plane of thought. This is one way that the process is reflective.

It is reflective in another way too. Reflecting an action onto another level calls for a reorganization of mental structures to integrate the new action with those already existing at this level. This process of reorganization establishes new relationships and new meanings not found at the lower level. For example, the child has to relate the counting of the pebbles to the action of increasing quantity. Counting to 10 always gives more objects than counting to 9. He has to relate the counting to the concept of sequencing: 5 is always counted after 4 and before 6. Counting must also be related to the notion of invariance of number. He sees that if he can count the objects in various ways and always get the same result, they must be the same number. In a sense, the child defines numerical equivalence in terms of his own actions. In reorganizing his actions of counting, he reflects on them, or contemplates his own actions, and comes to appreciate their wider implications and significance. In sum, reflective abstraction is "reflected" in two ways. The first consists of a projection, or reflection, of actions onto a higher level, and the second consists of a reflection upon and reorganization, or reworking, of both the projected and previous actions into a new and broader understanding.

In his later work, Piaget introduces a third type of abstraction, *pseudoempirical abstraction*. Pseudoempirical abstraction is found during the initial stages of the formation of logicomathematical knowledge, when the young child needs to use concrete objects as a support for such knowledge. The counting of pebbles is an example of pseudoempirical abstraction. Here the knowledge is not abstracted from the pebbles, and thus is not physical experience, but is attributed to them. The child could just as well have gained the understanding of number conservation from another set of objects, although some type of object is necessary at this beginning level. Later, when the child has gained sufficient mastery of counting, he will not need the pebbles, or his fingers, or any other objects as a support, and the abstraction will become truly reflective. Pseudoempirical abstraction is, therefore, a primitive form of reflective abstraction that occurs during the early part of the concrete operational period.

There are several notable aspects of logicomathematical experience. First, it relies on physical experience, although it goes beyond it. In the example cited, a child could not have discovered numerical equivalence if he had not accurately perceived the pebbles. Yet perception of the pebbles—physical experience—in itself was not sufficient, and had to be supplemented by reflection of and on the actions of counting. Second, logicomathematical experience results in harmony with the environment. As the child's physical knowledge becomes more accurate, his actions, and hence his logicomathematical knowledge, construct an increasingly objective interpretation of the real world. While the richness "of the subject's thought processes depends on the internal resources of the organism, the efficacy of these processes depends on the fact that the organism is not independent of the environment, but can only live, act, or think in interaction with it" (BK, p. 345).

Although different in nature, physical and logicomathematical knowledge are closely intertwined, particularly during the early years. In physical knowledge, the source of knowledge is exogenous or external to the person. It is in the object, or at least those aspects of the object that are perceived by the person. Piaget calls these aspects the *observables*. Observables, such as shape, color, or size, form the *content* of physical knowledge. However, this type of knowledge is extracted within a framework of mental instruments—schemes, concepts, and so on—that have been created by an endogenous or internal source, that of reflective abstraction. These instruments constitute the *form* of physical knowledge. In logicomathematical knowledge, the source of knowledge is endogenous and is found in the coordinations of the person's own actions, although at first the objects of the external world serve as the basis for this knowedge, as in the process of pseudoempirical abstraction. With development, logicomathematical knowledge becomes more and more removed from reality, as reflective abstraction continually leads to the construction of new operations, and of operations upon operations. The formal theories of logic, mathematics, or physics are examples of logicomathematical knowledge as it functions in a "pure" state. But, at the same time as becoming more detached from physical reality, logicomathematical knowledge provides conceptual tools which are able to grasp a deeper and more profound understanding of the physical environment.

Both physical and logicomathematical experience are important, but Piaget feels that they are not sufficient to explain development. One reason is because they omit social factors.

Social transmission.   A third factor influencing cognitive development is *social transmission*. This phrase is used in a very broad sense to refer to the influence of the culture on the child's thought. Social transmission may refer to a parent explaining some problem to a child, or to a child's obtaining information by reading a book, or to a teacher giving instruction in a class, or to a child discussing a question with a peer, or to a child's imitation of a model. Certainly, the social transmission of knowledge promotes cognitive development. The accumulated wisdom of a culture passes down from generation to generation, and enables the child to learn through the experience of others. Because of social transmission, the child need not completely reinvent everything for himself. The culture provides him with extraordinary cognitive tools—the counting numbers, a language, an alphabet. These tools enable him to do mathematics, to speak, to write—in sum, to participate in higher intellectual activities, particularly those of a literate nature.

But social transmission itself is not sufficient. Unless the child is prepared to understand the cultural wisdom, social transmission will not be effective. In other words, to appreciate the knowledge passed on by other individuals, the child must possess cognitive structures which can assimilate it. The 5-year-old cannot learn the calculus, however well it is transmitted, because he does not have the prerequisite structures.

Some American and Russian psychologists have proposed that one specific type of social factor, namely, the child's own language, is vital for the development of behavior and thought. In very general terms, their thesis is that at about the age of 4 or 5 years the child uses internal speech to control and organize his activities. Language "mediates" between external events and the child's response. Without an internal linguistic system, the child's responses are directly contingent upon external events; but with such a system the child can represent external events, delay responding to them, and can thereby control his own behavior.

Piaget's view, very different from the foregoing, attributes a lesser role to language. Piaget does not accept the proposition that language is the sole or primary device by which the child forms mental representations of external events. Representation takes many forms—mental imagery, symbolic play, drawing—in addition to language. Thus, mental images are often nonverbal. At 18 months of age, the infant has images of things and events even though he can hardly speak. According to Piaget, the infant's images and other representations derive from imitating persons and things and not from language. In brief, the representational function, and generally, the figurative aspect of thought, need not involve or depend on language.[3]

Piaget believes that the operative aspect of thought also need not involve language. In the case of classification, we have seen that the preoperational child in stage 1 cannot produce a hierarchical arrangement of objects and does not understand inclusion relations. This is so despite the

---

[3]Today, many psychologists are coming to agree with Piaget's thesis that thought shapes language far more than language shapes thought. See, for example, J. McNamara, "Cognitive Basis of Language Learning in Infants," *Psychological Review,* Vol. 79 (1972), pp. 1–13.

fact that the child can use all of the relevant words involved. He can say "blue triangles," or "red circles," or "more of these," or "some of these." Even though the language is available, the preoperational child cannot classify. This is not, however, to assert that language plays no role in the development of classification or other mental operations. For example, the presence of nouns in the language may stimulate the child to think in terms of discrete classes. Also, the ability to verbalize a thought structure, like class inclusion, may help to consolidate and generalize it. Nevertheless, for Piaget, thought involves more than language and is not dependent upon it.

This proposition is reinforced by the research of Sinclair (reported in Inhelder, Sinclair, and Bovet, 1974). She began by examining the language of two separate groups of young children, some of whom were unable to solve conservation problems and some of whom were successful. She found a correlation between the ability to conserve and the ability to talk about it. The conserving children used phrases comparing the variables, saying, for example, that one glass of water is "tall and thin," while the other is "short and fat." The nonconserving children, on the other hand, used "undifferentiated terms" to describe the situation; they said, for example, that one glass of water is "big" and the other is "fat." It would appear then—perhaps contrary to Piaget's views—that conservers and nonconservers are characterized by different types of linguistic ability.

But does the use of complex language cause the ability to conserve? To discover the answer to this question, Sinclair taught the nonconserving children to use the language of the conservers in describing the various problems. If language is crucial for conservation, these children should then have been able to conserve. Yet the results showed that they could not: the benefits of language training were quite limited. It appears, then, that language does not enable the child to conserve. In fact, the opposite seems true: the development of the thought structures underlying conservation enables the child to employ sophisticated forms of language to describe what he does and understands.

Further evidence supporting this proposition derives from Opper's (1979) research in Thailand. The Thai language contains certain built-in terms called "classifiers," which signify that an object is part of a higher-order class. Thus the word for *lotus* specifies both that the object is that particular flower known as a lotus *and* that it belongs to the larger class of flowers. The language itself virtually announces class inclusion. The question then becomes whether children exposed to such a language acquire class inclusion at a younger age than usual. Opper found that they did not. Despite the presence of linguistic mechanisms which would supposedly facilitate this development, Opper's work showed that Thai children did not acquire class inclusion earlier than Swiss children, whose mother tongue does not contain such mechanisms. This evidence also seems to support Piaget's proposition that thought involves more than language and that the former is not fully shaped by the latter.[4]

Consider now the role of formal schooling: Is this kind of social transmission crucial for intellectual development? Some psychologists believe that it is. Some years ago, on the basis of research in West Africa, Greenfield (1966) proposed that the Western style of schooling is necessary for the development of the stages of thought as described by Piaget. The main evidence for this assertion was the discovery that school children in Senegal did achieve the period of concrete operations, as judged from a test of conservation, whereas those children not in school remained at a lower level of thought. While this is an intriguing finding, the evidence in this area is by no means clear-cut. Some studies are directly contradictory, showing that schooling is not necessary for the development of concrete operations (Ashton, 1975; Dasen, 1972). At the present time, the weight of the evidence seems to support the Piagetian view that schooling, like other forms of social transmission, may accelerate intellectual development but is not necessary for it. Apparently, individuals growing up in "primitive" societies without schools nevertheless develop the basic thought structures described by Piaget. Perhaps the failure of some researchers to obtain this finding can be attributed to problems of measurement in strange cultures, where Western testing techniques and testing materials are often inappropriate. In any event, Piaget's view is that schooling and other forms of social transmission can contribute to intellectual growth but do not fully determine it.

Equilibration. A fourth factor affecting development is *equilibration*,[5] which in a way integrates the effects of the other three factors, none of which is sufficient in itself to explain mental development. Equilibration refers to the child's self-regulatory processes, by which he progressively attains higher levels of equilibrium throughout development. The equilibration process is the backbone of mental growth.

Let us begin by reviewing the concept of equilibrium. Piaget has borrowed this notion from physics and biology and has modified it to apply to human intelligence. The concept of equilibrium, which is not novel in psychology, refers to a state of balance or harmony between at least two

---

[4]These assertions concerning the role of language have not gone unchallenged. Beilin (1977) in particular has demonstrated that training in verbal rules can accelerate the pace of conservation, and in an address ("Language and Thought: Thistles Among the Sedums," Piaget Society, 1977) has elaborated on the role of language in the development of thinking.

[5]Piaget revised his concept of equilibration on several occasions. The present description is based on his last revision contained in works written between 1970 to 1980 and in particular in *The Equilibration of Cognitive Structures* (1985).

elements which have previously been in a state of disequilibrium. Freud, for example, makes use of a similar principle when he states that a person tends toward a release of tension. For Piaget (unlike Freud) equilibrium does not have the connotation of a static state of repose between a closed system and its environment. Rather, equilibrium, when applied to intellectual processes, implies an active balance or harmony. It involves a system of exchanges between an open system and its surroundings. The child is always active, and does not merely receive information from his environment like a sponge soaking up water. Rather, the child attempts to understand things, to structure experience, and to bring coherence and stability to the world. A cognitive system is never at rest, it continually interacts with the environment. The system attempts to deal with environmental events in terms of its structures (assimilation), and it can modify itself in line with environmental demands (accommodation). When in equilibrium, the cognitive system need not distort events to assimilate them, nor does it need to change very much to accommodate to new events.

Although the concept of equilibrium was taken from physics, Piaget stresses that physical and cognitive equilibrium are very different. Physical equilibrium seeks to maintain the stability of the system without change. Disequilibrium is overcome by a movement in the opposite direction which restores the original state of equilibrium. A thermostat, for example, maintains equilibrium by compensating for increases or decreases in heat with actions that restore the system to the original temperature. With intellectual development, however, there is both stability and change. Cognitive systems, as they progress, preserve past intellectual achievements but at the same time create new actions and novel responses which allow the person to gain more understanding. Equilibrium results from regulations that tend toward better forms of knowledge. There is an increase in knowledge rather than a return to an original state, and this requires a dynamic model of equilibrium. "It would not do, then, to conceive of equilibration as a simple process toward equilibrium since it always involves construction oriented toward *better* equilibrium" (*Equilibration of Cognitive Structures, ECS*, p. 26).

For Piaget, cognitive development consists of a succession of alternating equilibria and disequilibria. Each successive level of equilibrium reaches a better form of knowledge through the addition and reorganization of cognitive elements. These quantitative and qualitative changes result in new relationships, new understandings, and the solving of certain problems, but also open up the possibility of new questions and problems, of new imbalances and disequilibria. To reconcile both the stability and the changes that occur in cognitive development and to emphasize the dynamic aspect of this process, Piaget refers to it as *optimizing equilibration (équilibration majorante)*. Optimizing equilibration is the process that leads to the successive improvements in equilibrium that occur with development. Each new equilibrium becomes more powerful in its ability to comprehend the physical characteristics and relationships of the objects in the environment, and also to attribute causal, logical, and mathematical properties to them.

Piaget describes three types of equilibrium, all of which contribute toward achieving a balance between the person and his environment. The first is the equilibrium between a person and an object or event of the environment. Here the person encounters an object, assimilates it to a scheme, and accommodates the scheme to the particular object. If the scheme is appropriate, there is equilibrium; if not, there will be disequilibrium. A child who only has schemes for apple and oranges would have no trouble when encountering instances of these fruits, but would be in disequilibrium when presented with her first experience of a pineapple. This type of equilibrium depends upon the interaction between a person and the environment, that is, between assimilation and accommodation.

Another type of equilibrium is between the various cognitive subsystems. Here, the equilibrium is internal rather than external. Examples of this can be found in the research by Inhelder and colleagues into learning, discussed in the previous section, which indicated that very often the lack of understanding of a problem is caused by an imbalance due to differences in the speed of acquisition of different cognitive subsystems. For example, at a certain stage of development the child's acquisition of the subsystem of number is in advance of that of length and this creates a disequilibrium. Only when the two subsystems reach the same level and are in equilibrium is the child able to understand conservation of length problems. Assimilation and accommodation are also involved in this second type of equilibrium, but they are carried out internally by means of reciprocal assimilation and accommodation of the various cognitive subsystems.

A third type of equilibrium is between an overall cognitive system and its component subsystems, that is, between the whole and its parts. The overall system, by integrating the various elements, assumes various properties of its own which are not found in the individual subsystems. These subsystems do not cease to exist by virtue of being integrated, but continue to retain their own specific characteristics and thus be differentiated from each other. One example is the hierarchical class inclusion of animals. The category of animals integrates the various subcategories of lions, tigers, cats, dogs, and so forth. It incorporates certain characteristics of each of these, but has a broader application than any of them. The subcategories are clearly differentiated from each other even though they may have certain characteristics in common. The intension and extension of the class of animals does not duplicate entirely those of any of the subclasses, just as the intension and extension of each of these is distinct from those of any other subclass. Another example is the coordination at the level of formal operations of the two earlier types of reversibility, negation and reciprocity, within the overall INRC system. The INRC group provides more possibilities than either of the two types of reversibility encountered earlier in development although these continue to exist as distinct processes even when they have become integrated into the INRC system. This third type of equilibrium is between the processes of integration and differentiation, but also involves assimilation and accommodation. Integration is accomplished by assimilation, whereas accommodation is responsible for differentiation.

One fundamental question regarding the dynamics of this process of optimizing equilibration is this: What are the transition mechanisms that enable the progression from one level of equilibrium to another more powerful type of cognitive structure? Piaget believes that a major factor is reflective abstraction in its dual forms of projection and reorganization. Piaget also proposes some more specific principles to explain conceptual development: *differentiation and integration,* the *relativization of concepts,* and the *quantification of relations.*

Differentiation and integration are two complementary processes that play a major role in conceptual development. Differentiation is the process of constructing new schemes or elements on the basis of existing ones so as to meet the requirements of experience. As a result, finer and finer distinctions are made between and within schemes or concepts. Integration is the process of establishing links or connections between these elements so as to maintain their unity.

When faced with a familiar object or experience for which he already has a scheme available, the child uses this scheme to assimilate the familiar experience. If, however, he encounters a novel object or event, for which existing schemes are inadequate, a new scheme will need to be constructed. This new scheme will either be derived from an existing one that bears some similarity to the new experience, or may result from the reciprocal assimilation of two or more schemes that separately contain the characteristics of this experience. The new differentiated schemes that are created do not exist in isolation, but become related to, or integrated with, existing schemes into higher-order ones. By introducing new relationships and characteristics to concepts, differentiation and integration allow for the subsequent assimilation of more varied experiences and hence open up the possibility for further differentiation and integration.

Differentiation and integration are closely related to the intension and extension of concepts. Recall that the intension of a class or concept refers to the characteristics or properties of that class. For Piaget, this means the actions that a person can carry out, or the schemes that a person has available, relating to that class. The intension of an apple refers to the available schemes of red, round, or sweet. Extension refers to the members of the class, its field of application, or the objects to which these schemes apply. In the child, or in an adult for that matter, intension and extension are not static. On the contrary, they are constantly changing as the result of experience, and it is the processes of differentiation and integration that underly these changes. The first characteristics to be differentiated are the obvious superficial aspects of the physical environment that can be directly perceived. These refer to physical experience. Gradually, as the child reflects on his experiences of these objects, he goes beyond merely apprehending observable characteristics to draw inferences from them. Since inferences are processes of a logicomathematical nature, differentiation and integration now occur within a logicomathematical framework. Thus, knowledge moves from the periphery to the center of objects, from exogenous to endogenous processes. In this way differentiation and integration lead to an increasingly complex and deeper understanding of the world.

The development of the "cat" concept can serve as an illustration. For the very young child, the concept of "cats" initially refers to the actual cats that he encounters at home, in his neighborhood, or even in stories. At this stage his cat scheme is very general, and indeed there is often an overgeneralization of schemes. Its intension might be something with four legs, a tail, and fur, and its extension may even include squirrels, badgers, or other four-legged creatures with a tail and fur. With additional experience of cats of different colors such as ginger, black, or tabby, or with different eye colors, blue, green, or yellow, he will construct or differentiate subschemes of cats to account for these differences. Each subscheme has its own characteristics distinct from the others, but they are all interrelated and integrated within the overall scheme of cats.

Such differentiation and integration could continue indefinitely, depending upon the experiences, interests, and motivation of the person. The child starts with their physical characteristics or the actions that can be taken with cats, such as stroking or feeding. Later, the person considers features such as breed, personality traits, or genes that are not directly observable and require inferences. Thus a judge at a cat show, who needs to go far beyond just a superficial knowledge of the observable characteristics of cats, would have a highly differentiated and integrated concept of cats.

Piaget refers to this increasingly wide network of relations or links that are established between schemes and their elements by means of differentiation and integration as the *relativization of concepts*. The child initially understands objects, situations, or events in terms of a limited number of broad, undifferentiated categories or schemes. As she begins to create additional subschemes or elements to account for new differentiated characteristics, she establishes relationships and interdependencies between these elements. With an increased number of elements comes an

increase in the number of compositions, and hence of possible interrelationships between them. These relationships may cover the observable
characteristics of actions and objects, their physical features such as shape,
size, or color. Or they may cover *coordinations,* that is, inferences drawn
from the person's actions that construct spatial, causal, and logicomathematical relationships with other objects in the environment. The relativization of concepts underlies a movement from an initial, superficial, and
undifferentiated understanding of an object to a deeper and more varied
grasp of its various properties, functions, and relationships.

Consider the seriation of sticks task as an example of relativization.
The very young child divides the sticks into the two broad undifferentiated
schemes of "large" and "small." Relationships both within and between
the schemes are somewhat limited. The slightly older child begins to distinguish more characteristics of length and creates a new scheme of "me-
dium size." Already more relations need to be constructed because of the
larger number of schemes. Later the child will be able to seriate the sticks,
first, in a trial-and-error fashion, and then more systematically. When the
seriation is finally grasped, the child is able to set up relations and interdependencies between every element. Each of the sticks becomes linked or
related to every other one in an ordered system of graded lengths ranging
from shortest to longest.

One type of relation that the child slowly constructs is quantification.
The *quantification of relations* refers to the child's progressive move from an
initial focus on the qualitative features of a concept to reasoning on its
quantitative aspects. For example, in seriation, the young child first focuses on the qualities of "bigness" or "smallness." All the elements in the
"large" category are viewed as being similar to each other, they are all
large and different from those in the "small" one. The construction of a
third "middle-sized" category is still a qualitative approach, although it is
a move toward quantification. The addition of the middle calls for comparisons among the three categories in which the child focuses more specifically on, and becomes more sensitive to, the differences in length between the sticks.

With increasing sensitivity to these differences, the child comes to
recognize that, even within each category, the sticks are perhaps not quite
as similar as first believed. Indeed, there are differences among the various "large" sticks. Eventually, the child understands that all the sticks are
related in a quantifiable manner. Each stick, when compared with the others, is a little more, or less, "long" or "short." They are all now viewed as
variations along the single dimension of length. The implication is that the
child has now constructed a continuum with unlimited possibilities of including not only actual objects presented, but also any other possible variation along that same continuum. For example, the child could envisage

the possibility of including sticks that will never actually be presented but are only mentally conceived.

This continuum is a logicomathematical construction of which the actual sticks presented form only one part. Furthermore, at this point, the child also understands that "more" and "less" are reciprocally related. As the sticks become longer, or "more long," they also become "less short." A move in the positive direction of "more long" implicitly involves a corresponding move in the opposite, negative direction of "less short."

For purposes of simplicity, the present example has concentrated on the quantification of a single property, the "long-short" dimension of length. In real life, of course, the situation is far more complex. Objects vary along a number of dimensions. Apples are never identical. Each individual apple can be quantified along a number of dimensions: size, color, texture, sweetness, to name but the most obvious characteristics. All these differences can be placed along quantifiable continua that do not necessarily develop at the same pace. As quantification proceeds for these various differences, it allows for the possibility of an increasing number of relationships, and in this way not only contributes toward a more objective understanding of reality, but also toward better and better forms of equilibrium.

Inevitably, the study of equilibration and the successive levels of equilibrium along the path of development leads to the reverse of the coin, disequilibrium. As Piaget states, the existence of any positive instance necessarily implies the existence of its negation. Consequently the study of equilibrium leads to the study of disequilibrium. Piaget holds that disequilibrium is of crucial importance in the process of equilibration, since it is the prime motor of intellectual development. Disequilibrium motivates the search for better forms of knowledge, and thus provides the link between one level of equilibrium and the next.

Disequilibrium, or imbalance, occurs when a person encounters an object or event that he is unable to assimilate due to the inadequacy of his cognitive structures. In such situations, there is a discrepancy or a conflict between the child's schemes and the requirements of the experience. This is accompanied by feelings of unease. Piaget refers to this situation as a disturbance, perturbation, or conflict. Generally speaking, a disturbance is anything that prevents the person from assimilating an experience or achieving a goal. Since assimilation is involved in disturbances, and assimilation always occurs relative to an assimilatory scheme, the concept of disturbance is a relative one. What may be a disturbance to one person, because of the nature and type of schemes available, may not be so for another person, either because his schemes are not sufficiently developed for him even to perceive the event as disturbing, or because his schemes are so well organized that a particular event or experience is rapidly assimilated. In the conservation of liquids task, the very young child states with no feeling of unease or conflict that there is more liquid when it is poured into a tall thin container than when it is in a short fat one. For him, the situation is not disturbing. This same situation will, however, produce conflict in the slightly older child, who feels unease at stating that the same water is more, or less, depending upon the shape of the container. The even older child again feels no conflict because he can explain the situation in a logical way.

When faced with a disturbance, the person reacts with responses that attempt to regulate the conflict. These responses, or *regulations,* will differ depending upon what schemes are available. In most of the studies carried out in Geneva, three types of reactions to disturbances have been found, and Piaget calls them *alpha, beta,* and *gamma.*

Alpha reactions are generally found in the very young preoperational child who often, because he does not perceive the event as disturbing, simply ignores it. If he perceives it at all, it would be as a minor disturbance that requires only slight modification of his structures. On the other hand, he may deform the event completely so as to fit his schemes. In both cases, very little change occurs to the cognitive system. Alpha reactions, therefore, either modify the disturbing element so as not to interfere with existing cognitive structures or ignore the conflict altogether. The young child who has only schemes for squares and circles may assimilate a novel shape such as a triangle into the square scheme, thereby completely deforming the experience. Similarly, a child who, during the early stages of language development, refers to all animals as ''dogs,'' is not disturbed by feelings of unease. She assimilates all four-legged creatures into her underlying scheme of dogs, regardless of the extent to which reality is deformed to do this.

With *beta reactions,* which are usually found during the later preoperational and concrete operational stages, the child seeks to incorporate the conflicting event into his current cognitive system. To do this, he modifies and reorganizes this system so as to take account of the disturbance. The child of this level not only distinguishes circles from squares, but will create new schemes when he encounters triangles, rectangles, and so on. The disturbance introduces variations into the system by causing new schemes to be created that will exist alongside the original ones. The variations are partial because the child is able to create only a limited number of new schemes or subcategories. Beta reactions are nevertheless an improvement on alpha ones because they attempt to adapt the system to disturbances perceived in the environment.

Finally, *gamma reactions* are found at the formal operational level. Here the person constructs a system that allows him to anticipate all possible variations by means of inferences. The system becomes a closed one and the likelihood of disturbance is reduced. The original disturbing element becomes one possible variation within a whole system of possible transformations. The child at this level can anticipate the possibility of all sorts of shapes, both regular and irregular, even before he actually perceives them.

The alpha, beta, and gamma reactions are not necessarily confined to particular stages of development. Piaget believes that the same types of reactions are to be found in any area of knowledge, so that if an adult were exposed to a totally new topic, she too would exhibit the same sequence of alpha, beta, and finally gamma reactions when she masters the relevant knowledge.

In sum, disequilibrium, a major cause of cognitive development, is caused by disturbances, perturbations, or conflicts that occur when there is a discrepancy between the child's schemes, which determine what she is able to assimilate, and the requirements of certain experiences. Disequilibrium is relative to the child's developmental level. The child reacts to the conflict by regulations which Piaget categorizes as alpha, beta, or gamma, depending upon the schemes available.

Contradictions.   Closely related to cognitive conflict and disequilibrium is the notion of contradiction (see Piaget, *Experiments in Contradiction,* 1981a). One example is the conservation of liquids task, where liquid appears to be more when in a tall thin container than in a short fat one. The person starts to question this contradiction and, to resolve it, tries to discover its reasons or causes. In an attempt to explore the nature of contradiction and relate it to the equilibration process, Piaget and his colleagues have carried out a number of studies in this area.

In one of the tasks, the children were presented with a series of seven disks, referred to as A to G, each of which was imperceptibly larger than the previous one. The disks were attached to a board so that any single one could only be compared with those immediately before and after it. Thus disk A could be compared with B, B with C, and so on. The last and largest disk, G, was not attached, and could be compared with any other disk of the series. Since each disk was only very slightly larger than the previous one, the difference between each of the six attached disks was imperceptible, although it was evident that G was larger than A. The child was asked to explain the contradictory situation of an apparent equality between the first six disks, A = B, B = C, and so on, and the nonequality between G and A.

In this and other studies of the same nature, three stages were found in the child's understanding of contradiction. During an initial stage, the young child is not aware that there might be any contradiction in the situation, in this case of admitting that the first six disks are equal, that F is equal to G, and that G is larger than A. He also appears to feel no unease at stating at one point in the interview that F is the same size as G and later at another point that G is larger than F. Either he forgets his former statement, or he does not relate the two statements together, and thus does not recognize the contradiction. Children who remember their previous statements attempt to reconcile the contradiction but do so with inappropriate actions. Some of them say that G is the same as F, that F is the same as A, and that G is larger than A. As we have seen in the previous section, these are alpha reactions.

At the same time as exhibiting a lack of awareness of many contradictions, the young child of this initial stage provides examples of what Piaget calls *pseudocontradictions,* that is, he interprets as contradictory certain relationships or situations that are not so to the person at a higher level of development. For example, in the seriation task, a young child finds it contradictory that a stick can be simultaneously larger (than previous sticks) and smaller (than the ones to follow) or that a half-filled glass can be half full as well as half empty. He believes that a stick is either large or small, a glass either empty or full, but not both at the same time.

During a second stage, the child begins to be aware of the contradictions in his statements. He will search for solutions, but since he does not yet have the ability to overcome these contradictions, his solutions will be compromise ones. In the earlier disks experiment, he will set up two distinct classes: the "small" disks, A, B, and C, and the "large" ones, E, F, and G, but then he might have trouble deciding whether the boundary disk, D, should be in the "small" or "large" category and will move it back and forth between the two. Some children believe that disk G changes in size, and first say it is the same size as F, but then that it becomes larger when compared with A. Other children in this stage may create three classes, with an intermediate size between the small and large categories. For example, A and B would be small, C, D, and E intermediate, and F and G large. All these different reactions constitute beta behavior, or the creation of variations within the system.

Finally, at around 11 to 12 years, the stage 3 child understands that the disks form a seriation, with imperceptible differences between each successive disk. He has quantified the size relationship. By doing this he has created a new cognitive structure that is able to assimilate the disturbing element. This understanding of the situation resolves the imperceptible differences problem. It allows the child to explain the apparent contradiction and to anticipate the possibility of an unlimited number of disks.

Piaget states that the child's initial unawareness of contradiction occurs because he first concentrates on the observable features of a situation or the results of an action, on *affirmations,* and neglects the nonobservables, or what has been excluded by the action, the *negations.* The common feature of all contradictions is an incomplete compensation between affirmations and negations. For the young child, affirmations predominate over negations. This is because it is easier to apprehend positives than negatives. The perception of an absent object or characteristic involves *expectations* that go beyond the information actually provided by the objects. We can spontaneously think of red objects (affirmations), but we need to construct or infer the category of nonred ones (negations) since they are not given perceptually. Negation requires inference, that is, an internal construction, and the child needs time to build these internal constructions.

Only when the intension and extension of a concept have become sufficiently differentiated to cover negations will the child be able to overcome contradiction. The awareness of contradiction presupposes the ability to draw inferences. In the foregoing task, the young child concentrates on the observables or affirmations that "A is the same as B," "B is the same as C," and so on, until "F is the same as G" and "G is larger than A." To feel contradiction and to overcome it, the child must be able to infer two things. First, he must realize that the relationship "G is larger than A" (affirmation) implies that "A is not equal to G" (negation). Second, and more complex, the child must be able to infer, by using a scheme of transitivity, that "A is the same as F." Since only adjacent disks can be compared, this cannot be observed directly and is also a negation. It is only at quite an advanced stage of development that the child acquires transitivity and hence becomes capable of constructing this negation.

All this may seem contrived, artificial, and irrelevant to the study of normal intellectual development, but that is not so. On the contrary, Piaget believes that the concepts of affirmation and negation are of tremendous importance to the whole of cognitive development. This is because every action necessarily and implicitly contains both a positive and a negative aspect, both an affirmation and a negation. The class of red objects implies all the objects excluded from this class, or the class of nonred objects. Addition implies subtraction, and so on. Affirmations and negations are found at every level, in perception, sensorimotor actions, and mental operations. Initially, the young child grasps only affirmations. Only slowly and laboriously does he construct negations. His negations are systematically grasped only when the child is able to construct reversible operational structures in which there is a complete compensation of affirmations and negations.

Although Piaget reached these conclusions on affirmations and negations during the latter part of his career, he felt that they were such an important explanatory framework for intellectual development as a whole that he returned to many of his earlier studies, in particular the conservation tasks, in an attempt to explain past findings in terms of the child's initial primacy of affirmations and his subsequent construction of negations.

To end this section on equilibration, let us look at how Piaget incorporates the concepts of empirical and reflective abstraction, optimizing equilibration, equilibrium, and disequilibrium, into a model of cognitive

E   A   E'

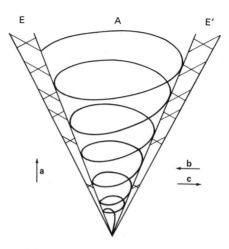

a   b
                                    ⟵
                                     c
                                    ⟶

FIGURE 18   The spiral of knowing. From *Adaptation Vitale et Psychologie de l'Intelligence: Selection Organique et Phénocopie,* by J. Piaget. Copyright 1974 by Hermann, Paris. Reprinted by permission of Hermann, Paris.

development which he calls the *spiral of knowing.* This spiral of knowing is symbolized by an inverted cone, as shown in Figure 18. The inner spiral of the cone, A, represents internal constructions in the form of reflective abstraction with its successive projections and reorganizations that are carried out within the optimizing equilibration process. The outer layers, E and E', represent interactions with the environment in the form of empirical abstraction within the framework of previous reflective abstraction. These two processes, A and E/E', are in constant interaction as new projections and reorganizations result from interactions with the environment. Three vectors, **a, b,** and **c,** determine the progress of cognition. Vector **a** represents the hierarchical succession of cognitive structures, starting with reflexes, moving through sensorimotor schemes, preoperational structures, concrete operations, finally to reach propositional operations. Vector **b** represents the modifications of the structures and disequilibria that result from interactions with the environment. Vector **c** represents explorations of the environment which lead to partial or complete reorganization of the structures.

The ever-widening but open circles of spiral A represent three major characteristics of equilibrium. First, there is the underlying *power* of the equilibrium. This refers to the number of actions that can be carried out and hence to the number of schemes available, or the *field of application* of the cognitive structures. As the field of application extends and schemes become more differentiated, more actions become possible, and equilibrium becomes more powerful. This increase in schemes, or in the field of application, is reflected in the widening of the circles.

The young child's classification system, for instance, would be relatively undifferentiated with few classes and subclasses. With only a few schemes and subschemes available, it would not be possible for him to carry out many actions, or to establish many links or relationships between them. This equilibrium would not be very powerful. For the older child who has already constructed a hierarchical classification system with numerous subclasses, the possibility of links and relationships becomes boundless. The equilibrium is therefore infinitely more powerful.

The power of a particular level of equilibrium is directly related to the degree of relativization and quantification of concepts as well as to differentiation and integration. Understanding becomes increasingly coherent as relationships and connections between schemes increase. Consequently an increase in power of equilibrium is accompanied by a growth in coherence.

Another characteristic of equilibrium is *stability,* which is defined as the capacity to compensate by actions or mental operations for changes in the environment without disturbing the whole structure. When a system is stable, the introduction of new elements does not destroy it. The structure easily incorporates the new elements and does not change. Stability is achieved when any action in one direction (affirmation) can be compensated for or canceled out by an action in an opposite direction (negation). With a stable equilibrium, affirmations are balanced by negations. In seriation, for instance, the young child who is able to construct a series only by trial and error will, when presented with additional sticks to insert, find it necessary to destroy the whole series and start from the beginning again, whereas the child with a mature seriation structure can incorporate an unlimited number of additional sticks without distorting the series. The latter has a more stable equilibrium. Perfect stability is achieved when the person is able to anticipate disturbances or conflict before they are actually encountered.

A third characteristic of equilibrium is its *openness,* which refers to the ability to incorporate new ideas and raise new questions and problems. These will lead to novel actions and responses to solve these problems. This openness is reflected in the upward movement of the spiral. Each successive level of equilibrium in the equilibration process solves previous problems and provides answers to previous questions, but at the same time opens up the possibility of new problems and new questions. It is this openness that ensures that cognition is continually developing. These three characteristics combined—power, stability, and openness—ensure that the equilibration process continually conserves past understanding and constructs new knowledge.

POSSIBILITY

Piaget was greatly concerned with the construction of new knowledge, a problem underlying the equilibration process and the spiral of knowing. How does the child create new responses or actions? What accounts for the openness of the spiral toward new possibilities of disequilibrium and reequilibration?

In a number of studies designed to investigate the development of the concept of possibility, children were required to come up with as many solutions as possible to certain problems. (See Piaget, *Le Possible et le Necessaire*, 1981b, 1983.) For example, they were asked to indicate all the different ways they could think of to place three dice on a piece of cardboard, to make a toy car go from point A to point B, or to cut up a paper square.

Findings of this type of study showed three main stages in the development of possibilities. The young child of 4 to 5 years comes up with a limited number of possible solutions, one or two at most. These few possibilities are often accompanied by a strong feeling of necessity, which Piaget calls *pseudonecessity*. This is the feeling that it is impossible to change reality or the impression that because this is how things are, this is how they necessarily have to be. Reality, as given in the few solutions suggested, is felt of necessity to be the only possibility.

In the study with the three dice, the very young children of 4 to 6 years were able to come up with only a few suggestions, and these were often generated by a process of analogy. For example, one child placed the three dice in the three angles of the square paper. When asked if there were other ways, he moved one of the dice to the fourth angle, then moved the three dice around the various angles, each time leaving a different angle without a die. Children of this level also believe that the best solutions are those that are similar to the first one proposed.

At the next stage the older children are able to increase the number of possible solutions suggested, and come up with a range of "co-possibles," the number of which increase with age. Children of 7 to 8 years produce four to five possible solutions, whereas by 9 to 10 years they can envisage thirty or more solutions, even though they themselves are not always able to describe all these possibilities. With the dice problem, children of 7 to 10 years suggested numbers ranging from twenty to ten thousand, although when the experimenter suggested ten thousand, one child felt that this number was too high. They realize that these many solutions exist as abstract co-possibles which someone else may be able to describe, even though they themselves cannot think of all of them. At this stage, the best solutions are considered to be those that differ the most from the ones that have already been suggested.

Finally, around 11 to 12 years, children infer more or less immediately that the number of possibilities is unlimited. The child realizes that any solution proposed is only a sample of such a vast number of solutions that it would not be possible to think of them all. At this point, an unlimited number of possibilities is conceptually deduced rather than actually observed.

The idea of an unlimited number of possibilities is obviously not something the child is able to observe in the environment, but is something that he constructs internally by making inferences from what is actually given in a situation. As we have seen, inferences require an internal construction that goes beyond observables. This explains why it takes so long for a child to acquire the concept of possibility.

Piaget maintains that the conquest of possibilities is a crucial mechanism of the equilibration process. Each new possibility opens up a field of virtual or potential new possibilities. As the child solves problems he begins to discover others, and to realize that each problem can generate a host of possible solutions, not all of which he is able to describe. It is this creation and multiplication of possibilities that provides the openness of equilibration, and explains the production of novelty which is one of the basic questions raised by Piaget in his genetic epistemology.

Studies were also conducted into the feeling of necessity in the child. Their results show that necessity follows a parallel development to possibility. Young children start with the feeling of pseudonecessity, which was found in the studies of possibility. Older children produce a small number of co-necessities and grasp the idea that each of the co-possibilities or solutions to a problem is equally necessary. Finally, around 11 to 12 years, the child explains that there are an unlimited number of co-necessities.

In his discussions on the relationship among possibility, necessity, and reality, Piaget states that in the early stages of development, there is a lack of differentiation among these three modalities. The young child, owing to his limited number of schemes, believes that the only possibilities are those that are observable. Moreover, these are conceived of as being necessary, which is in fact a pseudonecessity. As the child's schemes multiply, and as more connections between them are established, he becomes capable of going beyond observables and of drawing inferences about reality. It is these inferences that lead to the construction of a larger number of co-possibilities. Possibilities are the result of the differentiation of schemes. At the same time, with development, the initial regulations are changed into reversible operations. Operations are accompanied by feelings of necessity. As we have seen in the conservation tasks, necessity is one characteristic of logical reasoning processes which results from the integration of schemes and their transformation into operatory structures. Operations represent a synthesis of the possible and the necessary, as well as a synthesis between integration and differentiation which is characteristic of the third type of equilibrium.

Summary and Conclusions

Piaget distinguishes between development and learning in the narrow sense. Development is influenced by four factors. *Physical structures* both limit certain aspects of cognitive development and make others possible, but maturation in itself is not sufficient to explain mental development, partly because there are obvious cultural effects on cognitive functioning. A second factor is *experience*. Physical experience involves gaining knowledge of objects by observing them directly. Logicomathematical experience involves an internal coordination of the individual's actions which at the outset are performed on the objects, but later do not require this physical support. However, these two types of experience are not sufficient to explain development, because they omit, among other things, the effects of social influences. A third factor, *social transmission,* refers to the acquisition of knowledge by such techniques as reading or instruction. This factor is also insufficient to explain development, partly because it ignores the role of the cognitive structures which make social influences efficient or inefficient. A fourth factor is *equilibration.* This concept involves the child's self-regulatory processes which lead him through progressively more effective states of equilibrium. The notion of equilibrium refers to a system of exchanges between an open system and its surroundings. It implies a system that is in active balance with its environment. The degree of equilibrium is defined by a system's position on three dimensions: field of application, stability, and openness. The greater the degree of these qualities, the more perfect the equilibrium. Research stresses the central role of internal conflict in promoting equilibration. As equilibration proceeds, the child comes to appreciate the roles of possibility and necessity.

Piaget distinguishes between learning in the narrow sense and learning in the wider sense. The former involves the mere acquisition of specific responses to particular situations. Such learning is superficial: it is unstable, impermanent, and unlikely to generalize. Learning in the wider sense involves the acquisition of general cognitive structures. Indeed, these are used to give meaning to specific learning and often make it possible. Thus, development explains learning. Further, development occurs through a self-regulatory process involving the four factors, not through the acquisition of specific information or responses. Learning therefore cannot explain development.

Piaget's theory makes an enormous contribution in focusing on the processes of *self-regulated* development. Piaget continually stresses the child's contribution to the developmental process. It is the child who tries to assimilate the conservation problem into already available structures, and it is the child who feels a subjective lack of certainty about his solution. The child does not simply react to external events, but takes an active part in his own development. Piaget's notion of self-regulation is extremely valuable. It seems to capture a good part of the reality of children's development. It also serves as an alternative to human engineering views which stress the external shaping of responses and the modification of behavior.

EDUCATION

In the present section, we will consider some implications which Piaget's views hold for education. While Piaget has devoted relatively little attention to problems in this area, his work can make three types of contributions to educational practice. First, Piaget's theory provides some general principles for the conduct of education. Second, Piaget's studies of the development of specific logical, mathematical, and physical concepts in the child can assist the development of curricula and teaching practices in these areas. Third, Piaget's clinical interviewing technique can prove a valuable diagnostic and evaluative tool for the teacher. This section therefore will describe Piaget's thoughts with respect to education and will discuss these three types of potential contributions. The section closes by considering possible future directions for a Piagetian approach.

It should be emphasized at the outset that our intention is not to propose particular curricula or instructional practices on the basis of Piaget's work. As Sinclair (1976, p. 11) puts it,

> I'm not sure that much can be done with application of Piaget's theory in a detailed way by the Piagetian psychologist. . . . There are absolutely no [direct] practical indications in the work of Piaget with respect to education. . . . Piaget has very little to say with respect to specific problems such as how to teach reading and writing, and various other educational techniques.

Hence, we will be concerned with the major guiding principles which emerge from Piaget's work. Like Piaget, we feel that the implementation of these principles requires the special skills of the educator, who understands the distinctive conditions of the school setting, rather than the psychologist.

A Child-Centered Approach

One of Piaget's most significant contributions is his notion that the young child is quite different from the adult in several ways: in methods of approaching reality, in the ensuing views of the world, and in the uses of language. Piaget's investigations concerning matters such as the concept of number and verbal communication have enabled him to produce a change—indeed, one might almost say a metamorphosis—in our ways of understanding children. As a result of his work we have become increasingly aware that the child is not just a miniature although less wise adult,

but a being with a distinctive mental structure that is qualitatively different from the adult's. The child views the world from a unique perspective.
For example, the child below the age of 7 years truly believes that water,
when poured from one container to another, gains or loses in quantity,
depending on the shape of the second container. Or in the case of number,
the young child, although able to count to 20 or more, has no conception
of certain fundamental mathematical ideas. He may think, for example,
that a set of five elements is larger than a set of eight elements if the physical arrangement of the sets takes on certain forms.

These and many other unexpected discoveries lead to the surprising
recognition that the child's world is in many ways qualitatively different
from that of the adult. One reason for the child's distinctive view of reality
is a distinctive mental structure. The young child (below about 7 or 8
years of age) centers his attention on limited amounts of information; he
attends to states rather than transformations; he is egocentric, failing to
take into account other points of view; his concepts are relatively undifferentiated; and he is incapable of forms of thought, such as reversibility,
which allow symbolic manipulation of the data of experience. Even the
older child (between 7 and 11 years) is strongly tied to concrete situations
although he is capable of fairly subtle mental operations. The child reasons best about immediately present objects and fails to appreciate the
contradictions or possibilities inherent in a situation.

One result of the child's cognitive structure is a view of reality which
to the adult seems chaotic and unnatural. Another consequence is that the
young child's use of language is different from that of the adult. That is,
the words that the child uses do not hold the same meaning for him as they
do for the adult. Adults often overlook this point. We usually assume that
if a child uses a particular word, it automatically conveys the same meaning that it does when an adult uses that word. Adults often believe that
once a child has learned the linguistic label for an object, he has available
the underlying concept. But Piaget has shown that this often is not the
case. The child does learn his words from the adult, but assimilates them
into his own mental structure, which is quite different from the adult's.
The words "same amount to drink," for example, are interpreted in one
way by the 4-year-old, and in another way by the adult. Only after a period of cognitive development does the child use these words and understand them in the same way as the more mature person.

The implication of this very general proposition—that the young
child's thought and language are qualitatively different from the adult's—
is also very general: the educator must make a special effort to understand
the unique properties of the child's experience and ways of thinking. The
educator must try to adopt a child-centered point of view, and cannot assume that the child's experience or modes of learning are the same as his
own. For example, while the educator himself may learn a great deal by

reading a book or listening to a lecture, similar experiences may be far less useful for the young child. The educator may profit from an orderly sequence of material, but perhaps the child does not. While the educator may feel that a given idea is simple and indeed self-evident, the child may find it difficult. In short, it is not safe to generalize from the adult's experience to that of the child. The educator's assumptions, stemming as they do from an adult perspective, may not apply to children. The educator needs to improve his own capacity to watch and listen, and to place himself in the distinctive perspective of the child. Since the meaning expressed by the child's language is often idiosyncratic, the adult must try to understand the child's world by observing his actions closely. There are no easy rules or procedures to use to understand the child. What *is* necessary is considerable sensitivity—a willingness to learn from the child, to look closely at the child's actions, and to avoid the assumption that what is true or customary for the adult is also true for the child. The educator needs to interact with the child in a flexible way to gain insight into the latter's current level of functioning. With this attitude—a willingness to observe the child and to learn from him the educator can begin to understand the child and to tailor the educational experience to the child's needs. Education must stem from a child-centered perspective.

Activity

The concept that children—or individuals of any age—learn best from self-initiated activity is vital for the guidance of education. Throughout this book we have seen that Piaget places major emphasis on the role of activity—both physical and mental—in intellectual development. In Piaget's view, "to know an object, is to act on it" (Piaget, "Development and Learning," 1964, p. 8). Almost from birth, the infant touches objects, manipulates them, turns them around, looks at them, and through such activities gains an increasing understanding of their properties. It is through action, not passive observation, that he develops an understanding of the world. Indeed, there is a sense in which the child constructs reality. For the older child, too, the essence of knowledge is activity. Thus, when the preoperational child attempts to remember (retain his knowledge over time), he actively organizes the material by assimilating it to available schemes. Often, the child's understanding is not on a verbal level, which in fact usually takes a long time to develop. The adolescent's knowledge also involves activity: in trying to understand physical phenomena, he actively generates combinations of hypothetical possibilities and transforms them in thought. He does not simply respond to the immediate present. To summarize, in all cases—whether behavioral schemes, concrete operations, or formal structures are involved—the essence of knowledge is activity.

To promote genuine understanding, the teacher should therefore encourage the child's activity. When the teacher attempts to bypass this process in various ways—for example, by lecturing at a class of young children—the result is often superficial learning. Perhaps this is one reason why so much of what is taught in school is immediately forgotten after the school year ends. By contrast, genuinely active learning can lead to a more solid and long-lasting understanding.

A word of caution is needed in connection with this emphasis on activity. Sometimes teachers take it to refer solely to physical activity; they believe that the manipulation of objects automatically leads to learning. This may be true in some situations, but it is not always the case. Take, for example, a preschooler who is actively engaged in playing with the toys provided at school—swinging on the swings, or building castles in the sandpit. This child will probably learn something about the properties of toys, swings, or sand, and about his own relationships to these objects. This is important knowledge for the child at this stage. Take, on the other hand, the case of a high school student following a science lesson. First, the teacher carefully demonstrates a particular experiment to the class. The teacher then asks the pupils to carry out the same experiment, for which the procedure is given step by step on a certain page of the textbook. Is the pupil who carries out the correct physical actions as described in the book really learning? Not necessarily so, or at least he is not always learning the things that the teacher intended him to learn. If the pupil's physical actions are not accompanied by parallel mental activity, such as thinking of alternative types of results and their meaning, it is unlikely that much real and lasting learning will occur. At this stage, simply carrying out physical manipulations will not produce much learning.

As Piaget (*Science of Education and the Psychology of the Child,* 1970c) put it, "although the child's activity at certain levels necessarily entails the manipulation of objects, . . . at other levels the most authentic research activity may take place in the spheres of reflection, of the most advanced abstraction, and of verbal manipulation (provided they are spontaneous and not imposed on the child)" (p. 68).

Acceptance of the principle of active learning requires a considerable reorientation of beliefs concerning education. Teachers (and the public at large) usually consider that the aim of education is to impart existing knowledge, often of a factual type, as efficiently as possible to the pupil, who will then absorb it in the form presented. In this view, if students were allowed to design and conduct experiments, there would not only be chaos in the classroom, but there would also be no learning. According to Piaget's theory, these beliefs and attitudes are erroneous for several reasons. Teachers can in fact impose very little knowledge. It is true that they can convince the child to *say* certain things, but these verbalizations often indicate little in the way of real understanding. Moreover, it is seldom legitimate to conceive of knowledge as a *thing* which can be transmitted. Certainly the child needs to learn some facts, and these may be considered *things*. Sometimes, drill or programmed instruction may assist in learning of this type. But often the child does not learn even facts when imposed; the student may have to discover them himself.

In addition, facts are but a small portion of real knowledge. True understanding involves action, on both the motoric and conceptual levels. Consider for example the understanding of class properties. A traditional view might propose that the child can simply be taught some facts about classification, for instance, that a square is a geometric form. Piaget's view, on the other hand, argues that understanding of classification consists of a sequence of activities. First, the child physically sorts or otherwise manipulates objects. He feels various forms and in this way (among others), perceives the differences among them. He may put different forms in different places. Later, he can sort the objects solely on a mental level; now the child does not need to separate things physically. Later still, he can perform inclusion operations on imagined classes of objects and can consider that a hypothetical class includes and is "larger than" its constituent subclass. Thus, knowledge of classification does not merely involve facts but actions as well: physical sorting, mental sorting, mental inclusion operations. Furthermore, most of these actions are nonverbal.

Since learning occurs through the child's activity, structured teaching methods, such as programmed learning or audiovisual aids, should be deemphasized in favor of more "active" methods. Instead of attempting to impart truths, teachers should set up situations which will lead the child to question, to experiment, and to discover facts and relationships. Children need to be encouraged in their exploratory frame of mind. This occurs naturally in the very young child, who is constantly experimenting with objects, language, and situations to understand more about the world. Yet once he starts going to school, he seems to cease being an experimenter. What has happened to extinguish this desire for discovery? In school, exploration is often discouraged entirely. And when it does take place, the teacher—not the child—is usually the experimenter. Under these circumstances, the child learns very little, becomes disinterested, and loses motivation. Teachers should therefore present the child with materials and situations that encourage the design of his own experiments. This will in turn lead to a deeper and more long-lasting knowledge than will a rote memorization of facts presented by teachers or in textbooks.

We have seen that Piaget's theory stresses the role of activity in education. It should be clear that Piaget's intention is not to glorify activity for its own sake. Instead, it is to point out that activity, when channeled in certain directions, leads to the goal of genuine learning. As we shall see next, the notion of reinvention provides an understanding of the goal, genuine learning.

Reinvention

Suppose that the child has been encouraged to engage in active exploration and that the educator has taken pains to guide the process of equilibration in a manner sensitive to the child's cognitive abilities and needs. The goal of all this activity is to produce genuine understanding. As we have seen, this does not involve the mere repetition of simple facts. *Genuine understanding is instead a process of reinvention.* As Piaget puts it, "real comprehension of a notion or theory implies the reinvention of this theory by the subject" (Piaget, "Comments on Mathematical Education," 1977a, p. 731).

Piaget describes the reinvention process as follows. At first, the child engages in concrete activities involving a notion like cardinal number. For example, he may spontaneously count a line of objects first from left to right and then from right to left. Activities such as these, spontaneously generated by the child, lead to the understanding of key principles. He finds, for example, that if you count a set from right to left, you get the same number as when you count from left to right.

In the Piagetian view, we can say that the child has *reinvented* a key aspect of the principle of cardinality. The notion of reinvention is used since the concept was not simply transmitted from teacher to child; instead, the child was put in a position where his own spontaneous activity led to the creation of the concept. Thus, when the child gets the same number regardless of the direction of counting, he concludes *on his own* that directionality makes no difference for counting. This "concluding on his own" is the essence of reinvention.

The understanding which results from reinvention, Piaget maintains, is more genuine and powerful than is that provided through structured teaching and passive learning. One indication of the reinvented concept's power is that the child spontaneously uses it in new situations, as if he is testing its generality. The child who receives the concept in a passive fashion is less likely to engage in active generalization of this type.

At the same time, Piaget points out a key limitation to the child's reinvented understanding: "the pupil will be far more capable of doing and understanding in actions than of expressing himself verbally . . . a large part of the structures the child uses when he sets out actively to solve a problem are unconscious" (Piaget, 1977a, p. 731). So the child's reinvention leads to a genuine understanding, but one that is not yet capable of expression on a conscious, verbal level.

The achievement of a higher level of understanding should be delayed until a later time. As Piaget put it, "formalization [in mathematics] should be kept for a later moment as a type of systematization of the notions already acquired. This certainly means the use of intuitions before axiomatization" (in Piaget, 1977a, p. 732). In other words, formalization should be introduced only after the child has become comfortable with his "informal notions" and only with much assistance on the part of the teacher. Indeed, one of the teacher's main responsibilities is to help the child achieve an explicit consciousness, expression, and formalization of his "intuitive knowledge." In a later section (on curriculum), we shall explore the process of helping the child to make a transition between these different levels of understanding.

Individualized Learning

Piaget's theory stresses that current cognitive structures and new experiences interact to arouse interest and stimulate the subsequent development of understanding. Interest and learning are best facilitated if the experience presented to the child bears some relevance to what he already knows, but is at the same time sufficiently novel to present incongruities and conflicts. In other words, Piaget proposes that the child's interest is aroused when an experience is moderately novel (recall the discussion of the moderate novelty principle during infancy). This means that the experience is not so radically novel that the child cannot assimilate it into current cognitive structures, and it is not so familiar as to be immediately and effortlessly assimilated, and thus of little interest. The principle is relativistic: by itself an event does not possess some degree of interest. Rather, interest is derived from the interaction between the state of the child's mind and the properties of the thing to be known. At the same time, moderately novel experiences present the child with cognitive conflict. And according to the theory of equilibration, these conflicts serve as the basis for reorganization of cognitive structures and subsequent development.

The situation with regard to interest and conflict is complicated by the fact that there is considerable variation among children of the same age in their rate of development. We have seen that some children within a given culture acquire conservation, for example, at age 5 and others not until 8. Consequently, in any class of thirty to fifty children, there are wide differences among children in levels of cognitive functioning. Because these levels vary, the children's interests, which are determined by an interaction between the current level of cognitive functioning and experience, will also vary. The teacher is therefore inevitably faced with a wide variation among students in both cognitive level and interest.

To deal with this, there must be extensive changes in classroom practice. First, teachers should be aware of the child's current level of functioning. To some extent the teacher can rely on Piaget's discoveries for this information. But Piaget's work covers only a limited number of those topics usually studied in school. Therefore, the teacher himself must make an assessment of his students' capabilities. Once obtained, this knowledge will help the teacher to create situations intended to provoke the child to question and experiment. The teacher may also select suitable counterarguments which will encourage the child to clarify his thinking. Knowledge of students' functioning will also help the teacher to present the conflict situations that, as we have seen from the training research carried out in Geneva, are one important mechanism of conceptual growth.

The assessment of intellectual level is not an easy task. The evaluation must be different from the usual standard achievement tests which often measure only surface knowledge, rote memory, and other superficial aspects of learning. The teacher will have to evaluate not only the products of thought—correct or incorrect answers—but the process of students' thinking as well. The teacher will need to observe the children carefully and attempt to discover both their competencies and their weaknesses in any area. Without such evaluation, the teacher will find it difficult to judge between what is moderately novel and thus likely to arouse interest, between what is already known or too advanced for the pupil at this stage of development, and between what is or is not a conflict situation for each individual student. Once the teacher recognizes the child's current level of functioning he can create experiences which will promote interest, arouse conflict, and facilitate development for the student.

Second, teaching should be oriented more toward the individual student than the overall group. Since there are great individual differences in almost all areas of cognitive development, it is unlikely that any one task or lesson will arouse the interest of or promote learning in all members of the class. For some children, a specific task may be too easily assimilated into current mental structures, while for other students the same problem may require too great a degree of accommodation for them at their present stage of development. The result is boredom for the first group and confusion for the second. Third, children must also be given considerable control over their own learning. Some may need more time than others to deal with the same material; similarly, children may approach the same problem in different ways.

To promote interest and learning, then, the teacher should tailor the curriculum to the learner and try to individualize teaching as much as possible. This means that the large group should effectively be disbanded as the sole classroom unit, that children should often work on individual projects, and that they should be allowed a degree of freedom in their own learning. Several objections are usually raised to this sort of a proposal. Under an individual learning arrangement, would not children waste their time or engage in mere play? One may counter this argument by noting that the teacher may depend on a certain amount of spontaneous intellectual motivation in children, particularly younger ones. Piaget has shown that the child is quite active in acquiring knowledge, and that he learns about important aspects of reality quite apart from instruction in the schools. In the first two years of life, for example, the infant acquires a primitive understanding of causality, of the nature of objects, of relations, of language and of many other things—largely without the benefit of formal instruction or adult "teaching." One need only watch an infant for a short period of time to know that he is curious, interested in the world surrounding him, and eager to learn. The same can also be said of older children and is supported by the fact that some schools manage to operate individualized programs with a good deal of success. In addition, one must remember that individualized instruction does not require the abrogation of responsibility on the part of the teacher. Indeed, the more individualized the learning, the heavier the burden on the teacher. The teacher must assess the student's level, assign relevant learning experiences, and generally supervise the entire learning process. Getting children to work "on their own" requires a considerable contribution on the part of the teacher.

Indeed, the burden is so heavy that teachers often feel that the provision of individualized instruction in large classes (between twenty to fifty children) is an entirely unrealistic and impractical solution. It is true that in large classes no single teacher can effectively tailor a curriculum to meet the specific cognitive needs of every pupil at every moment of the teaching day. And from another point of view, it might not even be a good idea to have twenty, thirty, or fifty individual learners, all "doing their own thing" since some of the advantages of group learning would be lost in the process. Yet, when covering topics where there are obvious differences among children in their understanding of the material, teachers can divide the class into small groups of children at approximately the same level. For other topics, all children can work individually at their own level, while for still other topics the entire class can be joined together. The essential point is that teaching needs to be flexible; the teacher can employ a combination of group and individual instruction.

What the student needs, then, are opportunities to learn in a rich environment which contains many potentially interesting elements. The students needs a teacher who is sensitive to his affective and cognitive needs; who can judge what materials will challenge him at a given point in time; who is able to evaluate his level of functioning and present new ideas at a level consistent with the student's intellectual and linguistic development; who can present this knowledge in a way that arouses the child's interest and activity; and who can help the students when necessary and who has faith in the child's capacity to learn.

Social Interaction

In Piaget's view, physical experience and concrete manipulation are not the only influences on learning. Another factor that leads to the development of knowledge is social experience or interaction with other persons. While Piaget has not written extensively on this topic, his work contains a number of important implications concerning the role of peers in the educational process.

The effects of social experience, although almost negligible during the first few months of life, become increasingly important as the child grows older. We have pointed out earlier that one of the prime deterrents to an objective understanding of reality is the child's egocentric thought. At first, the child cannot view people, objects, or events in the surrounding world objectively because he can only perceive them as they relate to himself. The very young child assimilates external events directly into his own action schemes. Objects or events are only relevant to the extent that they concern the child's own private preoccupations. He cannot view objects or events from any perspective except his own, and this egocentrism of course prevents him from gaining an objective view of objects or of persons. Gradually, as the child becomes capable of decentering his attention, as he begins to focus simultaneously on various aspects of reality, and as he comes to understand another person's point of view, then he gains a more objective knowledge of reality.

One method which promotes the relinquishment of egocentrism is social interaction. When one child talks to another, he comes to realize that his way of viewing things is not the only perspective. The child sees that other people do not necessarily share his opinions. Social interaction inevitably leads to arguments and discussion: the child's views are questioned, and he must defend and justify his opinions. This action forces the child to clarify his thoughts, for if he wants to convince others of the validity of his own views, the child must present them clearly and logically. In addition, other people may not be as tolerant of his inconsistencies as is the child himself, and they do not hesitate to point them out. Thus social interaction helps the child to recognize the shortcomings in his thinking and forces him to see other points of view which may conflict with his own. Such conflicts in schemes or ideas are one of the mechanisms of progress. Therefore, we see that, in addition to the more commonly stressed affective side of social interaction—the need to get along with other people—there is also an important cognitive component. Social experience not only helps people to adjust to others at an emotional level, but it also serves to clarify a person's thinking and ultimately helps him to become more coherent and logical.

It should be made clear that social experience is not independent of physical experience. Verbal exchange of opinions, for example, is not feasible on certain subjects until the child has the experience of manipulating objects. During the early stages of development, physical experience is especially crucial. Yet once the child has acted on an object or a situation, language can then serve as a major tool to internalize the experience into a compact category. The child can also use language to communicate an understanding of experience to others. Indeed, the very attempt to communicate permits the child to make explicit certain aspects of experience which were at first understood only at the level of action. The child's activity and experience are of paramount importance during the early stages of development; later verbal communication and social interaction help to define and conceptualize this experience.

The implication of Piaget's view, therefore, is that social interaction should play a significant role in the classroom. Children should converse, share experiences and argue, for these are all major tools in the acquisition of knowledge.

Curriculum

In the preceding sections, we have reviewed various educational principles. Most refer to general aspects of the learning process and in themselves do not represent a completely novel approach to education. Many of these points have already been emphasized by educational philosophers. The role of activity in learning was discussed by Rousseau and Dewey, and the principle of individualized learning has some commonality with Skinner's concepts of programmed instruction. Piaget's research adds new empirical data in support of these principles, but the educational principles themselves are not new. The uniqueness of Piaget's contribution to education lies in other areas, particularly in his detailed description of the development of numerous physical, logical, and mathematical concepts in children, and in his account of the general development of thinking. This type of knowledge was not available to other educational theorists such as Rousseau or Dewey. A number of the concepts which Piaget has investigated are particularly relevant to education, since they are taught either directly or indirectly in schools. For example, while conservation of length is not usually taught in schools, it is a prerequisite for the understanding of measurement, which is taught. Knowledge of the child's cognitive level and of the child's understanding of particular concepts can be used to facilitate education in several ways.

Limits. On the one hand, research concerning the child's cognitive level demonstrates that there are limitations on what the child can learn. The child's thought develops through a series of stages, each showing both strengths and weaknesses. Any one stage is characterized by the ability to perform certain actions and, on the other hand, by the propensity to commit particular errors. One implication of the stage theory is in a way "pessimistic." Since intellectual development seems to follow an ordered sequence—a sequence which, until proof to the contrary, appears to be universal—the young child is incapable of learning certain kinds of concepts. It would serve no purpose, for instance, to try to teach a child of the preoperational period the principle of inertia, or any other abstract notion which requires the existence of reasoning at a formal operational level. Some things cannot be taught at any level, regardless of the method adopted. It is of course possible to accelerate some types of learning through the use of suitable environmental stimuli. For instance, if a child of the preoperational period is fairly close to achieving the structure of concrete operations, suitable physical experience may expedite the process, with the result that the structure may be acquired somewhat earlier than if no such experience had been presented. But as we have seen, such acceleration is possible only if the child is in a transitional stage.

Given these limitations on children's learning, the educator can respond in several ways. One strategy is to delay the teaching of certain subjects until children are presumed "ready" to understand them. To some extent, this strategy is obviously reasonable: it makes no sense to teach calculus to the 5-year-old. On the other hand, this approach can be applied in an overly-zealous manner. Thus, one might propose that since elementary school children cannot employ formal operations, science should not be taught until adolescence, when it is possible to reason in a hypothetico-deductive manner. Such a practice would be unfortunate because even young children can understand something of science on a level appropriate to their own cognitive abilities. For the concrete operational child, science could involve a good deal of physical experience which might lead to formal operational thought. Similarly, in mathematics, while preoperational children cannot fully understand equivalence, they can profit from considerable experience in the counting of concrete objects. Often such concrete activity is a prerequisite for more abstract understanding. In brief, while limitations in children's cognitive abilities prevent them from learning certain concepts, one should not forget that preparatory work, usually of a concrete nature, is often desirable and even necessary for later understanding. Hence, despite the limits, one should not give up on young children's learning of certain concepts, but should search out appropriate ways for them to engage in preparatory activities.[6]

Strengths. At the same time, there is a more "optimistic" side to Piaget's theory. At each stage of development, the child is capable of certain forms of thought, of specific concepts. For example, Piaget has found that concepts of topological geometry (distinctions between closed versus

---

[6]One important issue regards the teaching of reading to the young child. On the basis of Piaget's theory, what can one conclude concerning the desirability of teaching 4- or 5-year-olds to read? We believe that the theory has little if anything to say about reading, since Piaget has not studied it directly and since it is not clear how the intellectual skills which he has studied relate to reading. Our own experience is that there is no cognitive limitation which would prevent preoperational children from learning to read if they are motivated to do so.

open figures, etc.) develop in the child before those of Euclidean geometry (measurement of angles, distances, etc.) and projective geometry (measurement of perspectives, coordinates, etc.). Understanding of topological notions appears fairly early in life, whereas the child only begins to understand the notions of Euclidean and projective geometry at around 7 years of age. Thus, while the 5-year-old may be incapable of learning projective concepts, he has already developed an intuitive understanding of topological notions. Each stage of development is characterized by strengths as well as weaknesses. Knowledge of the strengths as well as of the limitations can be used to improve education in several ways. One possible improvement is a detailed evaluation and modification of existing curricula. This type of work is being carried out more and more extensively in several countries. For example, Shayer (1972; 1974) has worked with a number of science courses (chemistry, physics, biology) commonly given in the United Kingdom. He has tried, for each topic covered, to assess the minimum conceptual level required for a pupil to be interested in and to grasp the particular concept involved. Shayer attempts to determine how suitable the courses and specific concepts are in relation to the developmental levels of the students. As a result of these investigations, he suggests that many learning problems may be due to a mismatch between the conceptual level of the majority of pupils and the concepts being presented. Such work—assessing students' strengths and weaknesses in relation to the material taught—can eventually lead to the development of new and more effective curricula.

Knowledge of students' intellectual strengths can lead to the improvement of education in other ways, too. In particular, it can produce an optimistic view concerning students' potential and the creation of new learning opportunities. Piaget's theory shows that by the age of 5 or 6, when they are simultaneously entering school and the period of concrete operations, most children have developed remarkably sophisticated intellectual processes. By this age, most children already possess the intellectual prerequisites for understanding a good deal of what is taught in elementary school. For example, children's spontaneous concept of number is such that they should have no particular difficulty with the most notorious of school subjects, namely, arithmetic. As a result of natural development, they understand ideas of one-to-one correspondence, equivalence, additivity—that is, the concepts forming the foundation for a good deal of school arithmetic. In other words, Piaget's theory suggests that virtually all children possess the cognitive equipment for doing standard academic work. What is taught in school should easily be assimilated into the existing cognitive framework. Piaget feels that it is difficult to understand how students "who are well endowed when it comes to the elaboration and utilization of the spontaneous [patterns] of intelligence can find themselves handicapped in the comprehension" of academic subjects (Piaget,

Science of Education, 1970c, p. 4). The teacher should therefore seriously consider the notion that the education of children can rely on some already existing intellectual assets. Problems in learning are not likely to stem from fundamental intellectual deficits in the child. Given this notion, the educator can devise curricula which attempt to exploit the child's strengths. If, for example, the preoperational child is capable of understanding "functions," then the educator may elaborate on this concept. If the concrete operational child can deal with complex forms of equivalence, then the educator may try to exploit this informal knowledge. The natural course of development—the spontaneous appearance of intellectual capabilities—provides important opportunities for the fostering of academic knowledge and should therefore exert a strong influence on the nature of curriculum. The educator should also expect that children will have little difficulty in mastering school work because of their natural intellectual strengths.

Intuition and consciousness. We all know that despite children's intellectual strengths, the teaching of certain subjects does not go as smoothly as it might. Arithmetic is a prime example. Although children already possess spontaneous notions of basic mathematical ideas, they usually have a terrible time learning school arithmetic. Why should this be so? There are, of course, many different kinds of reasons, but perhaps Piaget's notion of different levels of understanding can shed some light on the issue.

The first of these levels is *motoric* or *practical* understanding. This is the level of action. The child can act directly on objects and manipulate them correctly, making the objects do what they are supposed to do. All this indicates that the child has "understood" objects at the level of motor responses. This knowledge is preserved in the form of schemes, which allow the actions to be repeated in identical situations and generalized to new ones. Another level of understanding is *conceptualization.* Here the child reconstructs internally the actions that were previously performed directly on objects, and at the same time adds new characteristics to these actions. He organizes the mental activities and provides logical connections. At the same time, much of the child's intellectual work remains unconscious. As we saw in reviewing Piaget's work on consciousness, the child is often capable of mental operations that he is not aware of and cannot express. A third level of knowledge involves *consciousness* and *verbalizations.* Now the child can deal with concepts on an abstract level and can express his mental operations in words. The child can reflect on his own thought.

At all stages of intellectual development, children find it easier to act—either behaviorally or mentally—than to achieve consciousness of their actions. Consciousness and verbalization are relatively late developments, and their emergence may depend on prior understanding at the lower levels.

The existence of different levels of understanding—practical, conceptual, and conscious—has important implications for education. We have already seen that at every stage of cognitive development the child possesses basic intellectual strengths. Usually these involve understanding at the unconscious levels, that is, motoric and conceptual understanding. By contrast, school learning typically operates at an exclusively verbal and formalized level. The child's spontaneous mathematics is informal and unconscious; the arithmetic taught in school is formal and highly verbalized. For Piaget, then, one of the key problems of education involves "finding the most adequate method for bridging the transition between these natural but nonreflective structures [that is, understanding of the first two types] to conscious reflection upon such structures and to a theoretical formulation of them" (*Science of Education*, 1970c, p. 47). Piaget recommends gradually building on what the child already knows—on the child's actions or unverbalized "intuitions"—to achieve a subsequent formalization.

Perhaps there is a paradox here: to foster true abstraction and consciousness, one must first encourage the concrete and unconscious. Of course, this does not mean that all learning must always involve the manipulation of concrete objects. The adolescent in the stage of formal operations may profit from verbal or written material, provided that in the course of development he has already acquired a good deal of motoric and conceptual knowledge corresponding to the abstraction in question. If, however, the formal operational learner encounters highly abstract material with which he has had no relevant previous experience, then for him (like the younger child) lower levels of understanding may help to serve as a foundation for consciousness. For most of us, truly abstract understanding can be achieved only through immersion in the concrete. In brief, one of the chief tasks of education is the elimination of the gap between the child's informal modes of understanding, which Piaget has described in some detail, and the formalities taught in school.

A caution.   A word of caution is necessary with regard to the use of actual Piagetian tasks or experiments in the school curriculum. Since conservation is an indicator that the child has reached a certain stage of development or has acquired a certain cognitive structure, some educators believe that the direct teaching of conservation will automatically promote the development of the child's underlying cognitive structure. Piaget's tasks are therefore being used as teaching devices, as basic subject matter in the curriculum. This seems to make little sense. Learning the correct responses to certain specific tasks does not mean that a child will reach the same intellectual level as another child who spontaneously gives the correct responses to the same task. The only result of instruction in Piagetian concepts is generally that the child acquires some very localized learning in the narrow sense, which does not promote general progress in other areas of cognition. Such instruction is therefore of rather limited value, especially since the cognitive structures normally develop in a spontaneous fashion, quite without the "benefit" of education.

Clinical Method

As we have seen in Chapter 1, it was very early in his career that Piaget rejected standard tests as a useful tool for the study of cognitive development. Such tests, he felt, fail to give a good indication of underlying cognitive processes. Piaget now feels that standard tests are not particularly useful for educational purposes, either. Indeed, he considers the tests to be a "veritable plague on education" (quoted by Elkind, 1976, p. 192). For Piaget the preferred method is the clinical interview. This technique is not merely preliminary, nor is it sloppy or unscientific. It is instead the most useful and "valid" method currently available for the study of thinking. The clinical method has an important role to play in education, too, particularly in the areas of assessment and diagnosis. By the use of suitable probing questions that attempt to reveal the underlying reasons for a child's initial statement or judgment, by presenting counter-suggestions to the child's arguments, and by providing conflict situations, the teacher who employs this method can discover a great deal about a child's cognitive functioning. In the clinical method, the interviewer must observe and listen to the child carefully and must adapt both the pace and the level of the questioning to the individual child who is interviewed. Standardization must be avoided. It is not the purpose of the interview to find out only whether a child is able to answer a certain question correctly or not, but to uncover underlying cognitive processes. Incorrect answers in particular provide the interviewer with an indication of the child's current state of knowledge.

The clinical method need not be restricted to Piagetian tasks, like conservation or seriation. The method can be used in any situation in which the objective is the exploration of the child's thought processes. Hence, it is quite appropriate, and we think very useful, to employ the method to examine the child's understanding of academic subject matter. For example, clinical interviewing has proved successful in the investigation of elementary school children's problems in learning arithmetic (Ginsburg, 1982). Teachers attempting to assess their pupils' functioning might therefore find the method a useful diagnostic tool in many areas of classroom learning. The technique is particularly valuable in identifying the intellectual difficulties which underlie learning problems.

Another and more indirect use of the method might be made in programs which attempt to train prospective teachers in questioning skills for use in teaching situations. There are many similarities between the clinical interview and the ''Socratic'' questioning technique in the classroom. For instance, in a group or individual setting, a skillful teacher does not simply ask questions which require the recall of correct answers; even more important, he asks provocative questions that stimulate the pupil to think, and to become aware of underlying causes. This requires questions that probe into the ''whys'' of situations. In addition, teachers need to adapt the level and pace of their questions to the understanding of pupils; teachers need to be able to listen and observe to understand the meaning of a response. These skills of questioning, sensitivity, and interpretation are all stressed in the clinical interview.

These, then, are two ways in which Piaget's clinical method can be used in education: first, as a means of assessment different from standard tests in both its flexible procedure and its aim of assessing cognitive structure, and, second, as a means of developing in the prospective teacher a sensitivity toward learners and the questioning skills essential for instruction.

Future Directions

During the period from 1960 to 1980, psychological and educational researchers carried out numerous studies based on the structural aspects of Piaget's theory, that is, the stages of cognitive development, concepts of conservation, classification, or seriation. Educators in particular believed that an overall theory of human intellectual development should be able to provide insights that would help them in their teaching in the classroom. These studies have resulted in a certain amount of perhaps predictable disenchantment and disappointment. Expectations were too high. It is difficult to see how a theory that emphasizes four broad stages of development could provide useful insights for a teacher who teaches children over the relatively short period of one year, just as it is difficult to imagine how the study of conservation, which is not a concept taught in school, could be of any direct benefit to the teacher. Piaget's later work into the processes of cognitive development and the mechanisms of learning offers more scope for both cognitive psychology and education. This later functional approach to cognitive development, however, like the early structural work, does not have *direct* applications to education. Before it can help the teacher in the classroom setting, a great deal of research is needed. But it provides a framework for the study and analysis of the processes by which learners acquire what it is teachers are trying to teach and could result in insights into classroom teaching and learning. Three main areas of this later work have potential applications to education.

The first is related to Piaget's distinction among three types of knowledge: social, physical, and logicomathematical. The different nature of each type calls for different types of teaching methods. Social knowledge calls for didactic methods; physical knowledge is best promoted through the manipulation, exploration, and discovery of objects; and logicomathematical knowledge requires construction, reinvention, and reflection on actions and coordinations. At present, teachers have a tendency not only to treat all knowledge as if it were of the same type, but in many cases to treat it as if it were social knowledge and best promoted through errorless learning. While this type of learning may be appropriate for social knowledge, it may not necessarily be suitable for the other two types. If, as Piaget claims, it is disequilibrium, disturbance, or conflict that motivates the search for better forms of knowledge, then the learning of physical and logicomathematical knowledge would call for situations with some element of conflict.

If a particular subject matter could be analyzed in terms of these three types of knowledge, and the kinds of conflict likely to lead to learning, then teaching appropriate to each type could be designed. This might result in more varied, interesting, and effective teaching methods than those currently adopted.

Another area of Piaget's theory with indirect application to education is that of the alpha, beta, and gamma reactions to disturbances. Here again, specific subject matters could be analyzed with these concepts in mind and appropriate teaching methods and situations designed for each level. Alpha reactions would require situations which enable the learner to become more aware of disturbing elements. Learners at the beta level need situations that help them to explore and construct variations and compromise solutions, whereas learners at the gamma level need to be helped to integrate their more mature understanding of one particular area of knowledge with other areas.

The third area in which Piaget's work can provide a heuristic framework for educational research covers specific principles of the equilibration process, such as differentiation and integration, and the relativization and quantification of concepts. For any specific area of academic learning, researchers could identify the processes involved, such as the type of differentiations and integrations that occur, the sequence and nature of relativizations, the characteristics that are quantified for any particular concept, the interrelationships between these quantifications, and so on. Understanding of the dynamics of these processes for an academic subject could then help educators to set up appropriate teaching-learning situations.

This approach to teaching and learning would be a radical change from past practices. If adopted, the educator, rather than looking at teaching from the point of view of the academic subject to be learned or at what has proved successful in the past, would approach the teaching-learning situation from the point of view of the learner and how this learner spontaneously acquires knowledge. We believe that this constructivist, genetic epistemological approach to the classroom setting, based on the functional aspects of Piaget's theory, could prove to be an extremely fruitful method of collaboration between psychology and education and could lead to important curriculum developments in the future.

Summary and Conclusions

We have reviewed some of the major implications of Piaget's views for educational practice. While Piaget has not been mainly concerned with schools, one can derive from his theory a number of general principles which may guide educational procedures. The first of these is that the child's language and thought are different from the adult's. The teacher must be cognizant of this and must therefore observe children very closely in an attempt to discover their unique perspectives. Second, children need to act on things to learn. Formal verbal instruction is generally ineffective, especially for young children. Activity constitutes a major portion of genuine knowledge; the mere passive reception of facts or concepts is only a minor part of real understanding. Third, children are most interested and learn best when experience is moderately novel. When a new event is both familiar enough so that it may be assimilated without distortion into current cognitive structure, and novel enough so that it produces some degree of conflict, then interest and learning are promoted. Since at a given age level children's cognitive structures differ, all children will not find the same new event interesting, nor will they learn from it. This implies that successful group instruction is almost impossible. Children should work individually, with freedom, at tasks of their own choosing. Piaget finds, too, that an important aspect of learning is self-regulation. Before entering school, and without adult instruction, the child learns in many ways. Fourth, children should have the opportunity to talk with one another in school, to argue and debate. Social interaction, particularly when it is centered on relevant physical experience, promotes intellectual growth.

Fifth, one of Piaget's major contributions to education lies in the provision of extensive data on the development in children of basic mathematical, logical, and scientific concepts, and thus on the general development of thinking. This information can be used to determine the limits on children's ability to learn, to evaluate curricula, to develop new learning experiences, and to eliminate the gaps between intuition and consciousness. Sixth, Piaget's clinical method can be used as an effective aid in diagnosis and assessment, and in helping teachers acquire the questioning skills useful for promoting genuine learning in the classroom. Finally,

Piaget's theory of equilibration has implications for the conduct of teaching.

   It should be clear that these views are at variance with many of the assumptions of traditional education. According to Piaget's evidence and theory, students of a given age level do not and cannot learn essentially the same material; they learn only in a minor way through verbal explanation or written exposition (concrete experience must come first); they can and do exert control over their own learning; and they should talk to one another. It should also be clear that these ideas are not particularly new. The "progressive" education movement has proposed similar principles for many years. Piaget's contribution is not in developing new educational ideas, but in providing a vast body of data and theory which provide a sound basis for a "progressive" approach to the schools.

   We would also like to point out that these educational ideas are not only "idealistic," but practical as well. Many primary schools in Great Britain and in the United States have been approaching education in line with the principles described above, and have drawn directly on Piaget's work for their inspiration. These schools represent a very promising experiment in educational innovation and have already achieved a good measure of success.

   We will close this section on education, and this book, with a quotation from Piaget, stating his educational goals and at the same time describing his own accomplishment.

> The principal goal of education is to create men who are capable of doing new things, not simply of repeating what other generations have done—men who are creative, inventive, and discoverers. The second goal of education is to form minds which can be critical, can verify, and not accept everything they are offered. The great danger today is of slogans, collective opinions, ready-made trends of thought. We have to be able to resist individually, to criticize, to distinguish between what is proven and what is not. So we need pupils who are active, who learn early to find out by themselves, partly by their own spontaneous activity and partly through material we set up for them; who learn early to tell what is verifiable and what is simply the first idea to come to them. (Piaget, "Development and Learning, 1964, p. 5)

References

Appleton, T., Clifton, R., and Goldberg, S. "The development of behavioral competence in infancy." In F. D. Horowitz (ed.), *Review of child development research*, Vol. IV. Chicago: University of Chicago Press, 1975.

Ashton, P. T. Cross-cultural Piagetian research: An experimental perspective. *Harvard Educational Review,* Vol. 45 (1975), pp. 475–506.

Beilin, H. "Dispensible and nondispensible elements in Piaget's theory." In J. Montangero (ed.), *Genetic epistemology: Yesterday and today.* New York: The Graduate School and University Center, City University of New York, 1985.

——— "Inducing conservation through training." In G. Steiner (ed.), *Psychology of the 20th century, Piaget and beyond,* Vol. 7. Zurich: Kindler, 1977.

Beth, E. W., and Piaget, J. *Mathematical epistemology and psychology.* Dordrecht, Holland: D. Reidel Publishing Company, 1966.

Dasen, P. R. Cross-cultural Piagetian research: a summary. *Journal of Cross-Cultural Psychology,* Vol. 3 (1972), pp. 23–29.

——— (ed.) *Piagetian psychology: Cross-cultural contributions.* New York: Gardner Press, Inc., 1977.

Elkind, D. *Child development and education.* New York: Oxford University Press, 1976.

Ennis, R. H. "Children's ability to handle Piaget's propositional logic: A conceptual critique." *Review of Educational Research,* Vol. 45 (1975), pp. 1–41.

Flavell, J. H. *Cognitive development,* 2nd ed. Englewood Cliffs, N.J.: Prentice-Hall, Inc., 1985.

Gallagher, J. M., and Reid, D. K. *The Learning theory of Piaget and Inhelder.* Austin, Tex.: Pro Ed, 1981.

GELMAN, R., and BAILLARGEON, R.   "A review of some Piagetian concepts." In P. H. Mussen (ed.), *Handbook of child psychology: Cognitive development,* Vol. III, 4th ed. New York: John Wiley & Sons, Inc., 1983.

——, and GALLISTEL, C. R.   *The young child's understanding of number.* Cambridge, Mass.: Harvard University Press, 1978.

GIBSON, E. J.   *Principles of perceptual learning and development.* Englewood Cliffs, N.J.: Prentice-Hall, Inc., 1969.

GIBSON, J. J.   *The senses considered as perceptual systems.* Boston: Houghton Mifflin Company, 1966.

GINSBURG, H. P.   *Children's arithmetic: How they learn it and how you teach it.* Austin, Tex.: Pro Ed, 1982.

——   "The clinical interview in psychological research: aims, rationales, techniques." *For the Learning of Mathematics,* Vol. 3 (1981), pp. 4–11.

——   and KOSLOWSKI, B.   Cognitive development. *Annual Review of Psychology,* Vol. 27 (1976), pp. 29–61.

GREENFIELD, P.   "On culture and conservation." In J. Bruner, R. R. Olver, and P. Greenfield. *Studies in cognitive growth.* New York: John Wiley & Sons, Inc., 1966.

HEBBELER, K.   Young children's addition. *Journal of Children's Mathematical Behavior,* Vol. 1 (1977), pp. 108–21.

HUNT, J. M.   *Intelligence and experience.* New York: Ronald Press, 1961.

INHELDER, B., SINCLAIR, H., and BOVET, M.   *Learning and the development of cognition.* Cambridge, Mass.: Harvard University Press, 1974.

KLAHR, D., and WALLACE, J. G.   "Class inclusion processes." In S. Farnham-Diggory (ed.), *Information processing in children.* New York: Academic Press, 1972.

KOFSKY, E.   A scalogram study of classificatory development. *Child Development,* Vol. 37 (1966), pp. 191–204.

KUHN, T. S.   *The structure of scientific revolutions,* 2nd ed. Chicago: University of Chicago Press, 1970.

LIBEN, L.   "Memory from a cognitive-developmental perspective: a theoretical and empirical review." In W. F. Overton and J. M. Gallagher (eds.), *Knowledge and development,* Vol. I. New York: Plenum Press, 1977.

LICKONA, T.   (ed.) *Moral development and behavior.* New York: Holt, Rinehart and Winston, 1976.

McNAMARA, J.   Cognitive basis of language learning in infants. *Psychological Review,* Vol. 79 (1972), pp. 1–13.

NEIMARK, E.   "Intellectual development during adolescence." In F. D. Horowitz (ed.) *Review of child development research,* Vol. IV. Chicago: University of Chicago Press, 1975.

NEISSER, U.   *Cognition and reality.* San Francisco: W. H. Freeman and Company, 1967.

——   *Cognitive psychology.* New York: Appleton-Century-Crofts, 1967.

OPPER, S.   "Concept development in Thai urban and rural children." In P. R. Dasen (ed.), *Piagetian psychology: Cross-cultural contributions.* New York: Gardner Press, Inc., 1977.

——   Cross-cultural studies in cognition and language: the acquisition of class inclusion by Thai and Swiss children, *Archives de Psychologie,* Vol. XLVII, Issue 183, (1979), pp. 293–308.

——   *Intellectual development in Thai children.* Unpublished doctoral dissertation, Cornell University, Ithaca, N.Y., 1971.

——   Piaget's clinical method. *Journal of Children's Mathematical Behavior,* Vol. 1 (1977), pp. 90–107.

PIAGET, J.   *Adaptation vitale et psychologie de l'intelligence: Sélection organique et phénocopie.* Paris: Hermann, 1974.

—— "Autobiography." In *History of psychology in autobiography*, E. G. Boring et al. (eds.), Vol. 4, pp. 237–56. Worcester, Mass.: Clark University Press, 1952a.

—— *Biology and knowledge*, trans. B. Walsh. Chicago: University of Chicago Press, 1971a.

—— *The child and reality: Problems of genetic psychology*, trans. A. Rosin. New York: Grossman, 1973a.

—— *The child's conception of movement and speed*, trans. G. E. T. Holloway and M. J. MacKensie. London: Routledge & Kegan Paul Ltd., 1970a.

—— *The child's conception of physical causality*, trans. M. Gabain. Totowa, N.J.: Little-field, Adams, and Co., 1960a.

—— *The child's conception of time*, trans. A. J. Pomerans. New York: Basic Books, Inc., Publishers, 1970b.

—— *The child's conception of the world*, trans. J. and A. Tomlinson, New York: Har-court, Brace & World, Inc., 1929.

—— *Classes, relations, et nombres*. Paris: Librarie Philosophique J. Vrin, 1942.

—— "Comments on mathematical education." In H. Gruber and J. Voneche (eds.), *The essential Piaget*. New York: Basic Books, Inc., Publishers, 1977a.

—— *Le comportement moteur de l'évolution*. Paris: Gallimard, 1976a.

—— *The construction of reality in the child*, trans. M. Cook. New York: Basic Books, Inc., Publishers, 1954.

—— "Correspondences and transformations." In F. B. Murray (ed.), *The impact of Piagetian theory: On education, philosophy, psychiatry, and psychology*. Baltimore: University Park Press, 1979.

—— "Development and learning." In R. E. Ripple and V. N. Rockcastle (eds.), *Piaget rediscovered*. Ithaca, N.Y.: Cornell University Press, 1964.

—— "Equilibration and the development of logical structures," in J. M. Tanner and B. Inhelder (eds.), *Discussions on child development*, Vol. IV. London: Tavistock Publications Ltd., 1960b.

—— *The equilibration of cognitive structures*, trans. T. Brown and K. J. Thampy. Chicago: University of Chicago Press, 1985.

—— *Essai sur les transformations des opérations logiques*. Paris: Presses Universitaires de France, 1952b.

—— *Etudes sociologiques*. Geneva: Librairie Droz, 1965. Also published in *Journal of Reserch in Science Teaching*, Vol. 2, Issue 3 (1965).

—— *Experiments in contradiction*, trans. D. Coltman. Chicago: University of Chicago Press, 1981a.

—— *The grasp of consciousness: action and concept in the young child*, trans. S. Wedgwood. Cambridge, Harvard University Press, 1976b.

—— *Insights and illusions in philosophy*, trans. W. Mays. New York: World Publishing Co., 1971b.

—— "Intellectual evolution from adolescence to adulthood." *Human development*, Vol. 15 (1972a), pp. 1–12.

—— *Introduction à l'epistémologie génétique*, Vol. I. *La pensée mathématique*, Vol. II. *La pensée physique*, Vol. III. *La pensée biologique, la pensée psychologique et la pensée sociologique*. Paris: Presses Universitaries de France, 1950a.

—— *Judgment and reasoning in the child*, trans. M. Warden. New York: Harcourt, Brace & World, Inc., 1926a.

—— *The language and thought of the child*, trans. M. Gabain. London: Routledge & Kegan Paul Ltd., 1926b.

—— *The mechanisms of perception*, trans. G. N. Seagrim. London: Routledge & Kegan Paul Ltd., 1969.

———— *The moral judgment of the child,* trans. M. Gabain, New York: Harcourt, Brace & World, Inc., 1932.

———— *On the development of memory and identity,* trans. E. Duckworth. Barre, Mass.: Clark University Press, 1968.

———— *The origins of intelligence in children,* trans. M. Cook. New York: International Universities Press, 1952c.

———— *Play, dreams, and imitation in childhood,* trans. C. Gattegno and F. M. Hodgson. New York: W. W. Norton & Co., Inc., 1951.

———— *Le possible et le nécessaire,* Vols. 1 and 2. Paris: Presses Universitaires de France. Vol. 1, 1981b; Vol. 2, 1983.

———— "Problems of equilibration." In M. H. Appel and L. S. Goldberg, *Topics in cognitive development,* Vol. 1. New York: Plenum Press, 1977b.

———— *Psychology and epistemology: Towards a theory of knowledge,* trans. P. A. Wells. Harmondsworth, England: Penguin Books, 1972b.

———— *The psychology of intelligence,* trans. M. Percy and D. E. Berlyne. London: Routledge & Kegan Paul Ltd., 1950b.

———— "Recent studies in genetic psychology." *Cahiers Fondation Archives Jean Piaget,* No. 1 (1980).

———— *Science of education and the psychology of the child,* trans. D. Coltman. New York: Orion Press, 1970c.

———— *Six psychological studies,* trans. A. Tenzer and D. Elkind. New York: Random House, Inc., 1967.

———— "Some recent research and its link with a new theory of groupings and conservations based on commutability." In R. W. Rieber and K. Salzinger (eds.), *The roots of American psychology: Historical influences and implications for the future.* Annals of the New York Academy of Sciences, Vol. 291 (1977c), 291, pp. 350–57.

———— *Structuralism,* trans. C. Maschler. New York: Basic Books, Inc., Publishers, 1970d.

———— *Success and Understanding,* trans. A. J. Pomerans. Cambridge, Mass.: Harvard University Press, 1978.

———— *To understand is to invent: The future of education,* trans. G. and A. Roberts. New York: Grossman, 1973b.

———— *Traité de logique.* Paris: Librarie Armand Colin, 1949.

————, and GARCIA, R. *Understanding causality,* trans. D. and M. Miles. New York: W. W. Norton & Co., Inc., 1974.

————, and INHELDER, B. *The child's construction of quantities: Conservation and atomism,* trans. A. J. Pomerans. New York: Basic Books, Inc., Publishers, 1974.

————, and INHELDER, B. *The child's conception of space,* trans. F. J. Langdon and J. L. Lunzer. London: Routledge & Kegan Paul Ltd., 1956.

————, and INHELDER, B. *The early growth of logic in the child,* trans. E. A. Lunzer and D. Papert. London: Routledge & Kegan Paul Ltd., 1964.

————, and INHELDER, B. *The growth of logical thinking from childhood to adolescence,* trans. A. Parsons and S. Seagrin. New York: Basic Books, Inc., Publishers, 1958.

————, and INHELDER, B. *Memory and intelligence,* trans. A. J. Pomerans. London: Routledge & Kegan Paul Ltd., 1973.

————, and INHELDER, B. *Mental imagery in the child,* trans. P. A. Chilton. London: Routledge & Kegan Paul Ltd., 1971.

————, and INHELDER, B. *The origins of the idea of chance in the child,* trans. L. Leake, P. Burrell, and H. D. Fishbein. London: Routledge & Kegan Paul Ltd., 1975.

————, and INHELDER, B. *The psychology of the child,* trans. H. Weaver. London: Routledge & Kegan Paul Ltd., 1969.

————, INHELDER, B., and SZEMINSKA, A. *The child's conception of geometry,* trans. E. A. Lunzer. London: Routledge & Kegan Paul Ltd., 1960.

————, and SZEMINSKA, A. *The child's conception of number,* trans. C. Gattegno and F. M. Hodgson. London: Routledge & Kegan Paul Ltd., 1952.

RESNICK, L. B. (ed.) *The nature of intelligence.* Hillsdale, N.J.: L. Erlbaum Associates, 1976.

ROSCH, E. H. "On the internal structure of perceptual and semantic categories." In T. E. Moore (ed.), *Cognitive development and the acquisition of language,* pp. 111–44. New York: Academic Press, 1973.

SAMUELS, M. T. "Scheme influences on long-term event recall in children." *Child Development,* Vol. 47 (1976), pp. 824–30.

SHAYER, M. Conceptual demands in the Nuffield O-level physics course. *School Science Review,* Vol. 186 (1972), pp. 26–34.

———— Conceptual demands in the Nuffield O-level biology course. *School Science Review,* Vol. 195 (1974), pp. 1–11.

SINCLAIR, H. Quoted in T. C. O'Brien, *Implications of Piagetian research for education: Interview with Elizabeth M. Hitchfield.* St. Louis, Mo.: Teachers Center, 1976, p. 11.

———— "Piaget's theory of development: the main stages." In M. F. Rosskopf, L. P. Steffe, and S. Taback. *Piagetian cognitive development research and mathematical education.* Washington, D.C.: National Council of Teachers of Mathematics, 1971.

TRABASSO, T. "Representation, memory, and reasoning." In A. D. Pick (ed.), *Minnesota symposia on child psychology,* Vol. 9. Minneapolis: University of Minnesota Press, 1975.

TULKIN, S. R., and KONNER, M. J. Alternative conceptions of intellectual functioning. *Human development,* Vol. 16 (1973), pp. 33–52.

TYLER, L. E. (ed.) *Intelligence: Some recurring issues.* New York: Van Nostrand Reinhold Company, 1969.

UZGIRIS, I. C. "Organization of sensorimotor intelligence." In M. Lewis (ed.), *Origins of intelligence.* New York: Plenum Press, 1976.

VIGOTSKY, L. S. *Thought and language.* Cambridge, Mass.: M.I.T. Press, 1962.

INDEX